THE
INSTITUTE CLAUSES
HANDBOOK

THE
INSTITUTE CLAUSES
HANDBOOK

By

N. G. Hudson, M.A. and J. C. Allen, F.C.I.I.
Members of the Association of Average Adjusters

LONDON   NEW YORK   HAMBURG   HONG KONG
LLOYD'S OF LONDON PRESS LTD.
1986

Lloyd's of London Press Ltd.
Legal Publishing and Conferences Division
26-30 Artillery Lane, London E1 7LX
Great Britain

U.S.A. AND CANADA
Lloyd's of London Press Inc.
817 Broadway
New York, NY 10003 USA

GERMANY
Lloyd's of London Press
PO Box 11 23 47, Deichstrasse 41
2000 Hamburg 11, West Germany

SOUTH EAST ASIA
Lloyd's of London Press (Far East) Ltd.
903 Chung Nam Building
1 Lockhart Road, Wanchai
Hong Kong

© N. G. Hudson and J. C. Allen

First published in Great Britain, 1986

British Library Cataloguing in Publication Data

Hudson, N.G.
The Institute clauses: a handbook.
1. Insurance, Marine—England
I. Title   II. Allen, J.C.
368.2'2'00942   HE964.5.G7

ISBN 1-85044-093-X

Text set 10 on 12 pt Times by
H. Charlesworth & Co. Ltd., Huddersfield
Printed in Great Britain by
St. Edmundsbury Press
Bury St. Edmunds

Contents

Acknowledgments

The authors and the publishers are grateful to the Institute of London Underwriters and Witherby & Co. Ltd. for their permission to copy the text of the Institute Clauses referred to herein and to the Association of Average Adjusters for their authority to reproduce Advisory Committee and Special Committee reports together with a number of the Rules of Practice of the Association.

ERRATUM

Page 105

Regrettably an error has crept into the figures in the example illustrating the practical effect of the adoption of the cross-liabilities method for assessing the claim on the policy.

These figures should have read as follows:

A sustains damage to the extent of <u>£10,000</u>
B sustains damage to the extent of <u>£ 6,000</u>

The actual settlement between the vessels will be as follows:

B is liable for 50% of A's damage	£ 5,000
A is liable for 50% of B's damage	<u>3,000</u>
Single liability of B to A	<u>£ 2,000</u>

If this were the basis of the claims under the respective policies, the position (ignoring policy deductibles) would be as follows:

Vessel A—P.A. damage	£10,000
Credit recovery from B	<u>2,000</u>
	<u>£ 8,000</u>

Vessel B—P.A. damage	£ 6,000
Three-fourths of single liability payment	<u>1,500</u>
	<u>£ 7,500</u>

The remainder of the figures in the example, showing the claims on the basis of cross-liabilities, are as printed at the bottom of page 105 and on page 106.

Table of Words and Phrases

The following abbreviations are used for the forms of the Clauses:

Abbreviation	*Form of Clause*
ICC	Institute Cargo Clauses
IFFC	Institute Frozen Food Clauses
IBOC	Institute Bulk Oil Clauses
INRC	Institute Natural Rubber Clauses
FOSFA S(1)	Institute FOSFA Supplementary Clauses (1)
IMDC	Institute Malicious Damage Clause
ITP+N-DC	Institute Theft, Pilferage and Non-Delivery Clause
ITCH	Institute Time Clauses, Hulls
ITCF	Institute Time Clauses, Freight
IAPC(H)	Institute Additional Perils Clauses—Hulls
IWC(C)	Institute War Clauses (Cargo)
ISC(C)	Institute Strikes Clauses (Cargo)
IWSC(H)	Institute War and Strikes Clauses—Hulls

Words and Phrases	*Clause*	*Page*
abandonment	ICC	30
according to the contract of affreightment and/or the governing law and practice	ICC	14
accidents in loading discharging shifting cargo or fuel	ITCH	95
adjusted or determined	ICC	14
All Risks	ICC(A)	10
any defective part which has caused loss or damage	IAPC(H)	160
any hostile act by or against a belligerent power	IWC(C)	190
arrest	IWC(C)	191
assured or their servants	ICC	21
attributable to	ICC	17
barratry of master officers or crew	ITCH	99
breakage of shafts	ITCH	95
breakdown of refrigerating machinery	IFFC(A)	48
breakdown of or accident to nuclear installations or reactors	ITCH	94
breakdown or collapse of proper stow	FOSFA S(1)	70
bursting of boilers	ITCH	95
capture	IWC(C)	190
civil commotions	ISC(C)	201
civil strife	IWC(C)	189
collision or contact . . . with any external object other than water	ICC(B)&(C)	38
collision with any other vessel	ITCH	103
confiscation or expropriation	IWSC(H)	208

Table of Cases

Table of Statutes

PART I

Introduction to the New Clauses

1. THE QUIET REVOLUTION

In November 1978 the Secretariat of the United Nations Conference on Trade and Development (UNCTAD) distributed a document entitled *"Marine Insurance — Legal and Documentary Aspects of the Marine Insurance Contract"*.[1]

This was a profound and well-researched study, the depth and objectivity of which was marred only by an unjustified assumption that commercial interests in the developing countries would prefer their contracts to be regulated in accordance with local, rather than international rules.

Some of the observations made by the UNCTAD Secretariat appear ingenuous — perhaps deliberately so. Thus, the Secretariat found that "the entire marine insurance industry had evolved historically from, and had largely retained, practices and conditions of cover which were formulated by insurers from developed countries". They recognised the ascendancy of the United Kingdom as "the international market centre of marine insurance", and consequently, as stated in the report, the Secretariat concentrated a large part of its investigation on the English marine insurance regime. In the course of this analysis, bouquets and brickbats were bestowed with equal largesse. Although the Lloyd's form of policy (the S.G. form) and many of the current clauses were criticised as antiquated and liable to be misunderstood, it was recognised that "English conditions offer a sophisticated set of widely known clauses ready for immediate use".

It would be a gross exaggeration to say that this document exploded like a bomb-shell in the London insurance market, or in any other insurance market, for that matter. Nevertheless, as UNCTAD is an inter-governmental body, representatives of the British insurance industry were invited to make their views known to Her Majesty's Government, and the process of consultation began. No doubt, at the outset, there were those who asked: "who

1. UNCTAD document TD/B/C14/ISL/27.

are these international civil servants, that they should interfere with the smooth running of our market?" However, as we may now recognise, the last-ditchers were eventually persuaded by the advocates for reform.

Marine underwriters at Lloyd's are represented by a body called Lloyd's Underwriters' Association, whereas the vast majority of insurance companies writing marine business in the United Kingdom are members of the Institute of London Underwriters. When working together, these bodies form joint committees, so called since they represent both Lloyd's and company underwriters. As a result of the groundswell for reform, Lloyd's Underwriters' Association and the Institute of London Underwriters set up a joint working party to consider what might be done in order to counter the criticisms made in the UNCTAD Report and to drag the standard policy forms into the twentieth century. In the words of an official document — "as a result it was recommended that the Lloyd's S.G. form should be replaced with a new form and the introduction of new cargo clauses". Thus, with typical British understatement, the quiet revolution was announced.

In fact, the review of policy conditions is one of the responsibilities exercised at all times by the Joint Cargo Committee and the Joint Hull Committee. When there are proposals to amend or update any of the standard forms, the drafting is undertaken by yet another joint committee, called the Technical and Clauses Committee. These are the bodies which undertook the major revision of the standard clauses which are reviewed in this book.

This work has been accomplished in an extremely thorough and competent manner. In the first place, as the result of the abolition of the old Lloyd's S.G. form, it has been necessary to transplant into each of the new sets of clauses the Perils Clause, the Sue and Labour Clause and the Waiver Clause, and at the same time to rephrase them in modern and (so far as possible) unambiguous language. On the other hand, other parts of Lloyd's S.G. form, such as the Memorandum and the paragraphs relating to the duration of risk, were already so out-dated that their provisions had for many years been varied or over-ridden in the forms of clauses attached to the policy. In the course of transplantation, some of the time-honoured expressions have been cast aside and replaced with entirely new wording. The old "Sue and Labour Clause" appears in an entirely new guise as the "Duty of Assured Clause", although its intention has been carefully preserved. On the other hand, to take one example, the words "perils of the seas" remain, obdurately ambiguous for those who are unfamiliar with the many English law cases which define that term, even though for the avoidance of one possible area of doubt, "the seas" have been joined by rivers, lakes or other navigable waters.

A great deal has however been done to render the new clauses more intelligible to an assured who enjoys only a nodding acquaintance with the English law relating to marine insurance. For example, the fact that the assured must have an insurable interest in the subject-matter insured at the time of the loss is expressly stated in the new forms of cargo clauses, although no attempt has been made to define what "insurable interest" means. Conversely, the effect of the expression "lost or not lost", as defined in Rule 1 of the Rules for Construction of Policy attached to the First Schedule of the Marine Insurance Act 1906, has been neatly reproduced for the assured to read and comprehend if he can. These and many other such provisions have been inserted into the new clauses for the sake of completeness and comprehension. Some critics might say that such additions to the new clauses are unnecessary, in view of the statement in all the new forms that the insurance "is subject to English law and practice", thereby importing the whole of the Marine Insurance Act 1906, as well as the effect of subsequent legal decisions, but there is no doubt in the minds of the authors that such declaratory provisions are valuable when the new clauses are employed in foreign markets.

Lastly, there are instances where the new clauses have introduced changes in the cover provided. There are many such instances — too many to mention in a general commentary — and the reader will have to delve further into this book to find out what they are.

2. THE MAR FORMS

With the abolition of Lloyd's S.G. form of policy, it was necessary to create a new formal document of contract. It was decided to do this in the simplest possible form of words consistent with the need to validate the existence of the contract and comply with the provisions of the Marine Insurance Act 1906.

Section 22 of the Marine Insurance Act provides:

> "Subject to the provisions of any statute, a contract of marine insurance is inadmissible in evidence unless it is embodied in a marine policy in accordance with this Act. The policy may be executed and issued either at the time when the contract is concluded or afterwards."

Section 23 used to set out a number of matters which the policy must specify by law, but now requires merely that the policy should specify the name of the assured, or of some person who effects the insurance on his behalf.[2]

Section 24 (1) of the Act provides:

> "A marine policy must be signed by or on behalf of the insurer, provided that in the case of a corporation the corporate seal may be sufficient, but nothing in this

2. The remainder of section 23, setting out other matters previously required to be specified was repealed in 1959, when stamp duty on marine insurance policies was abolished by the Finance Act 1959.

section shall be construed as requiring the subscription of a corporation to be under seal".

The form of the Institute of London Underwriters — Companies Marine Policy — reads as follows:

WE, THE COMPANIES, hereby agree, in consideration of the payment to us by or on behalf of the Assured of the premium specified in the Schedule, to insure against loss damage liability or expense in the proportions and manner hereinafter provided. Each Company shall be liable only for its own respective proportion.

IN WITNESS whereof the General Manager and Secretary of The Institute of London Underwriters has subscribed his name on behalf of each Company.

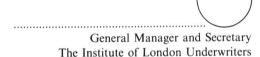

....
General Manager and Secretary
The Institute of London Underwriters

This Policy is not valid unless it bears the embossment of the Policy Department of The Institue of London Underwriters.

This insurance is subject to English jurisdiction.

Lloyd's Form of Marine Policy is similar, and provides that the liability of each underwriting member of any syndicate whose definitive number and proportion is set out in the list of syndicates forming part of the policy is limited to his share of that syndicate's proportion. The Lloyd's form is distinguished by the initial letters MAR in the bottom left hand corner, by reason of which these forms are now customarily referred to as the "MAR Forms".

This insurance is subject to English jurisdiction

These words were added to the Lloyd's and I.L.U. forms in order to remove any possible doubt there might be as to where any legal proceedings should be commenced. Of course, when the contract of insurance is concluded in England, the English courts may exercise jurisdiction, but this would not necessarily prevent an assured or an assignee who wished to do so from commencing legal proceedings in another country.

The inclusion of the English jurisdiction clause in the MAR form is to be contrasted with the provision contained in each of the various Institute Clauses which we shall examine later in this book, to the effect that the insurance is "subject to English law and practice". The reason for this is that whereas the MAR forms will only be used when the contract is concluded in the United Kingdom, the Institute Clauses may also be used in conjunction with a policy of insurance issued abroad providing for jurisdiction in the country of issue.

On the second page of each MAR Form is a schedule with a number of printed headings, as follows:

SCHEDULE

POLICY NUMBER

_____

NAME OF ASSURED

_____

VESSEL

_____

VOYAGE OR PERIOD OF INSURANCE

_____

SUBJECT-MATTER INSURED

_____

AGREED VALUE
  (if any)

_____

AMOUNT INSURED HEREUNDER

_____

PREMIUM

_____

CLAUSES, ENDORSEMENTS, SPECIAL CONDITIONS AND WARRAN-TIES

THE ATTACHED CLAUSES AND ENDORSEMENTS FORM PART OF THIS POLICY

PART II

Marine Cargo Forms

1. HISTORICAL PERSPECTIVE — CARGO INSURANCE FROM LLOYD'S FORM TO THE PRESENT DAY

The extent of cover provided

Until relatively recently all cargo insurance was written on restricted terms. Looking at the list of perils which the underwriters on Lloyd's S.G. form were "contented to bear and did take upon themselves", we find that they fall into two main categories:

Acts of God, but limited to perils "of the seas" and

Acts of men, but limited to:

(i) Acts performed maliciously, malevolently, fraudulently or with a hostile intent. In such category were enemies, pirates, rovers and even the master and crew when acting barratrously, that is to say in fraud of their employers and in breach of their duties.

(ii) General Average acts.

What is missing? The acts of men while performing their duties, however negligently they may have performed them.

The reason for this limitation on the extent of cover is not hard to seek. In the time when Lloyd's form of policy was being evolved, the carrier of the goods had full responsibility for the cargoes entrusted to his care and was answerable for all losses which might occur to those goods, other than those arising from acts of God, the action of enemies and like persons, or general average acts. From the consequences of these the carrier was exonerated by law and this therefore was the area in which the merchant required protection. For this protection the policy of insurance was evolved.

About 200 years ago it began to be asked whether the term "perils of the seas" comprehended those events such as stranding or collision which were brought about by some failure of the master or crew to perform their duties adequately, for example when they were negligent in navigation. The answer provided by the English courts was that if the loss or damage was caused "proximately" by the stranding or collision, as the case might be, the underwriter was liable to pay even though the stranding or collision was brought about by the negligence of master or crew. More or less concurrently with the unfolding of the doctrine of "proximate cause" came a clear elucidation of another important principle of insurance, namely that of subrogation, whereby in such an event the underwriter who had paid for the loss would be entitled to stand in the shoes of his assured and bring a legal action against the carrier for the consequences of his breach of the contract of carriage.

Later in the nineteenth century with the explosive expansion of commerce, and perhaps influenced also by the improvement in legal machinery, ship-owners began to feel in need of some protection against their potential liabilities. To this end, in so far as they were permitted within the principle of freedom of contract, they came to insert wide exoneration clauses in their bills of lading so as virtually to disclaim all responsibility for the goods in their care, and they also formed themselves into associations or clubs for their better protection and indemnity.

This brings us to the twentieth century in which, despite the Hague Rules, the Hague-Visby Rules and even (if they ever come into effect) the Hamburg Rules, the merchant adventurer stands in need of better protection by wider and more refined insurance cover.

Restrictions upon the losses paid for

It was not only in the list of perils that the traditional marine insurance policy was restricted. There was also a considerable limitation upon the extent of the losses which would be paid for. This limitation was expressed in what was called the Memorandum to Lloyd's form of policy, which read:

> "N.B. — Corn, fish, salt, fruit, flour and seed are warranted free from average, unless general, or the ship be stranded; sugar, tobacco, hemp, flax, hides and skins are warranted free from average, under five pounds per cent; and all other goods, also the ship and freight, are warranted free from average, under three pounds per cent, unless general, or the ship be stranded, sunk or burnt."

The reasons for this limitation were no doubt the lack of capacity in a market in an early stage of development and a desire to cut out small or contentious claims, coupled with a very real practical problem as to the proof of loss by insured perils. For example, in the event of goods being discharged at destination damaged by sea water, who could say whether the wet in the hold and the deteriorated condition of the cargo was due to an inevitable percolation of water through leaky seams in the side of the ship, or a failure on the part of the crew regularly to pump the bilges, or to a violent incursion of sea water which occurred in a storm?

So, in the case of those goods particularly susceptible to sea water damage enumerated in the first section of the Memorandum, the underwriters would pay no partial loss. Likewise, in the case of other commodities losses under five per cent or three per cent, as the case might be, were deemed to have come about through the normal incidents of the voyage and not by reason of perils of the seas. Only if the ship had stranded at some time during the voyage were underwriters prepared to take a generous view, and for this the reason is clear. The act of stranding places particular stresses on the hull of a wooden ship and even if on refloating she is found to have sustained no permanent damage, the very act of setting upon the ground would be likely to distort her timbers, disturb the caulking and open up the seams. Hence, if the ship had stranded during the voyage losses by sea peril would be payable irrespective of percentage.

The other significant exception to this limitation of underwriters' liability is in respect of general average contribution, which has always been responded for by underwriters on ships and cargoes.

Restricted conditions on the forms of 1.1.63: The Institute Cargo Clauses (W.A.) and the Institute Cargo Clauses (F.P.A.)

The initials stood for "with average" and "free of particular average" respectively.

These forms incorporated the "Memorandum" restrictions although with rather less severity than in the S.G. form. The assured had an option. He might elect to bear all the risk of partial loss (under the F.P.A. Clause), or the risk of small partial losses below three per cent or five per cent (the W.A. Clause), in either case except for those specified instances where the severity of the Memorandum wording was alleviated by the Average Clause.

The Average Clause (in the W.A. form)/The F.P.A. Clause (in the F.P.A. form)

By these clauses underwriters expressly agreed to pay certain classes of claim outside the average warranty. They were:

1. Claims for particular average irrespective of percentage for damage caused by any of the perils insured, if during the insured voyage the carrying vessel or craft was stranded, sunk or burnt. In the words of the old authorities these events "opened the warranty", and provided the insured goods were on board at the time of the event the assured was entitled to recover in full for any particular average damage sustained by insured perils whenever those perils had occurred — even if prior to the event which opened the warranty.
2. Packages totally lost in the course of loading, transhipment or discharge.

3. Loss or damage reasonably attributed to fire, explosion, collision or contact with an external substance (including ice).
4. Loss or damage reasonably attributed to discharging at a port of refuge or distress.
5. The F.P.A. Clause also covered special charges for landing, warehousing and forwarding to destination goods which had been discharged at an intermediate port subject to a proviso (rather curiously expressed) that the loss averted by such special charges would have been one which underwriters would be liable to pay under the W.A. Clause.

The area of additional cover granted by these exceptions to the average warranty was exactly the same in the F.P.A. Clause as in the W.A. Clause. Some of these extensions to underwriters' liability have now been transferred into the named risk sections of the new (B) and (C) Clauses.

The development of "All Risks" cover

About a hundred years ago, when iron and steel had largely displaced timber in the construction of the hulls of ships, and with other factors contributing to the safe carriage of goods by sea, underwriters were prepared to extend the area of cover which they granted to their assured. No doubt in the first instance such additions to the cover were made piecemeal, by adding such words as "including all risks of craft and/or lighterage to and from the ship", but for a merchant with a good claims record, who was prepared to pay a slightly higher rate of premium, the extra cover afforded by an "All Risks" insurance was — and still is — of great comfort.

2. INSTITUTE CARGO CLAUSES (A) — The "All Risks" form (1/1/82)

RISKS COVERED

The risks covered by this form are set out in Clauses 1, 2 and 3.

Clause 1 — Risks Clause

1   This insurance covers all risks of loss of or damage to the subject-matter insured except as provided in Clauses 4, 5, 6 and 7 below.

"All Risks"

The expression "All Risks" comprehends any loss or damage occasioned fortuitously, but not that which occurs inevitably. In that respect, the cover provided is less wide than an insurance to cover, for example, "all loss and damage, howsoever caused".

The leading case is *Gaunt* v. *British & Foreign Marine Insurance Co. Ltd.*[1] This was an insurance on bales of wool, subject to conditions "including ... all risks from sheeps back ... until safely delivered ...". On arrival it was found that many of the bales had been damaged by freshwater wetting, some of which must have occurred prior to shipment on the ocean steamer. The House of Lords held that the existence of fortuitous damage was sufficient evidence of a casualty, and that under an insurance against "all risks" it was not necessary to prove the exact nature of the casualty which had occasioned the loss. Lord Sumner said: "'All Risks' has the same effect as if all insurable risks were separately enumerated; for example, it includes the risk that when it happens to be raining the men who ought to use the tarpaulins to protect the wool may happen to be neglecting their duty. This concurrence is fortuitous; it is also the cause of loss by wetting."

Limitations on the expression "All Risks"

In the same case Lord Sumner said: "There are, of course, limits to 'all risks'. They are risks and risks insured against. Accordingly the expression does not cover inherent vice or mere wear and tear or British capture. It covers a risk, not certainty; it is something, which happens to the subject-matter from without, not the natural behaviour of that subject-matter, being what it is, in the circumstances under which it is carried. Nor is it a loss which the assured brings about by his own act, for then he has not merely exposed the goods to the chance of injury, he has injured them himself."

Proof of loss

The onus of proof remains upon the assured to show that, on the evidence, some accidental or fortuitous loss or damage has occurred during the duration of the risk as expressed by the policy. In the words of Lord Sumner, when a claimant "avers loss by some risk coming within 'all risks', as used in this policy, he need only give evidence reasonably showing that the loss was due to a casualty, not to a certainty or to inherent vice or to wear and tear. That is easily done. I do not think he has to go further and pick out one of the multitude of risks covered, so as to show exactly how his loss was caused. If he did so he would not bring it any the more within the policy."

By contrast, damage caused by moisture in the atmosphere would normally

---

1. *Gaunt* v. *British & Foreign Marine Insurance Co.* (1921) 26 Com.Cas. 247.

not be considered to be fortuitous. See *Whiting* v. *New Zealand Insurance Co.*[2]

"Loss of or damage to ..."

This expression comprehends all physical loss and damage to the goods. It does not include financial loss unaccompanied by any physical loss or damage, such as loss of market, even though the cause of the financial loss was a peril insured against.

Expense as such is not covered under this Clause 1, except for the charges customarily paid in the establishment of a claim upon the insurance. These comprise the expenses paid in order to ascertain the nature and extent of the loss and/or damage, e.g., stacking and sorting, separating sound and damaged lots and the cost of surveys and adjustment. (See Rule of Practice No. A9 of the Association of Average Adjusters.)

Certain classes of expenditure are however covered under Clauses 2, 3, 12 and 16.

"... to the subject-matter insured"

The Marine Insurance Act 1906 Act provides, by section 26:

"(1) The subject-matter insured must be designated in a marine policy with reasonable certainty.

(2) The nature and extent of the interest of the assured in the subject-matter insured need not be specified in the policy.

(3) Where the policy designates the subject-matter insured in general terms, it shall be construed to apply to the interest intended by the assured to be covered.

(4) In the application of this section regard shall be had to any usage regulating the designation of the subject-matter insured."

Provision is made for the declaration of the subject-matter insured in the schedule which is printed on the reverse of the MAR Policy Form (see page 5). Although there might be some argument that the Rules for Construction of Policy, which form part of the first schedule to the Marine Insurance Act, no longer apply to a policy consisting merely of the MAR Form and Institute Cargo Clauses, it is submitted that Rule 17 is a valid restatement of English law and, like the other Rules for Construction of Policy, continue to have effect, since the new wordings, although no longer incorporating Lloyd's S.G. form, constitute an "other like form".

Rule 17 states:

"The term 'goods' means goods in the nature of merchandise, and does not include personal effects or provisions and stores for use on board.

2. *Whiting* v. *New Zealand Insurance Co.* (1932) 44 Ll.L.Rep. 179.

> In the absence of any usage to the contrary, deck cargo and living animals must be insured specifically, and not under the general denomination of goods."

An example of a "usage to the contrary" would be "wood goods", meaning sawn timber, which by the custom of the trade is frequently carried on deck and which therefore need not be declared as "deck cargo".

Do packing materials form part of the subject-matter insured?

There is a "rule of thumb" in the London insurance market that unless the description of the subject-matter of the insurance is so clearly worded as to include the packing materials or containers, underwriters will not respond for any claim for damage sustained to the packing materials or containers, even when caused by a peril insured against.[3]

Such law as there is does not appear wholly to justify this practice. In *Brown* v. *Fleming*[4] the insurance was expressed to be upon "228 cases whisky". Survey at destination disclosed that in a large number of cases the straw in which the bottles were packed was sodden and discoloured by sea water and that many of the labels on the bottles had been damaged. There was nothing wrong with the whisky. The cases subject to damage were sold and the assured claimed the loss which they had sustained thereby. The underwriters declined the claim on the ground that the damage to the straw and labels was not covered by the policy. Bigham J., giving judgment for the assured, said:

> "The straw in which the bottles were packed and the labels upon the bottles are part of the subject of the insurance just as are the bottles and corks. Damage to the labels affects the selling value of the whisky on the market just as much as damage to the corks would."

In *Berk* v. *Style*[5] the policy was on a quantity of kieselguhr which was carried in heavy paper bags on a voyage from North Africa to London. On arrival in London it was found that a number of bags had split and it was therefore necessary to rebag a quantity of kieselguhr in order to enable it to be discharged ex lighters. The assured claimed the cost of rebagging and the underwriters denied liability on the ground that the bags were inadequate, and this inadequacy amounted to inherent vice. In argument for the underwriters counsel conceded that "if this had been a loss by a peril insured against, what the plaintiffs did would have been suing and labouring within the clause in the policy". In relation to the argument whether or not the rebagging was done in order to avert loss or damage to the goods, Sellers J. said: "I prefer the view accepted and alleged by the underwriters that the

3. See *Arnould on Marine Insurance*, 16th edn. (British Shipping Laws), footnote 62 appearing at the end of Section 280.
4. *Brown* v. *Fleming* (1902) 7 Com.Cas. 245.
5. *Berk* v. *Style* [1955] 2 Lloyd's Rep. 383.

subject-matter of the insurance was kieselguhr packed in paper bags ... I think it must be taken that both parties to the insurance contemplated that the goods would be packed for carriage and would not be carried in bulk."

On the other hand, in *Vacuum Oil Company* v. *Union Insurance Society of Canton*[6] where the policy was on "10,000 tins of petroleum", Roche J. said: "Here I hold on the facts that the policy covered petroleum in tins. The thing insured was not the tins but the petroleum. In other words, if all the petroleum was lost and the tins arrived, I should hold there was an actual total loss. If on the other hand the petroleum could be saved, although it had to be saved in other tins, I should hold that there was no loss."

It is submitted that this passage, which was obiter, is inconsistent with the principles followed in other cases.

It has been suggested that in the absence of clear words to describe the subject-matter of insurance, the packing will not form part of the subject-matter where the goods can, and commonly do, travel unprotected. Thus in *Lysaght* v. *Coleman*,[7] where the policy was on "galvanised iron", Lord Esher said: "I think I ought to say also that it is clear that the insurance was on the iron, so that no claim could arise in respect of damaged packing cases."

This would not be inconsistent with the principle suggested by *Berk* v. *Style* that where good commercial practice requires a certain standard of packaging for the transit, such packing does form part of the subject-matter insured, even if not specifically mentioned.

Clause 2 — General Average Clause

2   This insurance covers general average and salvage charges, adjusted or determined according to the contract of affreightment and/or the governing law and practice, incurred to avoid or in connection with the avoidance of loss from any cause except those excluded in Clauses 4, 5, 6 and 7 or elsewhere in this insurance.

Both general average and salvage charges are a species of ransom from total loss. Under English law, they are defined as follows:

General average

The Marine Insurance Act 1906, section 66(2) states:

"There is a general average act where any extraordinary sacrifice or expenditure is voluntarily and reasonably made or incurred in time of peril for the purpose of preserving the property imperiled in the common adventure."

Section 66(3) states how the charges are dealt with:

"Where there is a general average loss, the party on whom it falls is entitled,

6. *Vacuum Oil Company* v. *Union Insurance Society of Canton* (1925) 24 Ll.L.Rep. 188.
7. *Lysaght* v. *Coleman* (1895) 7 Asp.M.L.C. 552.

subject to the conditions imposed by Maritime Law, to a rateable contribution from the other parties interested, and such contribution is called a general average contribution."

Salvage charges

The Marine Insurance Act, section 65(2) states:

"'Salvage charges' means the charges recoverable under Maritime Law by a salvor independently of contract. They do not include the expenses of services in the nature of salvage rendered by the assured or his agents, or any person employed for hire by them, for the purpose of averting a peril insured against. Such expenses, where properly incurred, may be recovered as particular charges or as a general average loss, according to the circumstances under which they were incurred."

The chief distinction is that salvage charges have to do with the amount of the reward payable to a salvor, who is a "volunteer" from outside the common maritime adventure, whereas general average concerns the settlement of expenditure incurred and/or amounts made good for property sacrificed, as between the parties to the adventure *inter se*. Where the adjustment of general average is governed by the York/Antwerp Rules, 1974, Rule VI provides that the total of the payments made on account of salvage (including costs and other expenses incurred in connection therewith) will be admitted in general average whenever the salvage operation was undertaken for the common safety of all the interests at risk.

For a short summary of the similarities and differences between general average and salvage, see the authors' *Marine Claims Handbook*, Part III.

"adjusted or determined"

It is submitted that the word "adjusted" must be read as applying to general average, whereas the word "determined" (which is meaningless in the context of general average) has to be read as applying to salvage charges.

"according to the contract of affreightment and/or the governing law and practice"

The corresponding words in the previous Institute Clauses of 1/1/63 were "... according to Foreign Statement or to York/Antwerp Rules if in accordance with the contract of affreightment".

Some expansion is required, over and above a mere undertaking to pay general average and salvage charges, since by virtue of English law and practice (see Clause 19) it is implicit that underwriters will respond, even under the simplest form of policy (e.g., Lloyd's S.G. form without any other additions), for general average contributions and the proportion of salvage charges attaching to the insured interest, but only for such amounts as would be recognised as general average or "salvage charges" by English law and practice.

The vast majority of general average adjustments are drawn up in accordance with the York/Antwerp Rules, by virtue of a clause in the bill of lading or charter-party stipulating for such adjustment according to the current version of those rules. It is probably to be regretted that this Clause 2 in its present form does not accord recognition to this virtually universal practice. However, the same effect is achieved by the use of the words "according to the contract of affreightment", with the added advantage to the assured that if the general average clause in the bill of lading or charter-party should stipulate either for some other rule to apply (for example, the so-called Peking (Beijing) Rules) then the underwriters will respond (subject to the rule regarding under-insurance) for the general average contribution payable by their assured in accordance with such other rules.

If the bill of lading or charter-party should be silent as to the manner in which any general average should be adjusted, the law of all maritime countries is that the adjustment should be prepared in accordance with the law and practice obtaining at the port where the ship and goods part company.[8]

The words "the governing law and practice" apply not only to protect this principle in regard to the adjustment of general average when there is no relevant provision in the contract of affreightment, but also, it is submitted, to the "determination" of salvage charges if the same are not, as explained above, brought into a general average adjustment under Rule VI of the York/Antwerp Rules, 1974. An example would be when the efforts of a salvor have been directed not to all the property at risk, but merely to save some particular interests.

"incurred to avoid or in connection with the avoidance of loss from any cause except those excluded ..."

Under the (A) Clauses these words are merely declaratory of the principle set out in section 66(6) of the Marine Insurance Act, which states:

> "In the absence of express stipulation, the insurer is not liable for any general average loss or contribution where the loss was not incurred for the purpose of avoiding, or in connection with the avoidance of, a peril insured against."

Compare the position under Institute Cargo Clauses (B) and (C), where the corresponding provision has greater significance.

---

8. In English law, this principle was stated in *Simonds* v. *White* (1824) 2 B. & C. 811.

Clause 3 — "Both to Blame Collision" Clause

3   This insurance is extended to indemnify the Assured against such proportion of liability under the contract of affreightment "Both to Blame Collision" Clause as is in respect of a loss recoverable hereunder. In the event of any claim by shipowners under the said Clause the Assured agree to notify the Underwriters who shall have the right, at their own cost and expense, to defend the Assured against such claim.

In a collision action in the United States, the owners of cargo damaged by the collision may in principle proceed with their claim for damages against either the carrying vessel or the non-carrying vessel involved in the collision. Hence, if the carrier (as would be expected) is exempted from liability under the contract of carriage, the cargo owners will proceed to recover their losses in full from the owners of the non-carrying vessel, who can then in their turn claim as part of *their* damages the proportion of the claim they have paid to the cargo owners attaching to the degree of fault found against the carrying vessel. The "Both to Blame Collision Clause" has been inserted in bills of lading and charter-parties in an attempt to prevent this rule of American law from operating to saddle the owner of the carrying vessel with liability for the collision damages sustained by the cargo on board his own ship. In the United States, a carrier seeking to avoid liability for the damages sustained by the cargo on board his own ship by pleading the "Both to Blame Collision Clause" would fail, since the Supreme Court has held such a clause to be invalid in bills of lading on the grounds of public policy.[9] The clause may however be valid in charter-parties,[10] and the possibility also exists that the parties involved in a collision might agree to the American rules of settlement without invoking the jurisdiction of the United States.

If underwriters have already paid for the loss or damage sustained to the goods in consequence of the collision, then the benefit of any legal proceedings commenced by the assured against the non-carrying vessel would accrue to them by virtue of the doctrine of subrogation, and any diminution of their recovery resulting from the owner of the carrying vessel pleading the "Both to Blame Collision Clause" would be for the underwriters' account. However, the policy clause covers the contingency of an assured, having sustained a loss or damage by collision, seeking to recover for his own account from the non-carrying vessel, and being met by a valid "Both to Blame Collision Clause" in the contract of affreightment.

EXCLUSIONS

The exclusions are contained in Clauses 4, 5, 6 and 7.

---

9. *United States of America* v. *Atlantic Mutual Insurance Co* [1952] A.M.C. 659.
10. *American Union Transport Inc.* v. *United States of America* [1976] A.M.C. 1480.

Clause 4 — General Exclusions Clause

4   In no case shall this insurance cover
4.1   loss damage or expense attributable to wilful misconduct of the Assured

It is to be noted that *all* the exclusions apply to "expense" as well as to claims for loss or damage. Consequently a claim for the cost of forwarding charges under Clause 12, for example, would be defeated if the event giving rise to the need to forward arose through one of the exclusions.

". . . attributable to wilful misconduct of the Assured"

These words are a direct importation from the Marine Insurance Act — see section 55(1)(*a*).

"*attributable to*" is intentionally wider than "caused by" (the words employed in all the other exclusion clauses). A loss proximately caused by a peril insured would therefore appear to be defeasible if the wilful misconduct of the assured was a remote, but nonetheless effective cause.

"*wilful misconduct*" means a course of action undertaken either deliberately, knowing it to be wrongful so far as others are concerned, or recklessly, without caring whether it is wrongful or not.[11]

"*the assured*" means "the persons interested (in the subject-matter insured), the persons for whose benefit the insurance is made".[12]

Most of the English law cases on wilful misconduct concern ships which are allegedly cast away by their owners, and there have probably not been many instances where cargo underwriters have needed to avail themselves of this defence to a claim. It is however submitted that this exclusion would apply, for example, if a merchant insured goods, knowing that they were prohibited from importation in the country of destination, and they were destroyed or confiscated on the order of the customs authorities.

4.2   ordinary leakage, ordinary loss in weight or volume, or ordinary wear and tear of the subject-matter insured

"*Ordinary*" leakage or loss is to be contrasted with leakage or loss due to a fortuity, which would be covered within "all risks". It is submitted therefore that "ordinary" in its context means non-fortuitous or inevitable.

These exclusions, and that of wear and tear are, under English law, capable of being brought back within the policy cover by the use of express words. See Marine Insurance Act, section 55(2)(*c*).

"*Ordinary wear and tear of the subject-matter insured.*" This exclusion was not expressed in the Institute Cargo Clauses (All Risks) of 1/1/63. However, the effect of inserting these words into the Institute Cargo Clauses of 1/1/82

11. See *Arnould on Marine Insurance*, 16th edn. (British Shipping Laws), Section 786.
12. See *Ocean Iron Steamship Insurance Association* v. *Leslie* (1887) 6 Asp. M.L.C. 226.

is in fact to extend the cover granted to the assured, since the wear and tear excluded is limited to that "of the subject-matter insured" and does not extend to the wear and tear of the carrying vessel, barge or container. The limitation of this exclusion is more significant in the (B) Clauses — see the commentary on Clause 1.2.3 of those clauses on page 39.

> **4.3**   loss damage or expense caused by insufficiency or unsuitability of packing or preparation of the subject-matter insured (for the purpose of this Clause 4.3 "packing" shall be deemed to include stowage in a container or liftvan but only when such stowage is carried out prior to attachment of this insurance or by the Assured or their servants)

"... *insufficiency or unsuitability of packing*". Whether, in any particular case, the packing was insufficient or unsuitable, is often a nice question of fact. The test is whether the packing was adequate "to endure the ordinary contemplated handling and carriage".[13] It is submitted that if the type of packing is in accordance with the normal custom of the trade, this would raise a strong presumption that it was adequate.

"... *stowage in a container or liftvan*". It is to be noted that loss or damage due to bad stowage in a container or liftvan is not covered in two circumstances:

(a) When the stowage is carried out before the attachment of the insurance, or

(b) When it is the assured or his servants who carry out the stowage.

> **4.4**   loss damage or expense caused by inherent vice or nature of the subject-matter insured

A definition of inherent vice is: "the unfitness of the goods to withstand the ordinary incidents of the voyage, given the degree of care which the ship-owner is required by the contract to exercise in relation to the goods".[14] Also — "a loss by inherent vice is one which is proximately caused by the natural behaviour of the subject-matter insured, being what it is, in the circumstances in which it was expected to be carried".[15]

The exclusion is of considerable antiquity, and is recognised by the maritime law of all countries. In English law it is one of those events for which an underwriter will not be liable "unless the policy otherwise provides" — Marine Insurance Act, section 55(2)(*c*). For a case in which the policy did "otherwise provide", see *Soya G.m.b.H.* v. *White*[16] where the insurance was effected "to cover the risks of heat, sweat and spontaneous combustion only".

---

13. See *Berk* v. *Style* [1955] 2 Lloyd's Rep. 383, in which it was held that when the packing is included in the subject-matter insured, and is inadequate, this amounts to inherent vice.

14. *Scrutton on Charterparties*, 19th edn., art. 109.

15. *Per* Lord Sumner in *British & Foreign Marine Insurance Co.* v. *Gaunt* (1921) 7 Ll.L.Rep. 62, adapted by Scrutton L.J. in *Sassoon* v. *Yorkshire Insurance Co.* (1923) 16 Ll.L.Rep. 129 and approved by the Court of Appeal in *Soya G.m.b.H.* v. *White* [1982] 1 Lloyd's Rep. 136.

16. *Soya G.m.b.H.* v. *White* [1983] 1 Lloyd's Rep. 122 (H.L.).

4.5 loss damage or expense proximately caused by delay, even though the delay be caused by a risk insured against (except expenses payable under Clause 2 above)

"*. . . proximately caused by delay*". The word "proximately" is used in this clause, presumably in order to conform to section 55(2)(*b*) of the Marine Insurance Act, viz:

> "Unless the policy otherwise provides, the insurer on ship or goods is not liable for any loss proximately caused by delay, although the delay be caused by a peril insured against."

The leading English case is *Pink* v. *Fleming*.[17] In that case part of a cargo of fruit deteriorated owing to delay occasioned on the voyage by the ship requiring to be repaired on account of collision damage. In the United States, the rule is different,[18] and consequently a delay exclusion clause would be essential in a policy governed by American law if the underwriters wished to exclude a similar claim.

"(*except expenses payable under Clause 2 above*)". The only instance of claim for expenses consequent upon delay for which the insurers will respond arises when a ship has been detained in the circumstances envisaged in Rule XI of the York/Antwerp Rules or other similar provision affecting general average. In such a case, these words make it clear that the insurers will reimburse their assured for cargo's proportion of general average so settled, including the ship's detention expenses.

4.6 loss damage or expense arising from insolvency or financial default of the owners managers charterers or operators of the vessel

This clause was new in 1982 and its introduction caused a certain amount of resentment in some quarters. This clause was felt to bear particularly heavily upon the assured under an "all risks" policy, since it has been held that an unlawful detention of goods amounts to "conversion", thus founding a claim upon a policy against "all risks".[19]

In the light of the representations made to them, London Market underwriters agreed to ameliorate the severity of this clause in the standard forms which were negotiated with various trade associations.

"*insolvency or financial default*". A person is said to be insolvent when he is unable to pay all his debts in full. If that be the applicable definition in the context of this clause, "insolvency" would appear to be wider even than "financial default" and include the situation in which many shipowners or operators still manage to continue trading.

It appears that the intention of the draftsmen was to exclude all types of claim for recovery and forwarding of the goods arising from the abandonment of a voyage by shipowners or operators who run out of funds while the voyage was still in being.

17. *Pink* v. *Fleming* (1890) 25 Q.B.D. 396.
18. *Lanasa Fruit* v. *Universal Insurance Co.* (*The "Smaragd"*), 302 U.S. 556.
19. *London & Provincial Leather Processes* v. *Hudson* (1939) 64 Ll.L.Rep. 352.

4.7 loss damage or expense arising from the use of any weapon of war employing atomic or nuclear fission and/or fusion or other like reaction or radioactive force or matter.

"use of any weapon of war" presumably includes the testing of such weapons as well as their use in a war situation. If a ship and cargo were contaminated by fall-out from the test of a nuclear device intended to form the basis of a weapon, it is submitted the exclusion would apply. On the other hand, if the contamination occurred as a result of a radioactive emission owing to an accident at a nuclear power station, underwriters insuring on "All Risks" conditions would respond for the loss or damage so caused.

Clause 5 — Unseaworthiness and Unfitness Exclusion Clause

5 **5.1** In no case shall this insurance cover loss damage or expense arising from
   unseaworthiness of vessel or craft,
   unfitness of vessel craft conveyance container or liftvan for the safe carriage of the subject-matter insured,
   where the Assured or their servants are privy to such unseaworthiness or unfitness, at the time the subject-matter insured is loaded therein.

5.2 The Underwriters waive any breach of the implied warranties of seaworthiness of the ship and fitness of the ship to carry the subject-matter insured to destination, unless the Assured or their servants are privy to such unseaworthiness or unfitness.

Logically, Clause 5.2 has to be considered first. In the absence of such a waiver of the implied warranty of seaworthiness, the assured would have no claim at all if his goods were loaded on to an unseaworthy ship, since the Marine Insurance Act, section 40(2), provides:

"In a voyage policy on goods or other moveables there is an implied warranty that at the commencement of the voyage the ship is not only seaworthy as a ship, but also that she is reasonably fit to carry the goods or other moveables to the destination contemplated by the policy."

This rule bears very hard on an innocent assured, since very few owners of cargo are in a position to influence, still less control, the fitness of the carrying ship.

In previous editions of Institute Cargo Clauses underwriters' waiver of the implied warranty was expressed shortly by the words: "the seaworthiness of the vessel as between the Assured and Underwriters is hereby admitted".

It is submitted that the effect of Clause 5.2 is the same, since the fitness of the ship to carry the goods to destination is already imported into the definition of seaworthiness by section 40(2) of the Act, quoted above. The proviso — "unless the Assured or their servants are privy to such unseaworthiness or unfitness" — is new, and takes the place of a positive statement in the previous edition of Institute Cargo Clauses that in the event of loss the assured's right of recovery would not be prejudiced by the fact that the loss may have been attributable to the wrongful act or misconduct of the shipowners or their servants, committed without the assured's privity.

Clause 5.1 might appear at first sight to cover much the same ground as Clause 5.2, but the presumed intention of the draftsman was to clarify the position in regard to those cases where unseaworthiness of the ship or unfitness of the "vessel, craft, conveyance, container or liftvan" for the safe carriage of the goods was the *cause* of the loss, in contrast to those cases where, but for the waiver of the implied warranty of seaworthiness, the underwriters would have had a defence, on the ground of breach of warranty, against *any* claim for loss, however caused.

"Privy"

To be "privy" to something involves having actual positive knowledge of it or, being suspicious of the true situation, "turning a blind 'eye" to it and refraining from enquiry.[20]

"Of the Assured or their servants"

This state of knowledge, or "turning a blind eye", about the condition of the ship or, for example, a container, may be that of a cargo superintendent employed by the assured to supervise the operation of loading. In such a case, his knowledge would afford the underwriters a defence if he was employed by the assured, but not if he were employed by the assured's agents. On the other hand, the addition of the word "servants" broadens the scope of underwriters' defence beyond that provided for in the Marine Insurance Act in relation to a time policy on a ship, where, to afford underwriters a defence, the privity to the unseaworthiness has to be that of the assured personally or, in the case of a company, its *alter ego* or at least one of its top men.

The exclusion provided in Clause 5.1 is not likely in practice to apply very frequently in relation to the unseaworthiness of a ship, except in those instances where a shipowner or operator is loading goods for his own account. The exclusion does however place a heavy obligation upon the assured to ensure that the conveyances or containers into which the goods are loaded at the commencement of the transit are in a fit condition.

Clause 6 — War Exclusion Clause

6   In no case shall this insurance cover loss damage or expense caused by

    6.1   war civil war revolution rebellion insurrection, or civil strife arising therefrom, or any hostile act by or against a belligerent power

    6.2   capture seizure arrest restraint or detainment (piracy excepted), and the consequences thereof or any attempt threat

20. See the words of Lord Denning M.R. in *Compania Maritima San Basilio S.A.* v. *The Oceanus Mutual Underwriting Association* (*The "Eurysthenes"*) [1976] 2 Lloyd's Rep. 171.

6.3   derelict mines torpedoes bombs or other derelict weapons of war.

This War Exclusion Clause replaces the old Free of Capture and Seizure (F.C. & S.) Clause, the wording of which had become extremely convoluted owing to amendments having been made to it in the course of its history.

A commentary on the risks excluded by the clause appears in Part V of this book, where the various war risk covers are examined. However, two changes which were made in the 1/1/82 wording are particularly relevant to the cover afforded by the Institute Cargo Clauses (A):

"*Piracy*", by being excepted from the list of war exclusions, has been reinstated as a risk covered by Marine Underwriters when the (A) conditions apply. One definition of piracy, judicially approved,[21] is:

> "piracy is forcible robbery at sea, whether committed by marauders from outside the ship or by mariners or passengers within it. The essential element is that they violently dispossess the Master, and afterwards carry away the ship itself, or any of the goods, with a felonious intent."

Other old English law cases[22] have established that the term "pirates" includes passengers who mutiny and rioters who attack the ship from the shore (this being the partial definition contained in Rule for Construction of Policy No. 8 in Schedule 1 to the Marine Insurance Act).

In a more recent case, the judge considered the extent of force required to establish an act as piratical, and also the relevance of the place where the act was committed. He decided that the non-forcible entry of thieves on board a vessel moored in berth was not piracy, since the element of violence was absent, and the vessel was not "at sea".[23]

"*derelict mines torpedoes bombs or other derelict weapons of war*". Under previous editions of the Institute Clauses there was some doubt as to whether loss or damage caused by derelict weapons of war fell within Marine or War Risks.[24] Now the position has been clarified; such damage falls within the War Risks cover.

Clause 7 — Strikes Exclusion Clause

7   In no case shall this insurance cover loss damage or expense
   7.1   caused by strikers, locked-out workmen, or persons taking part in labour disturbances, riots or civil commotions

21. By Kennedy L.J. in *Republic of Bolivia* v. *Indemnity Mutual Marine Assurance Co.* (1909) 11 Asp.M.L.C. 218; 14 Com. Cas. 156.
22. See *Naylor* v. *Palmer* (1854) 10 Exch. 382 (mutiny of passengers) and *Nesbitt* v. *Lushington* (1792) 4 T.R. 783 (rioters from shore).
23. *Athens Maritime Enterprises Corporation* v. *Hellenic Mutual War Risks Association* (*The "Andreas Lemos"*) [1982] 2 Lloyd's Rep. 483, *per* Staughton J.
24. See *Costain-Blankevoort (U.K) Ltd.* v. *Davenport* (*The "Nassau Bay"*) [1979] 1 Lloyd's Rep. 395.

7.2 resulting from strikes, lock-outs, labour disturbances, riots or civil commotions

7.3 caused by any terrorist or any person acting from a political motive.

A fuller commentary is contained in the section of this book dealing with the Institute Strikes Clauses (see page 200).

However, it is worth noticing in this context that claims which arise from the activity of terrorists or persons acting from a political motive (which may well include agitators and hijackers) have been transferred from the Marine Risks cover to the Strike Risks cover.

DURATION

Clause 8 — Transit Clause

8   8.1   This insurance attaches from the time the goods leave the warehouse or place of storage at the place named herein for the commencement of the transit, continues during the ordinary course of transit and terminates either

8.1.1   on delivery to the Consignees' or other final warehouse or place of storage at the destination named herein,

8.1.2   on delivery to any other warehouse or place of storage, whether prior to or at the destination named herein, which the Assured elect to use either

8.1.2.1   for storage other than in the ordinary course of transit or

8.1.2.2   for allocation or distribution,
                or

8.1.3   on the expiry of 60 days after completion of discharge overside of the goods hereby insured from the oversea vessel at the final port of discharge,
            whichever shall first occur.

8.2   If, after discharge overside from the oversea vessel at the final port of discharge, but prior to termination of this insurance, the goods are to be forwarded to a destination other than that to which they are insured hereunder, this insurance, whilst remaining subject to termination as provided for above, shall not extend beyond the commencement of transit to such other destination.

8.3   This insurance shall remain in force (subject to termination as provided for above and to the provisions of Clause 9 below) during delay beyond the control of the Assured, any deviation, forced discharge, reshipment or transhipment and during any variation of the adventure arising from the exercise of a liberty granted to shipowners or charterers under the contract of affreightment.

This Clause 8 has to be read in close conjunction with Clauses 9 and 10 (q.v.) as all three of them have to do with the duration of the risk.

Clause 8 is in fact the old "Warehouse to Warehouse" clause, as it used to be called in previous editions of Institute Cargo Clauses. It defines the points at which the risk attaches and terminates, and adds (in Clause 8.3) comfortable words as to the circumstances in which it remains in force notwithstanding certain events beyond the control of the assured.

Clauses 9 and 10, however, are in effect exceptions, and they set out circumstances in which the assured must give notice to the underwriters if he wishes the cover to remain in force.

Commencement of the transit

"*. . . from the time the goods leave the warehouse . . .*" "leaving" involves physical movement of the goods with the intention to proceed on the transit. The mere loading into a lorry, which then remains on the premises, is not sufficient.

"*the place named herein for the commencement of the transit*". This may be anywhere in the interior, provided that the assured has accurately identified the place in his declaration, so that the same can be entered in the voyage description contained in the schedule to the MAR form.

Termination of the transit

Three possibilities are envisaged by the clause, and the insured transit will terminate as soon as any one of them occurs, even though the assured may intend to continue the transit notwithstanding such occurrence. Consequently, if an assured becomes aware that the insurance may terminate prematurely (so far as he is concerned), he must give notice to the underwriters and request a special extension of the risk. The events, any one of which will terminate the risk, are:

Delivery to the consignees' or other final warehouse or place of storage at the destination named in the policy. This is self-explanatory.

Delivery to a place of storage, which the assured intends to use "other than in the ordinary course of transit or for allocation or distribution". An example would be delivery to a customs warehouse where the goods remain for some period of time because the assured, not being in urgent need of the goods, elects to defer payment of the customs duty.

Expiry of 60 days after completion of discharge from the ocean vessel at the conclusion of the sea-leg of the transit. This 60 days is a limit, and at the same time an automatic cut-off. Even if the intended overland transit to ultimate destination cannot possibly be performed within 60 days, the insurance will terminate unless the assured has been able to negotiate special terms for its continuation.

Clause 8.2 sets out another circumstance when the insurance will terminate, which may be prior to any of the three termini provided in Clause 8.1. This is when, after having been discharged from the ocean steamer, the goods are "forwarded to a destination other than that to which they are insured hereunder". This clause is intended to deal with the situation of a resale to a customer of the assured, and to make it quite clear which insurance would be in force (that of the original assured or his customer), the clause provides for termination of the original insurance at the time when the new transit commences. Although this Clause 8.2 is widely worded, it is not intended to deal with the situation where the final destination is changed by the assured, say by reallocation of the goods to a different point of distribution. Such a circumstance is covered by Clause 10 (q.v.).

Clause 8.3 sets out the circumstances in which the underwriters are content to maintain the cover, notwithstanding that the listed circumstances add to the risks initially contemplated at the time the insurance was placed. Thus the insurance remains in force, without any obligation on the part of the assured to give notice to the underwriters, during delay beyond the assured's control, any deviation, forced discharge, reshipment or transhipment during the voyage and any permitted variation of the contract of carriage (but not its termination, which is dealt with in Clause 9). The circumstances envisaged would include, for example, the resort of the carrying vessel to a port of refuge to repair accidental damage to the ship, when those repairs were necessary for the safe prosecution of the voyage. In such a case, it might be necessary to discharge the cargo and store it ashore in order to effect the repairs to the ship. In such circumstances, the insurance would remain in force and continue to cover against "all risks", including those ashore.

Clause 9 — Termination of Contract of Carriage Clause

9   If owing to circumstances beyond the control of the Assured either the contract of carriage is terminated at a port or place other than the destination named therein or the transit is otherwise terminated before delivery of the goods as provided for in Clause 8 above, then this insurance shall also terminate *unless prompt notice is given to the Underwriters and continuation of cover is requested when the insurance shall remain in force, subject to an additional premium if required by the Underwriters,* either

    9.1   until the goods are sold and delivered at such port or place, or, unless otherwise specially agreed, until the expiry of 60 days after arrival of the goods hereby insured at such port or place, whichever shall first occur,

        or

    9.2   if the goods are forwarded within the said period of 60 days (or any agreed extension thereof) to the destination named herein or to any other destination, until terminated in accordance with the provisions of Clause 8 above.

This Clause 9 sets out one of the circumstances in which underwriters will require prompt notice to be given by the assured with a request for continuation of the cover, in order to maintain the insurance, subject to any additional premium that may be required. There are some small changes in the wording from that which applied in the previous edition of Institute Cargo Clauses, but the effect is the same. The clause contemplates either that the voyage is abandoned (with or without good cause) by the shipowner or other carrier, or that the adventure is frustrated, as for example occurred when ships were "locked in" the Suez Canal owing to its closure. However, the continuation of cover granted by the clause is fairly severely limited; it will end either when the goods are sold and delivered at the port or place where the transit has terminated, or on the expiry of 60 days if the goods have not been sold within that time, or, if the goods are forwarded within 60 days or any agreed extension of time, until delivery at either the original destination or a destination subsequently agreed to.

Clause 10 — Change of Voyage Clause

10 Where, after attachment of this insurance, the destination is changed by the Assured, *held covered at a premium and on conditions to be arranged subject to prompt notice being given to the Underwriters.*

This clause is a good deal more restricted than its predecessor in the 1/1/63 edition of Institute Cargo Clauses. In that edition it read:

"held covered at a premium to be arranged in case of change of voyage or of any omission or error in the description of the interest vessel or voyage".

What is a change of voyage? Section 45 of the Marine Insurance Act provides:

"(1) Where, after the commencement of the risk, the destination of the ship is voluntarily changed from the destination contemplated by the policy, there is said to be a change of voyage.

(2) Unless the policy otherwise provides, where there is a change of voyage, the insurer is discharged from liability as from the time of the change, that is to say, as from the time when the determination to change it is manifested, and it is immaterial that the ship may not in fact have left the course of the voyage contemplated by the policy when the loss occurs."

Since it is the shipowner or carrier who is most likely to order the carrying ship to sail to a different port, an innocent assured will be totally unable to influence the course of the voyage, and if it should be changed he may stand in even greater need of his insurance cover.

As we have seen, Clause 8.3 provides for continuation of the cover during any deviation of the ship (which is not the same thing as a "change of voyage"), and also during any "variation of the adventure" which the shipowners or charterers are permitted to undertake under the contract of affreightment. This Clause 10 appears only to apply when the destination is changed by the assured. It therefore appears to the authors that by oversight or deliberately, there is now no provision in the Institute Cargo Clauses to hold the assured covered in the event of an illegal change of voyage by a shipowner or other carrier. It is submitted that if these circumstances should occur, an assured should none the less give notice to his underwriters, arguing that it would be equitable for them to hold him covered on the grounds that such a change of voyage by the shipowner or charterer was an event, like a deviation or even a termination of the contract of carriage, entirely beyond his control.

Another restriction in this clause is the absence of the agreement previously granted by underwriters to hold the assured covered if there was any omission or error in the description of the interest (i.e., the subject-matter insured), the name of the vessel or the voyage. In a recent case under the 1/1/63 clauses, it was held that this concession by the underwriters could only be granted to an innocent assured, and was certainly not available to an assured who had wilfully misdescribed the goods.[25] Now that the concession has been withdrawn in the 1/1/82 clauses, an assured and his broker have to be even more careful to describe accurately the subject-matter to be insured.

CLAIMS

Clause 11 — Insurable Interest Clause

11   **11.1** In order to recover under this insurance the Assured must have an insurable interest in the subject-matter insured at the time of the loss.

11.2 Subject to 11.1 above, the Assured shall be entitled to recover for insured loss occurring during the period covered by this insurance, notwithstanding that the loss occurred before the contract of insurance was concluded, unless the Assured were aware of the loss and the Underwriters were not.

This clause closely follows section 6 of the Marine Insurance Act, which states:

"(1) the assured must be interested in the subject-matter insured at the time of the loss though he need not be interested when the insurance is effected:

Provided that where the subject-matter is insured 'lost or not lost', the Assured may recover although he may not have acquired his interest until after the loss, unless at the time of effecting the contract of insurance the Assured was aware of the loss, and the insurer was not.

(2) Where the Assured has no interest at the time of the loss, he cannot acquire interest by any act or election after he is aware of the loss."

The leading case in English law is *Anderson* v. *Morice*.[26] This case concerned a cargo of rice which the plaintiff had contracted to buy on terms under which the property did not pass to him until the whole cargo had been shipped. When about three-quarters of the rice had been loaded the ship sprang a leak and sank. The House of Lords held that as the property in the rice which was lost had not passed to the plaintiff at the time of the loss, he had no insurable interest. Furthermore, he did not obtain an insurable interest by agreeing after the loss had occurred to pay the seller for the part quantity which had been shipped.

Clause 11.2 reproduces the meaning of the words "lost or not lost" which appeared in Lloyd's S.G. form. The positive statement contained in this clause, which follows closely the wording of the proviso to section 6(1) of the Act, makes the old phraseology unnecessary.

25. *Liberian Insurance Agency Inc.* v. *Mosse* [1977] 1 Lloyd's Rep. 560.
26. *Anderson* v. *Morice* (1876) 3 Asp.M.L.C. 290.

Clause 12 — Forwarding Charges Clause

12 Where, as a result of the operation of a risk covered by this insurance, the insured transit is terminated at a port or place other than that to which the subject-matter is covered under this insurance, the Underwriters will reimburse the Assured for any extra charges properly and reasonably incurred in unloading storing and forwarding the subject-matter to the destination to which it is insured hereunder.
This Clause 12, which does not apply to general average or salvage charges, shall be subject to the exclusions contained in Clauses 4, 5, 6 and 7 above, and shall not include charges arising from the fault negligence insolvency or financial default of the Assured or their servants.

This clause recognises, as also does Clause 13, an important principle which has been expounded in a number of English law cases, namely, that what is insured is not merely the physical property of the goods, but also the voyage to which they are committed. In order to consider whether Clause 12 adds anything to the traditional cover, we should examine the circumstances in which underwriters would be liable to pay for forwarding charges on an insurance effected on Lloyd's S.G. form without any additional clauses attached:

1. If by the operation of an insured peril the voyage (what is now called the "insured transit") is terminated short of destination and the cost of recovering the goods, reconditioning them if necessary and forwarding them to destination would exceed their value on arrival, there is a constructive total loss. This proposition follows from the leading case of *Rosetto* v. *Gurney*,[27] and was put into statutory form in section 60(2)(iii) of the Marine Insurance Act 1906. This now appears as part of Clause 13 (Constructive Total Loss Clause).

2. If owing to the operation of an insured peril the insured transit is terminated short of destination and it is impossible or impracticable to forward the goods to destination, there is likewise a constructive total loss of the goods even though they are in sound condition.

This follows from the leading case of *Rodocanochi* v. *Elliot*,[28] in which cases of silk in transit from Shanghai to London were caught up in the Siege of Paris during the Franco-Prussian War of 1870. Even though the goods were undamaged and were non-perishable, it was held that the Restraint of Princes (in those days an included peril) was such as to destroy the object of the adventure and therefore the object of the insurance.

Another example would be goods which remain quite undamaged on board a ship which has stranded in a position from which salvage is impossible, either of the ship or the cargo still in her holds.

3. If by operation of an insured peril the voyage is terminated short of destination and it is possible to forward the goods to destination at an expense less than their value on arrival, there can be no total loss and any claim upon the policy can only be of a partial loss nature. The area of

27. *Rosetto* v. *Gurney* (1851) 11 C.B. 176.
28. *Rodocanochi* v. *Elliot* (1874) 2 Asp.M.L.C. 399.

protection afforded in these circumstances under the Suing and Labouring Clause was considered in three leading cases: *Great Indian Peninsular Railway* v. *Saunders*,[29] *Booth* v. *Gair*[30] and *Kidston* v. *Empire Marine Insurance Co.*[31] In all three cases the subject-matter was insured free of particular average and the decisions read together establish that the cost of forwarding cargo to destination will be recoverable under the clause only if incurred in order to avoid a risk of total loss.

4. If however the policy covered particular average in excess of a specified percentage, the cost of forwarding the cargo to destination after the abandonment of the voyage on account of insured perils will be recoverable under the Suing and Labouring Clause if the loss averted (measured by the loss on sale at the intermediate port) would have amounted to the specified percentage.

The origin of the Forwarding Charges Clause

In order therefore to encourage assureds to take steps to minimise their loss, underwriters came to insert a forwarding clause in F.P.A. policies on goods by which they agreed: "Also to pay Special Charges for landing warehousing and forwarding if incurred at an intermediate port of call or refuge, for which underwriters would be liable under the standard form of English marine policy with the Institute Cargo Clauses (W.A.) attached."

By this wording underwriters granted cover which was additional to their liability under the Suing and Labouring Clauses to respond for Special Charges which averted a total loss. However, such a clause would have no effect and indeed would not be necessary under a policy of insurance which paid particular average irrespective of percentage.

Clause 12 in the (A) Clauses would therefore seem to be largely declaratory, and its chief virtue may be in drawing attention to the fact that in the event of the voyage being abandoned by the carrier, it is the duty of the assured as well as being in his own interest to forward the goods to destination if possible.

Clause 13 — Constructive Total Loss Clause

13   No claim for Constructive Total Loss shall be recoverable hereunder unless the subject-matter insured is reasonably abandoned either on account of its actual total loss appearing to be unavoidable or because the cost of recovering, reconditioning and forwarding the subject-matter to the destination to which it is insured would exceed its value on arrival.

29. *G.I.P. Rly.* v. *Saunders* (1861) 2 B. & S. 266.
30. *Booth* v. *Gair* (1863) 33 L.J.C.P. 99.
31. *Kidston* v. *Empire Marine* (1866) L.R. 1 C.P. 535.

The clause closely follows English law as set out in section 60 of the Marine Insurance Act in that it provides that the subject-matter insured must be "reasonably abandoned" by reason of the circumstances specified in order to found a claim for a Constructive Total Loss. The circumstances specified are however more restrictively described than they are in the Act.

"Abandoned"

The word "abandoned", as used in the Act, "denotes the voluntary cession by the assured to the insurer of whatever remains of the subject-matter insured, together with all proprietary rights and remedies in respect thereof".[32] It is submitted that it has the same meaning in Clause 12.

Section 62 of the Marine Insurance Act provides that "where the assured elects to abandon the subject-matter insured to the insurer he must give notice of abandonment. If he fails to do so the loss can only be treated as a partial loss." While this requirement technically applies to any claim for a Constructive Total Loss under these clauses (because of Clause 19 — the English Law and Practice Clause), it is submitted that there is a class of case, applicable only to policies of insurance on goods, when claims are settled as for a Constructive Total Loss, either without the necessity of notice of abandonment, or when the presentation of the claim constitutes such notice. This is the class of case known as a "salvage loss", when goods are sold or otherwise disposed of at a port or place short of destination, either because they are deteriorating to the extent that they would be worthless on arrival at destination, or because the cost of getting them to destination would exceed their value on arrival. Such claims are in practice settled on the basis of the insured value less the proceeds of sale.

The circumstances giving rise to a claim for Constructive Total Loss

By Clause 13 these circumstances are either:

> "on account of its actual total loss appearing to be unavoidable".

An example would be the deterioration, by perils insured against, of a perishable commodity such that, by the time it was brought to market, it would either have no value or would cease to be a "thing of the kind insured". When such a commodity ceases to be merchantable as a thing of the kind originally insured, it is said to have lost its species, and in those circumstances it has been held that there is an actual total loss of the goods. Or

> "because the cost of recovering, reconditioning and forwarding the subject-matter to the destination to which it is insured would exceed its value on arrival".

32. Chalmers' *Marine Insurance Act*, 9th edn., p. 95.

This is a purely objective test which would strictly speaking have to be proved by figures showing that the estimated costs involved would be greater than what the goods were worth at their destination.

"*value on arrival*" also involves an estimation of what the goods would sell for in whatever condition they would be in on arrival at destination.

An additional circumstance (not mentioned in Clause 13) which may also found a claim for a Constructive Total Loss, is set out in section 60(2)(i) of the Marine Insurance Act: "where the assured is deprived of the possession of his ship or goods by a peril insured against, and (a) it is unlikely that he can recover the ship or goods ..., or (b) the cost of recovering the ship or goods would exceed their value when recovered". While it is conceded that there may not be many cases in which these circumstances would apply (except under a War or Strikes Risks cover), the omission is regrettable. After' all, conversion or other tortious detention of the goods by a third party is one of the perils which are protected by an insurance against "All Risks".

Clause 14 — Increased Value Clause

14 14.1 If any Increased Value insurance is effected by the Assured on the cargo insured herein the agreed value of the cargo shall be deemed to be increased to the total amount insured under this insurance and all Increased Value insurances covering the loss, and liability under this insurance shall be in such proportion as the sum insured herein bears to such total amount insured.

In the event of claim the Assured shall provide the Underwriters with evidence of the amounts insured under all other insurances.

14.2 **Where this insurance is on Increased Value the following clause shall apply:**
The agreed value of the cargo shall be deemed to be equal to the total amount insured under the primary insurance and all Increased Value insurances covering the loss and effected on the cargo by the Assured, and liability under this insurance shall be in such proportion as the sum insured herein bears to such total amount insured.

In the event of claim the Assured shall provide the Underwriters with evidence of the amounts insured under all other insurances.

This clause did not appear in the 1/1/63 version of the Institute Cargo Clauses. While it appears to make good common sense, the real object of the clause is not to provide any additional advantage to the assured, but to regulate the position *inter se* between original and increased value underwriters, and to negate the unfortunate effect, under English law, of the judgment in the case of *Boag* v. *Standard Marine Insurance Co. Ltd.*[33] In that case the original underwriters had insured only part of the real value of the cargo, the balance being insured with Increased Value underwriters. During the voyage the shipment was jettisoned for the common safety, and the general average adjustment showed the whole amount to be made good in general average, less the contribution attaching to it. This calculation reduced the net credit balance to less than the amount insured by the original underwriters, and the court held that they were entitled to all of it. The intention of the draftsman is to ensure that all claims are divided *pro rata* over original

33. *Boag* v. *Standard Marine Insurance Co. Ltd.* (1937) 57 Ll.L.Rep. 83.

and Increased Value underwriters, and that all recoveries shall be dealt with likewise.

Clause 15 — Not to Inure Clause

15   This insurance shall not inure to the benefit of the carrier or other bailee.

This clause has been standard in Marine Cargo Insurance for many years. The object of the clause is to prevent a carrier or other bailee contracting out of his liability by inserting a clause in the contract of affreightment, or other agreement, claiming the benefit of insurance.

MINIMISING LOSSES

Clause 16 — Duty of Assured Clause

16   It is the duty of the Assured and their servants and agents in respect of loss recoverable hereunder

16.1   to take such measures as may be reasonable for the purpose of averting or minimising such loss, and

16.2   to ensure that all rights against carriers, bailees or other third parties are properly preserved and exercised

and the Underwriters will, in addition to any loss recoverable hereunder, reimburse the Assured for any charges properly and reasonably incurred in pursuance of these duties.

This clause seeks to amalgamate the wording of the "Bailee Clause" in previous editions of Institute Cargo Clauses with the time-honoured provisions of the Suing and Labouring Clause which appeared in Lloyd's S.G. form.

The words of the old Suing and Labouring Clause — once described by an enthusiast as "sheer poetry" — were:

> "And in case of any loss or misfortune it shall be lawful to the Assured, their factors, servants and assigns, to sue, labour, and travel for, in and about the defence, safeguards, and recovery of the said goods and merchandises, and ship, &c., or any part thereof, without prejudice to this insurance; to the charges whereof we, the assurers, will contribute each one according to the rate and quantity of his sum herein assured."

"Sue", incidentally, did not mean "commence legal proceedings"; neither did "travel" mean to go on a journey: it was in fact a transliteration of "travail".

There is authority[34] for the proposition that when an insurance policy spells out the obligations of the assured to avert or minimise any loss which would otherwise fall upon the underwriters, it is implicit that the underwriters will be bound to reimburse the assured for the expense he has incurred. It will, of course, not be necessary to rely upon any such implied bargain

34. *Emperor Goldmining Co. Ltd.* v. *Switzerland General Ins. Co.* [1964] 1 Lloyd's Rep. 348 (Sup.Ct. NSW).

under the Institute Cargo Clauses, since the obligation of the underwriters to reimburse the assured for any such expenses incurred by the assured, their servants or agents, is made quite explicit. Indeed, the draftsman is to be congratulated for restating in modern English the effect of the archaic wording in the Suing and Labouring Clause, and at the same time giving verbal expression to the provisions of sections 78(1), (3), and (4) of the Marine Insurance Act. Given that the object was clarity of expression, it was necessary to draft the clause in such a way that its provisions could be read and acted upon without reference to section 78(1) of the Marine Insurance Act which is stated to apply "*where* the policy contains a Suing and Labouring Clause ..."; for the reason that although this Clause 16 reproduces the effect of the Suing and Labouring Clause, it is *not* the Suing and Labouring Clause.

"... the duty of the Assured and their servants and agents"

This expression is wider than appears at first sight. Under English law the master of a ship is invested with wide duties and responsibilities to take care of the goods entrusted to his charge. These duties derive in part under the law of bailment, since a shipowner who receives the goods for carriage is a bailee for reward and the master of the ship is the person responsible for exercising the duties of care which follow from that legal relationship. In some of the law cases dealing with this subject the master is said when exercising this authority to be acting as an "agent of necessity" for the owners of the property entrusted to his care.

In the event of a serious casualty, a shipowner may be responsible for the payment of substantial sums for the preservation and care of cargo, all of which (in the absence of his actionable fault) he will be entitled to recover as Special Charges on Cargo.[35]

"for the purpose of averting or minimising such loss"

This means a loss (or damage) for which the underwriters would respond under the policy, thus reproducing the effect of section 78(3) of the Marine Insurance Act, which states:

"expenses incurred for the purpose of averting or diminishing any loss not covered by the policy are not recoverable under the Suing and Labouring Clause".

A recent case[36] concerned the measures taken by an assured to recover their property (containers) from the premises of their lessees who had gone bankrupt. The insurance was against all risks of loss or damage to the

35. See N. G. Hudson: "Special Charges on Cargo" [1981] LMCLQ 315 (part 1) and 471 (part 2).

36. *Integrated Container Service Ltd.* v. *British Traders Insurance Co. Ltd.* [1981] 2 Lloyd's Rep. 460 and [1984] 1 Lloyd's Rep. 154.

subject-matter insured, but the underwriters argued that the expense incurred by the assured had not been undertaken with the object of averting or minimising losses for which the insurers would have responded. The court held that when the lessees ceased to trade they were no longer capable of taking care as bailees of the plaintiff's property; consequently the plaintiff's containers "were exposed to the risk of theft, misuse, enforcement of a lien — in other words to the risk of loss or damage from some cause or another". The court considered the extent of the measures taken by the assured to recover their containers, and the probability that in the absence of those measures, a loss would have occurred, and found in favour of the assured on both points. The assured were thus entitled to recover the payments which they had made in respect of customs and storage charges in order to secure the release of containers, the cost of their transhipment from where they lay to their own depots, the travelling expenses of those engaged in this operation and legal fees incurred in the same connection.

"rights against carriers, bailees and other third parties"

On payment of a loss underwriters are by section 79 of the Marine Insurance Act subrogated to all rights and remedies of the assured in respect of the loss so paid for. However, owing to the lapse of time that may occur between the happening of the loss and the claim being paid, it is essential that rights and remedies against third parties should be preserved. Sub-Clause 16.2 (previously called the Bailee Clause) places a duty upon the assured to preserve and exercise the rights to which underwriters have, or will become entitled by subrogation. Expenses reasonably incurred by the assured in pursuance of this duty will be met by the underwriters, and this is now spelled out in the clause, even though the underwriters' obligation to reimburse the assured for such expenses is implicit.[37]

Clause 17 — Waiver Clause

17 Measures taken by the Assured or the Underwriters with the object of saving, protecting or recovering the subject-matter insured shall not be considered as a waiver or acceptance of abandonment or otherwise prejudice the rights of either party.

This clause has commonly been inserted in marine insurance policies for many years. Its purpose is to preserve the position of both assured and

37. In *The Netherlands Insurance Co. Est. 1845* v. *Karl Ljunberg & Co.* (judgment delivered 23 April 1986 — not yet reported) the Judicial Committee of the Privy Council held that in the 1/1/63 edition of Institute Cargo Clauses a term must be implied in order to give business efficacy to the contract, that expenses incurred by an assured in performing his obligations under the second limb of the bailee clause shall be recoverable by him from the insurers in so far as they relate to the preservation or exercise of rights in respect of loss or damage for which the insurers are liable under the policy.

underwriter in the event of measures being taken to recover the property by either party after notice of abandonment has been given. Any steps taken by the assured "in saving, protecting or recovering the subject-matter insured" shall not constitute a waiver or withdrawal of the notice of abandonment which he has given; and similarly, the underwriters are free to take such steps without their being regarded as an acceptance of the abandonment which had been previously declined.

AVOIDANCE OF DELAY

Clause 18 — Reasonable Despatch Clause

18 It is a condition of this insurance that the Assured shall act with reasonable despatch in all circumstances within their control.

This clause is also of considerable antiquity and its purpose is self-evident.

LAW AND PRACTICE

Clause 19 — English Law and Practice Clause

19 This insurance is subject to English law and practice.

This clause is common to all the new Institute Clauses issued from 1/1/82 onwards, except those intended to be attached to American Forms. As will be appreciated from the commentary on some of the more important clauses in this and other forms, the fact that these forms have to stand by themselves, instead of being attached to Lloyd's S.G. form of policy, means that, in several important particulars, the benefit of the interpretation pronounced in the U.K. Marine Insurance Act 1906 would be lost, if nothing was inserted in the new forms to preserve it. Hence the necessary rewording of many of the clauses to incorporate the more important provisions of the Marine Insurance Act; and hence, likewise, the reference to English law and practice in order to incorporate as much as possible of the body of jurisprudence which has been built up over many centuries.

That is the end of the numbered clauses. There then appears:

NOTE:— It is necessary for the Assured when they become aware of an event which is "held covered" under this insurance to give prompt notice to the Underwriters and the right to such cover is dependent upon compliance with this obligation.

This note appears at the foot of all Institute Clauses covering goods. It is not only sound advice: it also states the existing law, since it is an implied term of any contract of marine insurance that the assured will be unable to invoke a "held covered" provision unless within a reasonable time after knowing of the event he has given notice to the underwriter. As Scrutton L.J. said in *Hood* v. *West End Motor Car Parking Co.*[38]: "There is a tendency on the part of the assured to wait in order to see what may turn up, and he often omits to pay the extra premium until a loss has actually occurred. It is to meet that tendency that this implied term is introduced into the contract."

3. INSTITUTE CARGO CLAUSES (B) and (C) — The restricted perils forms (1/1/82)

These are the new forms for restricted conditions which were issued at the same time as Institute Cargo Clauses (A) on 1/1/82. They may be said to replace the previous W.A. and F.P.A. Clauses, but with certain important differences. The W.A. and F.P.A. Clauses insured against the traditional risks enumerated in Lloyd's S.G. form (with some extensions set out in the Average Clause and F.P.A. Clause, respectively), but the quantum of recovery varied.[39] Under the (B) and (C) Clauses the restrictions apply to the list of the perils insured against, but in the event of loss or damage by one of the named perils the underwriters will pay any claim, however small it may be.

RISKS COVERED

The risks covered are set out in Clauses 1, 2 and 3.

Clause 1 — Risks Clause

1   This insurance covers, except as provided in Clauses 4, 5, 6 and 7 below,
  1.1   loss of or damage to the subject-matter insured reasonably attributable to
    1.1.1   fire or explosion

"fire"

The expression "fire" includes damage by heat through proximity to something which is on fire, but it does not include deterioration due to the chemical changes involved in the heating up of some commodity by natural causes nor spontaneous combustion, both of which are excluded by Clause 4.4 as being caused by inherent vice or nature of the subject matter insured. Loss or damage reasonably attributable to fire also comprehends damage caused

38. *Hood* v. *West End Motor Car Parking Co.* (1917) 23 Com.Cas. 112, following *Thames & Mersey Marine Insurance Co.* v. *Van Laun*, a case heard by the House of Lords in 1905, but not reported until *Hood's* case.
39. See Section 1, Historical Perspective, on p. 8.

by the act of extinguishing fire or reasonably taken in order to avoid the spread of fire — see *Symington* v. *Union Insurance Society of Canton*,[40] and in acts taken in anticipation of and to prevent the outbreak of fire — see *The "Knight of St. Michael"*.[41]

"Explosion"

In the recent case of *Commonwealth Smelting Ltd.* v. *Guardian Royal Exchange Assurance*[42] the judge concluded that the word "explosion" in a policy of insurance denoted "an event that is violent, noisy and caused by a very rapid chemical or nuclear reaction, or the bursting out of gas or vapour under pressure". In that case it was held that the violent disintegration of a moving part revolving at high speed, causing fragments to fly outwards under considerable force and with a lot of noise, was not an explosion; it was centrifugal disintegration.

1.1.2 vessel or craft being stranded grounded sunk or capsized

These words are slightly wider than the corresponding words in the Average and F.P.A. Clauses. The addition of the word "grounded" makes it unnecessary to consider the limitations which were applied in a long series of law cases to the word "stranded" when it appeared alone in the Memorandum. "Stranded or grounded", read together, comprise any fortuitous taking of the ground by the carrying vessel or craft, for however short a period of time. It is also submitted that an intentional taking of the ground, for example in a mud berth where it is customary for ships to lie aground at low tide, will also be covered, if in consequence the insured goods sustain damage, since it is the causation of damage which constitutes the fortuity in what would otherwise have been a normal and uneventful situation.

The addition of the word "capsized" is new. It is submitted that the effect of its inclusion in the list of risks covered will mean that such a loss as took place in the case of *The "Stranna"*,[43] when goods fell into the sea as a result of the carrying ship taking a totally unexplained list whilst in port, will be settled by the underwriters.

1.1.3 overturning or derailment of land conveyance

This is an entirely new risk, which has not featured previously in any standard forms of policy covering restricted conditions. It is therefore to be expected that underwriters and claims practitioners will interpret both these words in their ordinary, everyday sense, without resorting to niceties of

40. *Symington* v. *Union Insurance Society of Canton* (1928) 34 Com.Cas. 23.
41. *The "Knight of St. Michael"* (1888) 8 Asp.M.L.C. 360.
42. *Commonwealth Smelting Ltd.* v. *Guardian Royal Exchange Assurance* [1984] 22 Lloyd's Rep. 608.
43. *The "Stranna"* [1938] P. 69.

interpretation. It is however the opinion of the authors that by use of the words "reasonably attributable to" in the preamble, the extent of loss or damage consequential upon these events should be afforded a reasonably wide construction. For example, if in consequence of derailment, the goods in the railway wagon have to be hurriedly unloaded and dumped by the side of the railway track in order to enable the wagon to be lifted back on to the rails, loss or damage caused by this operation should be responded for by the underwriters as well as the damage caused by the direct shock of the derailment.

1.1.4   collision or contact of vessel craft or conveyance with any external object other than water

The contact must be with something external to the carrying vessel, craft or conveyance. Hence if goods fall to the quay or the ship's deck whilst slung from the ship's derrick, because the derrick boom hits a gantry on the quay, the consequent loss or damage will be recoverable under this section, but not if the derrick boom hits a part of the ship's superstructure. In that event, a total loss of an individual package will be recoverable as having been dropped whilst loading or unloading within section 1.3 in the (B) Clauses, but if the assured has opted for the (C) Clauses, he will recover nothing.

Under the old Average Clause, the expression used was "any external substance (ice included) other than water", but it is suggested that this does not imply any change in meaning. The authors submit that contact with an iceberg or ice-floe is within the meaning of "any external object".

Collisions and contacts by vehicles on the land are included.

"Conveyance" in this section (and also in section 1.2.3) comprehends any type of vehicle customarily used during the insured transit including, for example, a hovercraft or an amphibious vehicle.

1.1.5   discharge of cargo at a port of distress,

This is a relatively minor area of risk, since in practically every case where cargo is discharged at a port of refuge the cost of discharging the cargo is admissible in general average by virtue of Rule X(b) of the York/Antwerp Rules 1974 and when that is the case any damage or loss of cargo caused in the process of discharging is likewise admitted under Rule XII. However in a small minority of instances the discharge of cargo at a port of refuge may be for a purpose unconnected with general average; for example for the purpose of examining the goods themselves for suspected damage or after the shipowner had validly abandoned the voyage, and in these circumstances it is reasonable that the assured should be similarly covered.

1.1.6   earthquake volcanic eruption or lightning,

These risks appear in the (B) Clauses but not in the (C) Clauses. They are a welcome addition to the cover.

1.2 loss or damage to the subject-matter insured caused by
1.2.1 general average sacrifice

This is merely declaratory. Any insurance subject to English law and practice (see Clause 19) will pay for general average, and in accordance with section 66(4) of the Marine Insurance Act 1906 an underwriter on property is liable to pay the whole of any general average loss without his assured having exercised his right to call for a general average contribution from other parties. Having paid the general average sacrifice in full, underwriters are then entitled under the doctrine of subrogation to require their assured to procure an adjustment of general average in order that he should be paid the contributions due from the other parties to the adventure. Under English law an owner of cargo sacrificed has the right to compel the shipowner to have the general average adjusted — see *Crooks* v. *Allan*.[44] Similar rights exist in most maritime countries, but it may well be that the English law and practice clause will similarly extend underwriters' subrogative rights when the policy is written outside the United Kingdom.

The next clause appears in different forms in the (B) and (C) Clauses.

In the (B) form it reads:

1.2.2 jettison or washing overboard

In the (C) form it reads:

1.2.2 jettison.

Jettison is a peril specifically covered under the old Lloyd's S.G. form of policy. It means the lawful throwing overboard of goods whether in circumstances which make it general average or not. This could extend, for example, to the deliberate dumping overside of packages condemned as hazardous by a local authority, unless (by exclusion 4.1) the assured was guilty of wilful misconduct in shipping them. The deliberate damage exclusion (4.7) would not apply in such a case, since the throwing overboard would be entirely lawful. Washing overboard is a species of loss by sea peril and was covered under the W.A. and F.P.A. Clauses subject to the average warranty.

1.2.3 entry of sea lake or river water into vessel craft hold conveyance container liftvan or place of storage,

This appears in the (B) Clauses only. Most of the risk covered here was also covered, subject to average, as sea peril under the old clauses but the risk now clearly extends beyond the ocean transit. Suppose that during the overland leg of the transit a lorry driver loses his way and drives his lorry containing the insured goods into the middle of a river; underwriters will be liable for the damage due to their immersion.

The entry of sea water into the hold of a ship may also cause damage to

44. *Crooks* v. *Allan* (1880) 4 Asp.M.L.C. 216.

one commodity, for example hides, which, becoming putrid, cause further damage to adjoining goods affected by taint or contagion. Under the authority of *Montoya* v. *London Assurance*,[45] the assured can recover the damage by taint.

> **1.3**   total loss of any package lost overboard or dropped whilst loading on to, or unloading from, vessel or craft.

This appears in the (B) Clauses only. As it was in both the W.A. and F.P.A. Clauses, its exclusion from the (C) Clauses has to be recognised as a positive diminution of the cover.

Clause 2 — General Average Clause

> **2**   This insurance covers general average and salvage charges, adjusted or determined according to the contract of affreightment and/or the governing law and practice, incurred to avoid or in connection with the avoidance of loss from any cause except those excluded in Clauses 4, 5, 6 and 7 or elsewhere in this insurance.

The reference to the avoidance of loss from any cause except those specifically excluded in the insurance, which is merely declaratory under the (A) Clauses in view of section 66(6) of the Marine Insurance Act 1906, is necessary when the insurance is on restricted conditions, since otherwise general average contribution payable by the insured cargo would only be recoverable if the general average act were undertaken to avoid one of the limited named perils.

Take two packages, both insured with the (C) Clauses, being carried by a small schooner which is blown by a gale out of her course into waters infested with marauding pirates. One of the packages (the heavy one) is thrown overboard to lighten the schooner to enable her to escape from a pirate crew. This is a general average sacrifice. As such, and also as jettison, it is payable by the underwriters under the (C) Clauses. Piracy — the peril avoided — is not however covered; yet it is surely reasonable that the underwriters on the package saved should reimburse their assured for the general average contribution he has to pay towards the loss of the package jettisoned. And so they will, because the general average clause provides that the loss avoided shall be from any cause except those specifically excluded, and piracy — although not covered — is not specifically excluded.

Clause 3 — "Both to Blame Collision" Clause

> **3**   This insurance is extended to indemnify the Assured against such proportion of liability under the contract of affreightment "Both to Blame Collision" Clause as is in respect of a loss recoverable hereunder. In the event of any claim by shipowners under the said Clause the Assured agree to notify the Under-

---

45. *Montoya* v. *London Assurance* (1851) 6 Exch. 451.

writers who shall have the right, at their own cost and expense, to defend the Assured against such
claim.

The same as in the (A) Clauses — see commentary on page 16.

EXCLUSIONS

The exclusions are contained in Clauses 4, 5, 6 and 7

Clause 4 — General Exclusions Clause

4   In no case shall this insurance cover

    4.1 loss damage or expense attributable to wilful misconduct of the Assured

    4.2 ordinary leakage, ordinary loss in weight or volume, or ordinary wear and tear of the subject-matter insured

    4.3 loss damage or expense caused by insufficiency or unsuitability of packing or preparation of the subject-matter insured (for the purpose of this Clause 4.3 "packing" shall be deemed to include stowage in a container or liftvan but only when such stowage is carried out prior to attachment of this insurance or by the Assured or their servants)

    4.4 loss damage or expense caused by inherent vice or nature of the subject-matter insured

    4.5 loss damage or expense proximately caused by delay, even though the delay be caused by a risk insured against (except expenses payable under Clause 2 above)

    4.6 loss damage or expense arising from insolvency or financial default of the owners managers charterers or operators of the vessel

    4.7 deliberate damage to or deliberate destruction of the subject-matter insured or any part thereof by the wrongful act of any person or persons

    4.8 loss damage or expense arising from the use of any weapon of war employing atomic or nuclear fission and/or fusion or other like reaction or radioactive force or matter

All these exclusions, other than that contained in Clause 4.7, are the same as
in the (A) Clauses — see commentary on pages 17–20.

On the other hand Clause 4.7, which does not appear in the (A) Clauses,
is of some importance in the (B) and (C) Clauses. It excludes deliberate
damage or deliberate destruction of the subject-matter insured by the wrongful act of any person. By this wording certain acts of man are excluded
which would, under the traditional wording of Lloyd's S.G. form, have
founded a legitimate claim; for example:

(a) barratry of the Master and crew, that is to say wrongful acts in prejudice of their employment and/or in breach of their duties,

(b) arson, or sabotage causing the ship to sink,

(c) scuttling of the carrying ship or craft by its owner in fraud of his
insurers, and

(d) a jettison of the goods without reasonable cause.

However, this cover can be reinstated and extended, on payment of an
additional premium, by attachment of a separate clause to the policy. This is
the Institute Malicious Damage Clause (see page 79). It is, of course, not
necessary when the goods are insured with the Institute Cargo Clauses (A).

Clause 5 — Unseaworthiness and Unfitness Exclusion Clause

5   5.1   In no case shall this insurance cover loss damage or expense arising from
   unseaworthiness of vessel or craft,
   unfitness of vessel craft conveyance container or liftvan for the safe carriage of the subject-matter insured,
   where the Assured or their servants are privy to such unseaworthiness or unfitness, at the time the subject-matter insured is loaded therein.

   5.2   The Underwriters waive any breach of the implied warranties of seaworthiness of the ship and fitness of the ship to carry the subject-matter insured to destination, unless the Assured or their servants are privy to such unseaworthiness or unfitness.

The wording of the clause and its effect is the same as in the Institute Cargo Clauses (A). See commentary on pages 20–21.

Clause 6 — War Exclusion Clause

6   In no case shall this insurance cover loss damage or expense caused by

   6.1   war civil war revolution rebellion insurrection, or civil strife arising therefrom, or any hostile act by or against a belligerent power

   6.2   capture seizure arrest restraint or detainment, and the consequences thereof or any attempt thereat

   6.3   derelict mines torpedoes bombs or other derelict weapons of war.

The wording is similar to the War Exclusion Clause in the (A) Clauses, with one important exception. This is that whereas in the (A) Clauses the risk of piracy is excepted from the list of war perils — "capture seizure arrest restraint or detainment" — listed in Clause 6.2, piracy is not so excepted under the (B) and (C) Clauses. The effect is that the merchant is protected against a loss by piracy if insured with the (A) Clauses, but he does not have this protection in the (B) or (C) Clauses. Moreover, since piracy is not included as one of the perils covered by the Institute War Clauses (Cargo) — see page 188 — a merchant who opts for the (B) or (C) Clauses for marine perils plus the standard Clauses for War Risks will, perhaps to his astonishment, find himself unprotected against the risk of piracy.

Clause 7 — Strikes Exclusion Clause

7   In no case shall this insurance cover loss damage or expense

   7.1   caused by strikers, locked-out workmen, or persons taking part in labour disturbances, riots or civil commotions

   7.2   resulting from strikes, lock-outs, labour disturbances, riots or civil commotions

   7.3   caused by any terrorist or any person acting from a political motive.

This is the same as in the Institute Cargo Clauses (A). See commentary on page 22.

CLAUSES RELATING TO THE DURATION OF THE RISK

Clause 8 — Transit Clause

8 **8.1** This insurance attaches from the time the goods leave the warehouse or place of storage at the place named herein for the commencement of the transit, continues during the ordinary course of transit and terminates either

8.1.1 on delivery to the Consignees' or other final warehouse or place of storage at the destination named herein,

8.1.2 on delivery to any other warehouse or place of storage, whether prior to or at the destination named herein, which the Assured elect to use either

8.1.2.1 for storage other than in the ordinary course of transit or

8.1.2.2 for allocation or distribution,

or

8.1.3 on the expiry of 60 days after completion of discharge overside of the goods hereby insured from the oversea vessel at the final port of discharge,

whichever shall first occur.

Clause 9 — Termination of Contract of Carriage Clause

9 If owing to circumstances beyond the control of the Assured either the contract of carriage is terminated at a port or place other than the destination named therein or the transit is otherwise terminated before delivery of the goods as provided for in Clause 8 above, then this insurance shall also terminate *unless prompt notice is given to the Underwriters and continuation of cover is requested when the insurance shall remain in force, subject to an additional premium if required by the Underwriters*, either

9.1 until the goods are sold and delivered at such port or place, or, unless otherwise specially agreed, until the expiry of 60 days after arrival of the goods hereby insured at such port or place, whichever shall first occur,

or

9.2 if the goods are forwarded within the said period of 60 days (or any agreed extension thereof) to the destination named herein or to any other destination, until terminated in accordance with the provisions of Clause 8 above.

Clause 10 — Change of Voyage Clause

10 Where, after attachment of this insurance, the destination is changed by the Assured, *held covered at a premium and on conditions to be arranged subject to prompt notice being given to the Underwriters.*

These Clauses 8, 9 and 10 are all the same as in the Institute Cargo Clauses (A). See commentary on pages 23–27.

CLAIMS

Clause 11 — Insurable Interest Clause

11 **11.1** In order to recover under this insurance the Assured must have an insurable interest in the subject-matter insured at the time of the loss.

11.2 Subject to 11.1 above, the Assured shall be entitled to recover for insured loss occurring during the period covered by this insurance, notwithstanding that the loss occurred before the contract of insurance was concluded, unless the Assured were aware of the loss and the Underwriters were not.

This is the same as in the Institute Cargo Clauses (A). See commentary on page 27.

Clause 12 — Forwarding Charges Clause

12 Where, as a result of the operation of a risk covered by this insurance, the insured transit is terminated at a port or place other than that to which the subject-matter is covered under this insurance, the Underwriters will reimburse the Assured for any extra charges properly and reasonably incurred in unloading storing and forwarding the subject-matter to the destination to which it is insured hereunder.
This Clause 12, which does not apply to general average or salvage charges, shall be subject to the exclusions contained in Clauses 4, 5, 6 and 7 above, and shall not include charges arising from the fault negligence insolvency or financial default of the Assured or their servants.

Whilst the wording of this clause is precisely the same as in the Institute Cargo Clauses (A), the effect of it is much more limited, by reason of the words "as a result of the operation of a risk covered by this insurance". As the Institute Cargo Clauses (A) cover All Risks, all the events which are likely to bring to an end the insured transit at an intermediate port or place are covered, except for some event arising from insolvency or financial default of the owners, managers, charterers or operators of the vessel (exclusion 4.6) or unseaworthiness of the vessel, to which the assured or their servants are privy at the time of loading the cargo (exclusion 5.1).

Under the Institute Cargo Clauses (B) and (C), however, the risks covered are limited to the named perils which we have considered under Clause 1. Under the laws of virtually all maritime countries relating to the carriage of goods by sea (and certainly under English law), the carrier is entitled to abandon the voyage without liability attaching to him if in consequence of excepted perils under the contract of carriage the ship has sustained such damage that the cost of making her fit to continue the voyage would exceed the value of the ship when repaired. While this would clearly constitute a risk insured under an "All Risks" policy, it would not, strictly speaking, be a risk covered under the Institute Cargo Clauses (B) or (C) except under Clauses 1.1.2 and 1.1.4 which in terms presuppose some damage sustained to the carrying vessel.

This construction, if correct, would render this Clause 12 under the (B) and (C) Clauses much narrower than the corresponding obligation to pay special charges for landing, warehousing and forwarding which were contained in the old W.A. and F.P.A. Clauses. Representatives of London market underwriters have, however, gone on record as saying that the intention of this Clause 12 is to provide coverage for forwarding charges which would correspond in practice with the cover previously granted. Such an interpretation would involve an implication (not expressly stated in the clauses) that the risks insured against included a loss of voyage by the carrying vessel arising from traditional sea perils.

In view of the uncertainty which exists as to the correct interpretation of this Clause 12, it is suggested that if there is a termination of the contract of carriage or of the insured transit at an intermediate port or place, the assured under Institute Cargo Clauses (B) or (C) should, at the same time as giving prompt notice to his underwriters requesting a continuation of the cover under Clause 9, also request that the underwriters will grant him a liberal interpretation of Clause 12 to cover any forwarding charges that he may reasonably incur.

Clause 13 — Constructive Total Loss Clause

13 No claim for Constructive Total Loss shall be recoverable hereunder unless the subject-matter insured is reasonably abandoned either on account of its actual total loss appearing to be unavoidable or because the cost of recovering, reconditioning and forwarding the subject-matter to the destination to which it is insured would exceed its value on arrival.

While the wording of this clause is the same as in Institute Cargo Clauses (A), it will be appreciated that its effect is limited to those instances where the abandonment of the goods is reasonably made on account of one of the risks covered under Clause 1.

Clause 14 — Increased Value Clause

14 14.1 If any Increased Value insurance is effected by the Assured on the cargo insured herein the agreed value of the cargo shall be deemed to be increased to the total amount insured under this insurance and all Increased Value insurances covering the loss, and liability under this insurance shall be in such proportion as the sum insured herein bears to such total amount insured.
In the event of claim the Assured shall provide the Underwriters with evidence of the amounts insured under all other insurances.
14.2 Where this insurance is on Increased Value the following clause shall apply:
The agreed value of the cargo shall be deemed to be equal to the total amount insured under the primary insurance and all Increased Value insurances covering the loss and effected on the cargo by the Assured, and liability under this insurance shall be in such proportion as the sum insured herein bears to such total amount insured.
In the event of claim the Assured shall provide the Underwriters with evidence of the amounts insured under all other insurances.

This is the same as in Institute Cargo Clauses (A). See commentary on page 31.

Clause 15 — Not to Inure Clause

15 This insurance shall not inure to the benefit of the carrier or other bailee.

The wording and effect is the same as in Institute Cargo Clauses (A). See commentary on page 32.

Clause 16 — Duty of Assured Clause

16 It is the duty of the Assured and their servants and agents in respect of loss recoverable hereunder
16.1 to take such measures as may be reasonable for the purpose of averting or minimising such loss, and

16.2 to ensure that all rights against carriers, bailees or other third parties are properly preserved and exercised

and the Underwriters will, in addition to any loss recoverable hereunder, reimburse the Assured for any charges properly and reasonably incurred in pursuance of these duties.

This clause is in the same terms as in Institute Cargo Clauses (A). However, because Clauses (B) and (C) are against the risks of named perils, it has to be borne in mind that "loss recoverable hereunder" is limited to any claim for loss or damage caused by those named perils.

As an example, if a package containing goods belonging to the assured falls overboard whilst being discharged from the carrying steamer at the port of destination, it will be the duty of the assured to try and recover it, and underwriters under the (B) Clauses will reimburse the assured for the cost of its recovery and safe landing, even if the contents are landed completely undamaged. No doubt a prudent assured under the (C) Clauses will also attempt to recover the package in the same circumstances, but in so doing he will be acting entirely for his own account as a "prudent uninsured owner" since the (C) Clauses afford no cover for loss in discharging, except at a port of distress.

Clause 17 — Waiver Clause

17   Measures taken by the Assured or the Underwriters with the object of saving, protecting or recovering the subject-matter insured shall not be considered as a waiver or acceptance of abandonment or otherwise prejudice the rights of either party.

This clause and its effect are the same as under Institute Cargo Clauses (A). See commentary on page 34.

Clause 18 — Reasonable Despatch Clause

18   It is a condition of this insurance that the Assured shall act with reasonable despatch in all circumstances within their control.

This is the same as in the (A) Clauses.

Clause 19 — English Law and Practice Clause

19   This insurance is subject to English law and practice.

See the observations under the (A) Clauses on page 35.

NOTE:— It is necessary for the Assured when they become aware of an event which is "held covered" under this insurance to give prompt notice to the Underwriters and the right to such cover is dependent upon compliance with this obligation.

This is the standard form of note which appears at the foot of all Institute Clauses covering goods. The observations on page 35 also apply here.

COMPARISON IN THE COVER AFFORDED BY THE INSTITUTE
CARGO CLAUSES (B) AND (C), 1/1/82 AND THE COVER
PREVIOUSLY AVAILABLE UNDER THE INSTITUTE CARGO CLAUSES
(W.A.) AND (F.P.A.), 1/1/63

The main change under the 1/1/82 clauses is that the risks insured have been limited to a number of named perils, and in return for that curtailment of the cover, the assured is entitled to claim for each and every loss which occurs during the insured transit as a result of those perils, however small such claims may be.

The perils no longer covered under the restricted conditions of Clauses (B) and (C) are:

1. Certain effects of "perils of the seas", viz:-
    (a) Damage resulting from the breaking of stowage due to heavy weather.
    (b) Damage consequential upon measures taken to avoid the effects of heavy weather, for example sweat damage through forced closure of ventilation — as in *Canada Rice Mills* v. *Union Marine*.[46]
    (c) Commixture and contagion damage, unless resulting from the entry of water into the hold or compartment in which the adjacent goods are stowed. (See Clause 1.2.3.)
2. Certain acts of man:
    (a) Theft, albeit only theft accompanied by violence, as previously covered in Lloyd's S.G. form.
    (b) "Takings at sea" — an expression of some antiquity whose limited meaning has now been established by the House of Lords in the case of *The "Salem"*.[47]
    (c) Barratry of the master and crew, that is to say wrongful acts in prejudice of their employment and/or breach of their duties.

COMPARISON IN THE COVER AFFORDED BY THE INSTITUTE
CARGO CLAUSES (B) AND THE INSTITUTE CARGO CLAUSES (C)

The only difference consists in the list of the risks insured in Clause 1.

The following are the risks covered by the (B) Clauses which do *not* appear in the (C) Clauses:

1.1.6   earthquake volcanic eruption or lightning,
1.2.2   (part), washing overboard,
1.2.3   entry of sea lake or river water into vessel craft hold conveyance container liftvan or place of storage,

46. *Canada Rice Mills* v. *Union Marine* [1941] A.C. 55.
47. *Shell International Petroleum* v. *Gibbs* (*The "Salem"*) [1983] 1 Lloyd's Rep 342.

1.3   total loss of any package lost overboard or dropped whilst loading on to, or unloading from, vessel or craft.

4. INSTITUTE CLAUSES FOR PARTICULAR COMMODITIES

In certain instances, where noted, these clauses have been agreed with the trade associations concerned. In the commentary which follows, only those clauses are mentioned which differ from the standard Institute Cargo Clauses.

A. INSTITUTE FROZEN FOOD CLAUSES (A)
(Excluding Frozen Meat) (1/8/82, re-issued 1/1/86)

Clause 1 — Risks Clause

1   This insurance covers, except as provided in Clauses 4, 5, 6 and 7 below,
   1.1   all risks of loss of or damage to the subject-matter insured, other than loss or damage resulting from any variation in temperature howsoever caused,
   1.2   loss of or damage to the subject-matter insured resulting from any variation in temperature attributable to
   1.2.1   breakdown of refrigerating machinery resulting in its stoppage for a period of not less than 24 consecutive hours
   1.2.2   fire or explosion
   1.2.3   vessel or craft being stranded grounded sunk or capsized
   1.2.4   overturning or derailment of land conveyance
   1.2.5   collision or contact of vessel craft or conveyance with any external object other than water
   1.2.6   discharge of cargo at a port of distress.

It is to be noted that the Risks Clause is not quite as wide as "All Risks", since claims for loss or damage resulting from variation in temperature are limited to those attributable to the causes set out in Clauses 1.2.1 to 1.2.6.

Of the perils causing variation in temperature, the most important is:

"1.2.1 breakdown of refrigerating machinery resulting in its stoppage for a period of not less than twenty-four consecutive hours".

It has been held that the expression "breakdown of machinery", by itself, does not necessarily involve the machinery coming to a full stop.[48] Hence the addition of the words "resulting in its stoppage" which has the effect of excluding claims arising from variation in temperature due to the mere malfunction of the refrigerating machinery. It is also to be noted that in order to found a claim under this clause the assured must be able to show, presumably by evidence obtained from the carrier, that the stoppage of the refrigerating machinery extended for a continuous period of not less than 24 hours.

48. *Giertsen* v. *Turnbull*, 1908 S.C. 1011.

The other listed perils from which "variation in temperature" claims may arise are the same as set out in Institute Cargo Clauses (C), Clause 1.1. These are the same as in previous Frozen Food Clauses, but with the addition of the overturning or derailment of any land conveyance.

Clause 2 — General Average Clause

Clause 3 — "Both to Blame Collision" Clause

These clauses are the same as in the Institute Cargo Clauses.

Clause 4 — General Exclusions Clause

4   In no case shall this insurance cover

    4.1   loss damage or expense attributable to wilful misconduct of the Assured

    4.2   ordinary leakage, ordinary loss in weight or volume, or ordinary wear and tear of the subject-matter insured

    4.3   loss damage or expense caused by insufficiency or unsuitability of packing or preparation of the subject-matter insured (for the purpose of this Clause 4.3 "packing" shall be deemed to include stowage in a container or liftvan but only when such stowage is carried out prior to attachment of this insurance or by the Assured or their servants)

    4.4   loss damage or expense caused by inherent vice or nature of the subject-matter insured (except loss damage or expense resulting from variation in temperature specifically covered under Clause 1.2 above)

    4.5   loss damage or expense proximately caused by delay, even though the delay be caused by a risk insured against (except expenses payable under Clause 2 above)

    4.6   loss damage or expense arising from insolvency or financial default of the owners managers charterers or operators of the vessel

    4.7   loss damage or expense arising from the use of any weapon of war employing atomic or nuclear fission and/or fusion or other like reaction or radioactive force or matter

    4.8   loss damage or expense arising from any failure of the Assured or their servants to take all reasonable precautions to ensure that the subject-matter insured is kept in refrigerated or, where appropriate, properly insulated and cooled space

    4.9   any loss damage or expense otherwise recoverable hereunder unless prompt notice thereof is given to the Underwriters and, in any event, not later than 30 days after the termination of this insurance.

Exclusions 4.1, 4.2, 4.3, 4.4, 4.5, 4.6 and 4.7 correspond with (and carry the same numbering as) the exclusions contained in the Institute Cargo Clauses (A).

Exclusion 4.4 — the Inherent Vice exclusion — differs from the usual form, the words in parenthesis being added to make it clear that underwriters will not raise this defence against any claim resulting from variation in temperature which has come about through one of the specific causes mentioned in Clause 1.2.

There follow two exclusions which are particular to the Frozen Food Clauses. They are:

Exclusion 4.8 exempts the underwriters from liability for any claim arising from the failure of the assured, or the assured's servants, to take reasonable precautions to ensure that the goods are kept in properly refrigerated or cool and insulated spaces.

Exclusion 4.9 is unusual. It provides in effect that no claim under the policy will be recoverable if prompt notice of it has not been given to the underwriters within 30 days after the termination of the insurance. Although a claims "cut-off" clause, such as this, is sometimes thought to be a harsh provision, it reinforces the good sense of the proposition which every dealer in frozen food would recognise, that it is prudent for the receiver to ascertain as soon as possible after arrival of the goods into his cold store that they are in proper condition.

Clause 5 — Unseaworthiness and Unfitness Exclusion Clause

Clause 6 — War Exclusion Clause

Clause 7 — Strikes Exclusion Clause

These clauses are the same as the corresponding clauses, so numbered in the Institute Cargo Clauses — see pages 20–23 for commentary.

Clause 8 — Transit Clause

8 **8.1**   This insurance attaches from the time the goods are loaded into the conveyance at freezing works or cold store at the place named herein for the commencement of the transit, continues during the ordinary course of transit and terminates either

8.1.1   on delivery to the cold store or place of storage at the destination named herein,

8.1.2   on delivery to any other cold store or place of storage, whether prior to or at the destination named herein, which the Assured elect to use either

8.1.2.1   for storage other than in the ordinary course of transit or

8.1.2.2   for allocation or distribution,

or

8.1.3   on the expiry of 5 days after discharge overside of the goods hereby insured from the oversea vessel at the final port of discharge,

whichever shall first occur.

8.2   If, after discharge overside from the oversea vessel at the final port of discharge, but prior to termination of this insurance, the goods are to be forwarded to a destination other than that to which they are insured hereunder, this insurance, whilst remaining subject to termination as provided for above, shall not extend beyond the commencement of transit to such other destination.

8.3   This insurance shall remain in force (subject to termination as provided for above and to the provisions of Clause 9 below) during delay beyond the control of the Assured, any deviation, forced discharge, reshipment or transhipment and during any variation of the adventure arising from the exercise of a liberty granted to shipowners or charterers under the contract of affreightment.

This clause differs in a number of respects from the corresponding clause in Institute Cargo Clauses, viz:

(a) The insured transit commences at the time the goods are loaded into the conveyance, whatever it may be, for the first leg of the journey. This is one stage earlier than is provided in the Institute Cargo Clauses, under which the insurance does not attach until the time the goods leave the warehouse or place of storage. Thus a loss caused by insured perils which occurs after the goods have been loaded into a lorry while it remains on the premises where the goods were loaded and before it begins its journey, will be covered under the Institute Frozen Food Clauses, whereas it would not be covered under Institute Cargo Clauses.

(b) The words "warehouse or place of storage" are replaced in the Institute Frozen Food Clauses by "freezing works or cold store" to describe the location where the goods are loaded, and by "cold store or place of storage" at destination.

(c) The transit "cut-off" is a mere five days after discharge of the goods from the ocean steamer, instead of the period of 60 days which is provided in Institute Cargo Clauses.

Clause 9 — Termination of Contract of Carriage Clause

9   If owing to circumstances beyond the control of the Assured either the contract of carriage is terminated at a port or place other than the destination named therein or the transit is otherwise terminated before delivery of the goods as provided for in Clause 8 above, then this insurance shall also terminate *unless prompt notice is given to the Underwriters and continuation of cover is requested when the insurance shall remain in force, subject to an additional premium if required by the Underwriters,* either

    9.1 until the goods are sold and delivered at such port or place, or, unless otherwise specially agreed, until the expiry of 30 days after arrival of the goods hereby insured at such port or place, whichever shall first occur,
        or

    9.2 if the goods are forwarded within the said period of 30 days (or any agreed extension thereof) to the destination named herein or to any other destination, until terminated in accordance with the provisions of Clause 8 above.

This clause is in the same form as the corresponding clause, so numbered, in Institute Cargo Clauses, except that in the event of the termination of the contract of carriage in the circumstances set out in the clause, and subject to prompt notice being given to the underwriters requesting a continuation of cover, the period of time for which such extension may be granted (without any further extension being asked for) is *30 days*, instead of 60 days as provided in the Institute Cargo Clauses.

Clauses 10 to 19

Clauses 10 to 19 are the same as in Institute Cargo Clauses (A). So is the usual Note which appears at the foot of the 1/8/82 form. See pages 26 to 35 for commentary.

An additional Special Note was added when the Institute Frozen Food

Clauses were reissued on 1/1/86. It reads:

SPECIAL NOTE:— This insurance does not cover loss damage or expense caused by embargo, or by rejection prohibition or detention by the government of the country of import or their agencies or departments, but does not exclude loss of or damage to the subject-matter insured caused by risks insured hereunder and sustained prior to any such embargo rejection prohibition or detention.

The purpose of this note is to make it clear that if the goods have sustained no loss or damage by insured perils, the fact that they may be rejected from importation by government regulation (for example, by not attaining some standard prescribed by a sanitary authority) or made subject to an embargo, will not give the assured a right to claim under the policy. In a word, there is no "Rejection" cover under this form.

B. INSTITUTE FROZEN FOODS CLAUSES (C)
(Excluding Frozen Meat) (1/8/82, reissued 1/1/86)

As the title implies, these are the restricted conditions clauses available for the frozen food trade.

Clause 1 — The Risks Clause

This clause is in the same terms as the corresponding clause in Institute Cargo Clauses (C). See page 36 for text and commentary.

Clause 4 — General Exclusions Clause

Incorporates Clauses 4.1 to 4.8, the exclusions contained in Institute Cargo Clauses (C), together with the special exclusions 4.9 and 4.10 applying to the trade, which have been commented upon in connection with the Institute Frozen Food Clauses (A).
   The following may be observed:

"4.4 loss damage or expense caused by inherent vice or nature of the subject matter insured".

This exclusion is not limited by the exception of claims resulting from variation in temperature (as is the corresponding exclusion in the Institute Frozen Food Clauses (A)), since there is no specific reference to coverage in the Risk Clause for losses so caused. In the authors' opinion, this does not necessarily mean that every claim based upon deterioration of the frozen goods by reason of loss of refrigeration will be caught by the "nature of the subject matter insured" exclusion. The question whether the assured will be able to recover for such deterioration will depend upon the application of the doctrine of proximate cause to the circumstances of the loss. For example, if in consequence of a collision, the refrigeration machinery is rendered totally inoperable, and the ship being disabled is unable to attain a port of refuge where the frozen goods could be discharged into a cold store until such time as the goods have deteriorated, it is submitted that there is an unbroken chain of causation between the collision and the consequential deterioration of the refrigerated goods.

"4.7 deliberate damage to or deliberate destruction of the subject matter insured or any part thereof by the wrongful act of any person or persons"

This exclusion does not appear in the (A) form of the Institute Frozen Food Clauses. It does however appear in the Institute Cargo Clauses (C). See commentary on page 41.

Clause 8 — Transit Clause

Clause 9 — Termination of Contract of Carriage Clause

These clauses are in the same terms as the (A) form of the Institute Frozen Food Clauses. See above.

Clauses 2, 3, 5–7, 10–19, Note and Special Note

Clauses 2, 3, 5–7 inclusive, 10–19 inclusive and the note at the foot of the form are the same as the Institute Cargo Clauses (C).

In the 1/1/86 form the Special Note printed at the foot of the form is the same as in the (A) form.

C. INSTITUTE COAL CLAUSES (1/10/82)

These clauses form a welcome addition to the Institute's portfolio. They replace an old (undated) non-Institute form entitled "Clauses on Coal Shipments", which contained some curious provisions and had become outdated.

Clause 1 — Risks Clause

1   This insurance covers, except as provided in Clauses 4, 5, 6 and 7 below,
  1.1   loss of or damage to the subject-matter insured reasonably attributable to
  1.1.1   fire explosion or heating, even when caused by spontaneous combustion, inherent vice or nature of the subject-matter insured
  1.1.2   vessel being stranded grounded sunk or capsized
  1.1.3   collision or contact of vessel with any external object other than water
  1.1.4   discharge of cargo at a port of distress
  1.1.5   earthquake volcanic eruption or lightning,
  1.2   loss of or damage to the subject-matter insured caused by
  1.2.1   general average sacrifice
  1.2.2   jettison or washing overboard
  1.2.3   entry of sea lake or river water into vessel hold container or place of storage.

The risks covered are those contained in Institute Cargo Clauses (B) with the following notable differences:

"1.1.1 Fire explosion or heating, even when caused by spontaneous combustion, inherent vice or nature of the subject-matter insured".

This express provision displaces the time-honoured rule of construction laid down in section 55(2)(c) of the Marine Insurance Act 1906 that the insurer is not liable for inherent vice or nature of the subject-matter insured. It is in line with, and the wording is an improvement upon, a similar provision in the Clauses on Coal Shipments.

This is an important extension of underwriters' liability, and its inclusion carries with it a number of substantial benefits to both assured and underwriters:

(i) It renders unnecessary, for the purpose of establishing whether there is claim upon the policy, any investigation into the cause of the heating or combustion. As was stated in *Soya G.m.b.H.* v. *White*,[49] a policy against the risk of heating is like an insurance against fire, in that evidence of heating is sufficient proof of the casualty.

(ii) It precludes what would otherwise be an extremely difficult question of fact to be determined, namely, where in each case to draw the dividing line between the extent of deterioration caused by heat alone and the loss/deterioration caused by a subsequent fire.

(iii) It encourages the assured to take timely and active steps to prevent the heating of a cargo from getting out of hand. The case of *The "Knight of St. Michael"*[50] illustrates the necessity of prompt action to avert the outbreak of fire in a coal cargo which has become heated. Although the coal was never in a state of combustion, the vessel had properly put into a port of refuge, where part of the coal was discharged and sold, the remainder

49. *Per* Lloyd J. in the Commercial Court, *Soya G.m.b.H.* v. *White* [1980] 1 Lloyd's Rep. 491. The decision in this case was upheld in the Court of Appeal [1982] 1 Lloyd's Rep. 136, and the House of Lords [1983] 1 Lloyd's Rep. 122.
50. *The "Knight of St. Michael"* (1888) 8 Asp.M.L.C. 360; 3 Com.Cas. 62.

being carried on and delivered at destination. The claim was brought by the ship owners under their policy of insurance on freight for the loss which they sustained in respect of the part cargo sold at the port of refuge, and Barnes J. held that the underwriters were liable. He said: "I have found that fire did not actually break out, but it is reasonably certain that it would have broken out, and the condition of things was such that there was an existing state of peril by fire, and not merely a fear of fire. ... The danger was present, and, if nothing were done, spontaneous combustion and fire would follow in natural course."

Because of the limited duration of the risk (see Clause 8 below), there is no need to bring into the Risks Clause the perils which may occur only when the cargo is on board craft or land conveyances. Hence the omission of the perils of overturning and derailment of land conveyance and stranding, etc., of craft, and the limitation of the perils of the entry of sea, lake or river water into the vessel, hold, container or place of storage. Furthermore, as we shall see, "place of storage" in the context of this insurance can mean only such storage as is arranged after a forced discharge of the cargo.

Clause 2 — General Average Clause

Clause 3 — "Both to Blame Collision" Clause

These clauses are the same as in Institute Cargo Clauses.

Clause 4 — General Exclusions Clause

4   In no case shall this insurance cover
   4.1   loss damage or expense attributable to wilful misconduct of the Assured
   4.2   ordinary leakage, ordinary loss in weight or volume, or ordinary wear and tear of the subject-matter insured
   4.3   loss damage or expense proximately caused by delay, even though the delay be caused by a risk insured against (except expenses payable under Clause 2 above)
   4.4   loss damage or expense arising from insolvency or financial default of the owners managers charterers or operators of the vessel
   4.5   deliberate damage to or deliberate destruction of the subject-matter insured or any part thereof by the wrongful act of any person or persons
   4.6   loss damage or expense arising from the use of any weapon of war employing atomic or nuclear fission and/or fusion or other like reaction or radioactive force or matter.

The list of exclusions is shorter than those contained in Institute Cargo Clauses. There is no need to refer to "insufficiency of packing" since this is not relevant to a cargo of coal in bulk. The usual exclusion of inherent vice and nature of the subject matter insured is also omitted, since these risks are included by Clause 1.1.1.

Clause 5 — Unseaworthiness and Unfitness Exclusion Clause

This is in the same terms as in the Institute Cargo Clauses, although the references to craft, conveyance or container are unnecessary.

Clauses 6 and 7

Clause 6 and Clause 7 contain the War and Strikes Exclusions in the same terms as in the Institute Cargo Clauses.

Clause 8 — Transit Clause

8   8.1   This insurance attaches as the subject-matter insured is loaded on board the oversea vessel at the port or place named herein for the commencement of the transit, continues during the ordinary course of transit and terminates as the subject-matter insured is discharged overside from the oversea vessel at the destination named herein.

8.2   This insurance shall remain in force (subject to termination as provided for above and to the provisions of Clause 9 below) during delay beyond the control of the Assured, any deviation, forced discharge, reshipment or transhipment and during any variation of the adventure arising from the exercise of a liberty granted to shipowners or charterers under the contract of affreightment.

It is to be noted that the duration of the risk is limited, and except when the cargo is forced discharged at port of refuge, it extends only to the period of time that the cargo is on board the "oversea vessel". The risk attaches "as the subject-matter insured is loaded on board". The use of these words signifies that if only part of the cargo has been loaded at the time of a loss, the risk will attach in respect of the cargo which is on board the oversea vessel, but not in respect of the part cargo which remains on the shore. Likewise, the risk terminates "as the subject-matter insured is discharged overside" at destination, and similar considerations apply.

If the cargo is forced discharged during the ocean transit, the "shore risks" will be covered by the insurance, subject to Clause 9, below.

Clause 9 — Termination of Contract of Affreightment Clause

This in similar terms to Clause 9 of Institute Cargo Clauses, except that in the event of prompt notice being given to the underwriters for a continuation of the cover after termination of the contract of affreightment, the period of time for which underwriters will agree to continue the cover (subject to any agreed extension) is limited to fifteen days, compared with 60 days under Institute Cargo Clauses.

Clauses 10 to 19 and Note

Clauses 10 to 19 inclusive and the Note at the foot of the form are the same as in Institute Cargo Clauses.

D. INSTITUTE BULK OIL CLAUSES (1/2/83)

This is another new addition to the Institute portfolio of clauses. Previously, the only clauses available for oil cargoes was a form of Bulk Oil Clauses (SP—13C of January 1962) which had its origin in the United States. Although in terms of cover provided, it might be argued that the Institute Bulk Oil Clauses are less wide than the SP—13C Form, in terms of drafts-manship and clarity of expression they are infinitely superior.

Clause 1 — Risks Clause

1   This insurance covers, except as provided in Clauses 4, 5, 6 and 7 below,
- **1.1** loss of or contamination of the subject-matter insured reasonably attributable to
- **1.1.1**   fire or explosion
- **1.1.2**   vessel or craft being stranded grounded sunk or capsized
- **1.1.3**   collision or contact of vessel or craft with any external object other than water
- **1.1.4**   discharge of cargo at a port or place of distress
- **1.1.5**   earthquake volcanic eruption or lightning,
- **1.2** loss of or contamination of the subject-matter insured caused by
- **1.2.1**   general average sacrifice
- **1.2.2**   jettison
- **1.2.3**   leakage from connecting pipelines in loading transhipment or discharge
- **1.2.4**   negligence of Master Officers or Crew in pumping cargo ballast or fuel,
- **1.3** contamination of the subject-matter insured resulting from stress of weather.

This list of perils insured is generally in line with the provisions of Institute Cargo Clauses (B). However, the following variations may be noted:

(a) Where the Institute of Cargo Clauses refer to damage, the Bulk Oil Clauses substitute "contamination".

(b) As will be seen from the clauses which define the duration of the risk, overland transit (other than by pipeline) is not provided for, and consequently there is no reference to "conveyance", other than by vessel or craft.

(c) Two additional perils are specifically included:

"1.2.3 leakage from connecting pipelines in loading shipment or discharge". The words used express two limitations upon the risk of "leakage": (i) the leakage must occur in the course of loading shipment or discharge of the cargo, (ii) the leakage must be from "connecting pipelines". There is some ambiguity in this expression, but the authors submit that it must mean leakage from any of the pipelines which connect the shore tanks at the place of loading or discharging with the ship, thus excluding any leakage from an associated pipeline (not connected with the ship) which is simultaneously put "on flow" by the pumping operation.

"1.2.4   Negligence of Master Officers or Crew in pumping cargo ballast or fuel." It is to be noted that in order to found a claim under this sub-clause, the loss or contamination has to be caused by the negligence of those concerned "in pumping". This expression imports a limitation similar to that conveyed by the words "accidents in loading discharging or shifting cargo or fuel" in Clause 6.2.1. of the Institute Time Clauses Hulls — see page 95.

There is, of course, some overlap in the way in which these two perils are expressed, in that a leakage from a pipeline caused by the negligence of the crew in operating the ship's pump in the course of loading, shipment or discharge will be covered by both sub-clauses, but the leakages covered by Clause 1.2.3 will include those occurring through any cause in these operations, whereas Clause 1.2.4 covers not only loss, but also contamination caused by the ship's crew in any pumping, including transfers from tank to tank on board the ship.

(d) In place of "entry of sea water etc" in the Institute Cargo Clauses, the Bulk Oil Clauses covers "contamination ... from stress of weather". This can include, e.g., claims for depreciation in value of an oil cargo of a specific quality which becomes contaminated with the residues which normally lie inert at the bottom of the ship's tanks, through abnormal movement of the ship in severe weather.

Clause 2 — General Average Clause

Clause 3 — "Both to Blame Collision" Clause

These are in the same terms as the clauses so numbered in the Institute Cargo Clauses.

Clause 4 — General Exclusions Clause

4   In no case shall this insurance cover
    4.1   loss damage or expense attributable to wilful misconduct of the Assured
    4.2   ordinary leakage, ordinary loss in weight or volume, or ordinary wear and tear of the subject-matter insured
    4.3   loss damage or expense caused by inherent vice or nature of the subject-matter insured
    4.4   loss damage or expense proximately caused by delay, even though the delay be caused by a risk insured against (except expenses payable under Clause 2 above)
    4.5   loss damage or expense arising from insolvency or financial default of the owners managers charterers or operators of the vessel
    4.6   loss damage or expense arising from the use of any weapon of war employing atomic or nuclear fission and/or fusion or other like reaction or radioactive force or matter.

These exclusions correspond to those which are set out in Clauses 4.1, 4.2, 4.4, 4.5, 4.6 and 4.8 of the Institute Cargo Clauses (B). However, it may be noted:

(a) There is no exclusion in respect of insufficiency of packing, since this would clearly be irrelevant; and

(b) whereas Clause 4.7 of the Institute Cargo Clauses (B) — and, for that matter, all the other Institute Clauses providing for restricted cover — stipulate for the exclusion of "deliberate damage to or deliberate destruction of the subject-matter insured . . . by the wrongful act of any person or persons", this does not appear in the Bulk Oil Clauses. One is tempted to see in this omission a gesture of repentance on the part of underwriters, in favour of that part of the judgment in the case of *The "Salem"*[47] under which underwriters were held liable to make good the loss of the remainder of the oil cargo which went down with the ship when she was scuttled by the deliberate act of the now infamous conspirators.

Clauses 5, 6 and 7

Clauses 5, 6 and 7 — the Unseaworthiness and Unfitness Exclusion Clause and the War and Strikes Exclusion Clauses are the same as in the Institute Cargo Clauses.

Clause 8 — Transit Clause

8 **8.1** This insurance attaches as the subject-matter insured leaves tanks for the purpose of loading at the place named herein for the commencement of the transit, continues during the ordinary course of transit and terminates either

8.1.1 as the subject-matter insured enters tanks on discharge to place of storage or to storage vessel at the destination named herein,

or

8.1.2 on the expiry of 30 days after the date of arrival of the vessel at the destination named herein, whichever shall first occur.

8.2 If, after discharge from the oversea vessel into craft at the final port or place of discharge, but prior to the termination of this insurance under 8.1 above, the subject-matter insured or any part thereof is to be forwarded to a destination other than that to which it is insured hereunder, the insurance on the subject-matter insured or such part thereof shall not extend beyond the commencement of transit to such other destination, *unless otherwise agreed by the Underwriters upon receipt of prompt notice from the Assured.*

8.3 *Subject to prompt notice being given to the Underwriters and to an additional premium if required by them,* this insurance shall remain in force (until terminated under 8.1 or 8.2 above and subject to the provisions of Clause 9 below) during delay beyond the control of the Assured, any deviation, forced discharge, reshipment or transhipment and during any other variation of the adventure provided such other variation is beyond the control of the Assured.

47. *Shell International Petroleum* v. *Gibbs (The "Salem")* [1983] 1 Lloyd's Rep 342.

The definition of the duration of the risk is of importance in insurances on bulk oil, for two reasons:

(a) because of the number of losses which occur during the operations of loading and discharging cargo, and

(b) because the assessment of any claim for shortage necessarily starts with the determination of the quantity of cargo at the risk of the assured at the commencement of the cover.

In short the duration of the risk is from shore tank to shore tank, although provision is impliedly made for part of the transit to be performed by lighters or vessels of smaller capacity than the ocean tanker.

"leaves tanks for the purpose of loading ..." These words are deliberately wide enough to cover the movement of oil from one or more initial storage tanks in the tank farm at the place of loading into another tank or tanks for the purpose of loading onto the ship.

The period of "cut-off" after the date of arrival of the vessel at the place of destination is 30 days, compared with 60 days as provided in the Institute Cargo Clauses.

Clause 9 — Termination of Contract of Carriage Clause

This is in the same terms as the corresponding clause in Institute Cargo Clauses, except that in the event of the termination of the contract of carriage in the circumstances set out in the clause, and subject to prompt notice being given to the underwriters requesting a continuation of cover, the period of time for which such extension may be granted (without any further extension being asked for) is 30 days, compared with 60 days as provided in the Institute Cargo Clauses.

Clauses 10 to 14 and 16 to 20 and Note

Clauses 10 to 14 inclusive and 16 to 20 inclusive are the same as the clauses numbered 10 to 19 inclusive in the Institute Cargo Clauses.
Likewise the Note at the foot of the form.

Clause 15 — Adjustment Clause

15   Claims for leakage and shortage recoverable under this insurance are to be adjusted as follows:—

    15.1 The amount recoverable shall be the proportionate insured value of the volume of oil lost, to be ascertained by a comparison of the gross volume certified as having left tanks for loading on to the vessel with the gross volume certified as having been delivered to tanks at the termination of the transit, except that where the contract of sale is based on weight and not on volume the amount recoverable may be calculated on a weight basis from such certified quantities.

The term "gross volume" in this Clause 15.1 means total volume without deduction of sediment and water content and free water, except to the extent that the amount of water can be shown by the Assured to have increased abnormally during the insured transit as a result of the operation of a risk covered by this insurance.

15.2 Adjustment shall be made to the calculation under 15.1 above to eliminate any change in volume caused by variation in temperature and any apparent change in quantity arising from the use of inconsistent procedures in determining the certified quantities.

15.3 Where this insurance provides for an excess to be applied to claims for leakage or shortage, such excess shall be deemed to include ordinary loss in weight or volume except when caused by variation in temperature or settling out of water. Where there is no such provision, the amount recoverable in accordance with Clauses 15.1 and 15.2 shall be subject to reduction for any ordinary loss excluded by Clause 4.2 above.

This clause has been designed to eliminate as far as possible claims for "paper losses" occurring as a result of the incompatibility of documents recording quantities loaded and discharged, and the well-known difficulties of measuring liquid cargoes. A typical claim for shortage, adjusted in accordance with the above clause would be as follows:

Facts

A quantity of 650,497 bbls Crude Oil is ascertained by meter readings to have been loaded from shore tanks to the vessel. Sediment and water content is established by analysis to be 340 bbls. A bill of lading is issued, based on shore tank figures, for 650,497 bbls gross — 650,157 bbls nett.

The consignment is insured for US$9,752,355 under Institute Bulk Oil Clauses, with claims for shortage subject to a deductible of 0.50% on the whole shipment.

At destination, the quantity ascertained to have been discharged to shore tanks is:

	645,100 bbls
Water drained from shore tanks is	1,384 bbls
	643,716 bbls
S & W content by analysis is	324 bbls
Quantity of oil available to the Assured	643,392 bbls

The Assured might submit his claim as follows:

Shipped	650,157 bbls	
Received	643,392 bbls	
	6,765 bbls	
Less deductible 0.50% on 650,157 bbls	3,251 bbls	
Amount Claimed	3,514 bbls	*Insured Value*
		US$52,710

However, by reference to this Clause 15, the liability of underwriters is to be ascertained as follows:

Received from shore tanks, gross	650,497 bbls
Delivered to shore tanks, gross	645,100 bbls
	5,397 bbls
Less deductible 0.50% on *whole* shipment 650,497 bbls	3,252 bbls
Amount Recoverable	2,145 bbls
Insured Value	*US$32,175*

E. INSTITUTE COMMODITY TRADES CLAUSES (A) (B) (C) (5/9/83)

Agreed with the Federation of Commodity Associations for the insurance of shipments of cocoa, coffee, cotton, fats and oils not in bulk, hides and skins, metals, oil seeds, refined sugar and tea.

These clauses are available in each of the (A) (B) (C) Forms. In each of these forms, Clause 1 — Risks Clause — is in exactly the same terms as the corresponding Clause 1 of the Institute Cargo Clauses (A) (B) and (C). In fact the only difference between these clauses and the Institute Cargo Clauses is that underwriters have agreed to ameliorate the severity of the "insolvency clause" and the Unseaworthiness and Unfitness Exclusion Clause, viz:

Clause 4.6 — "insolvency clause"

In no case shall this insurance cover

4.6 loss damage or expense caused by insolvency or financial default of the owners managers charterers or operators of the vessel where, at the time of loading of the subject-matter insured on board the vessel, the Assured are aware, or in the ordinary course of business should be aware, that such insolvency or financial default could prevent the normal prosecution of the voyage

This exclusion shall not apply where this insurance has been assigned to the party claiming hereunder who has bought or agreed to buy the subject-matter insured in good faith under a binding contract.

Clause 5 — Unseaworthiness and Unfitness Exclusion Clause

5 **5.1** In no case shall this insurance cover loss damage or expense arising from

5.1.1   unseaworthiness of vessel or craft or unfitness of vessel or craft for the safe carriage of the subject-matter insured, where the Assured are privy to such unseaworthiness or unfitness, at the time the subject- matter insured is loaded therein

5.1.2   unfitness of container liftvan or land conveyance for the safe carriage of the subject-matter insured, where loading therein is carried out prior to attachment of this insurance or by the

Assured or their servants.

5.2   Where this insurance has been assigned to the party claiming hereunder who has bought or agreed to buy the subject-matter insured in good faith under a binding contract, exclusion 5.1.1 above shall not apply.

5.3   The Underwriters waive any breach of the implied warranties of seaworthiness of the ship and fitness of the ship to carry the subject-matter insured to destination.

In comparison with the standard wording contained in Institute Cargo Clauses, there are three major concessions:

(a)   The exclusion of loss damage or expense caused by insolvency or financial default of the owners, managers, charterers or operators of the ship is limited to instances where the assured was or should have been aware that there was a risk that the voyage might be frustrated or interrupted on that account.

(b)   Both the "insolvency exclusion" (Clause 4.6) and the unseaworthiness and unfitness exclusion (Clause 5.1) are agreed not to apply to a purchaser in good faith under a binding contract, to whom the insurance has been assigned. This is, of course, particularly important in trades where it is customary to supply customers with goods under a c.i.f. contract.

(c)   By Clause 5.3, the underwriters agree to waive any breach of the implied warranties of seaworthiness or "cargo-worthiness". This agreement used to be expressed in virtually all previous forms of cargo insurances by such words as "the seaworthiness of the vessel as between the assured and the underwriters is hereby admitted", the absence of which has been commented upon on page 20.

Conversely, under the Institute Commodities Trade Clauses, the assured undertakes a somewhat heavier obligation in regard to the fitness of containers, liftvans and land conveyances for the safe carriage of the goods. Under these clauses, any claim arising from such unfitness will be excluded if the goods had been loaded therein by the assured or his servants, whereas under Institute Cargo Clauses the exclusion only applies when the assured or his servants are privy to the unfitness.

F. INSTITUTE JUTE CLAUSES (1/1/84)

Clause 1 — Risks Clause

1   This insurance covers, except as provided in Clauses 4, 5, 6 and 7 below,

1.1   loss of or damage to the subject-matter insured reasonably attributable to

1.1.1   fire or explosion

1.1.2   vessel or craft being stranded grounded sunk or capsized

1.1.3   overturning or derailment of land conveyance

1.1.4   collision or contact of vessel craft or conveyance with any external object other than water

1.1.5   discharge of cargo at a port of distress,

1.2 loss of or damage to the subject-matter insured caused by

1.2.1 general average sacrifice

1.2.2 jettison or washing overboard

1.2.3 entry of sea lake or river water into vessel craft hold conveyance container liftvan or place of storage,

1.3 total loss of any package lost overboard or dropped whilst loading on to, or unloading from, vessel or craft.

The list of perils insured under these clauses corresponds with the list of perils insured under Institute Cargo Clauses (B) except for the risk of earthquake, volcanic eruption and lightning (Clause 1.1.6 in the Institute Cargo Clauses (B)) which are omitted from the Institute Jute Clauses.

Clause 2 — General Average Clause

Clause 3 — "Both to Blame Collision" Clause

Both are the same as in the Institute Cargo Clauses.

Clause 4 — General Exclusions Clause

Clause 5 — Unseaworthiness and Unfitness Exclusion Clause

Both these clauses appear in the same form as the corresponding clauses in the Institute Commodity Trades (A). It may therefore be noted:

(a) The underwriters have agreed to the same concessions, ameliorating the severity of the "insolvency clause" (Clause 4.6) and the Unseaworthiness Clause (Clause 5.1), as we have noted above on page 63.

(b) Although the Institute Jute Clauses are on restricted conditions, the risks covered being slightly more limited than under Institute Cargo Clauses (B), they do not contain the "deliberate damage" exclusion common to virtually all the cargo forms on restricted conditions.

Clauses 6 and 7 — the War and Strikes Exclusion Clauses

These are the same as in the Institute Cargo Clauses.

Clause 8 — Transit clause

Clause 9 — Termination of Contract of Carriage Clause

These are the same as in the Institute Cargo Clauses, except that:

(a) The "cut-off" period after the completion of discharge of the goods at the final port of discharge is 30 days compared with 60 days under Institute Cargo Clauses,

(b) in the event of the termination of the contract of carriage in the circumstances set out in the clause, and subject to prompt notice being given to the underwriters requesting a continuation of cover, the period of time for which such extension may be granted (without any further extension being asked for) is 15 days, instead of 60 days as provided in the Institute Cargo Clauses.

Clauses 10 to 19 inclusive and Note

Clauses 10 to 19 inclusive and the Note at the foot of the form are the same as in Institute Cargo Clauses.

G. INSTITUTE NATURAL RUBBER CLAUSES (Excluding Liquid Latex) (1/1/84)

Clause 1 — Risks Clause

1   This insurance covers, except as provided in Clauses 4, 5, 6 and 7 below,
   1.1   loss of or damage to the subject-matter insured reasonably attributable to
   1.1.1   fire or explosion
   1.1.2   vessel or craft being stranded grounded sunk or capsized
   1.1.3   overturning or derailment of land conveyance
   1.1.4   collision or contact of vessel craft or conveyance with any external object other than water
   1.1.5   discharge of cargo at a port of distress
   1.1.6   earthquake volcanic eruption or lightning,
   1.2   loss of or damage to the subject-matter insured caused by
   1.2.1   general average sacrifice
   1.2.2   jettison or washing overboard
   1.2.3   water or condensation
   1.2.4   hooks, spillings or leakage of any substance or liquid, other cargo (excluding rubber), or moisture from wet or damp dunnage
   1.2.5   theft pilferage or non-delivery.

The list of perils corresponds with the list of the perils insured under Institute Cargo Clauses (B) from Clause 1.1 through Clause 1.2.2, inclusive. Clauses 1.2.3, 1.2.4, 1.2.5 are particular to the Natural Rubber Clauses.

"1.2.3   water or condensation"

It is to be noted that there is no limitation upon the nature or the cause of the water or condensation damage which may be recovered under this clause. It is submitted that as in the risks of fire or heating, evidence of damage by wetting is sufficient proof that a casualty has occurred.

"1.2.4   hooks, spillings or leakage of any substance or liquid, other cargo (excluding rubber), or moisture from wet or damp dunnage"

"hooks"

Instances of damage by hooks used to be far more frequent in the days when the majority of packaged cargo was individually handled by stevedores, and it became common to add the risk of damage by hooks to the lists of perils insured in many cargo policies in order to displace the assumption (which was probably justified in many instances) that a certain amount of hook damage was either inevitable and/or excluded from recovery by reason of section 55(2)(*c*) of the Marine Insurance Act 1906, which excluded "ordinary leakage and breakage" as one of the risks for which the insurer was not liable in the absence of a specific provision in the policy.

"spillings or leakage of any substance or liquid"

"Leakage" is not used here in the normal sense of a loss of liquid by its escape from its container. What is intended to be covered by this expression is damage to rubber by its coming into contact with any liquid or substance which leaked or spilled, and is, in effect, where it should not be.

"other cargo"

Damage by other cargo may result from direct physical contact, as, for example, when the rubber is overstowed by heavy goods, or indirectly, by its being affected in some other way, e.g. by leakage, moisture, heat, fumes, gas or any other form of emanation from the other cargo. It is not necessary that the two parcels of cargo should have been stowed next to each other.

The question may also arise whether damage sustained by the rubber through its being stowed on top of the remnants of previous cargoes should be considered as coming within the words "other cargo" in terms of this clause. The practice of adjusters is against so extending the meaning of the words "other cargo".

"1.2.5   theft, pilferage or non-delivery"

These words import the terms of the Institute Theft Pilferage and Non-delivery Clause which is set out and commented upon on page 79.

Clause 2 — General Average Clause

Clause 3 — "Both to Blame Collision" Clause

These are in the same form as in Institute Cargo Clauses

Clause 4 — General Exclusions Clause

4   In no case shall this insurance cover

    4.1   loss damage or expense attributable to wilful misconduct of the Assured

    4.2   ordinary loss in weight or volume, or ordinary wear and tear of the subject-matter insured

    4.3   loss damage or expense caused by insufficiency or unsuitablility of packing or preparation of the subject-matter insured (for the purpose of this Clause 4.3 "packing" shall be deemed to include stowage in a container or liftvan but only when such stowage is carried out prior to attachment of this insurance or by the Assured or their servants)

    4.4   loss damage or expense caused by inherent vice or nature of the subject-matter insured

    4.5   loss damage or expense proximately caused by delay, even though the delay be caused by a risk insured against (except expenses payable under Clause 2 above)

    4.6   loss damage or expense caused by insolvency or financial default of the owners managers charterers or operators of the vessel where, at the time of loading of the subject-matter insured on board the vessel, the Assured are aware, or in the ordinary course of business should be aware, that such insolvency or financial default could prevent the normal prosecution of the voyage

    This exclusion shall not apply where this insurance has been assigned to the party claiming hereunder who has bought or agreed to buy the subject-matter insured in good faith under a binding contract

    4.7   loss damage or expense arising from the use of any weapon of war employing atomic or nuclear fission and/or fusion or other like reaction or radioactive force or matter.

The exclusions follow the standard pattern, but the following variations from the wording employed in Institute Cargo Clauses (B) should be noted:

(a) Clause 4.2 does not refer to "ordinary leakage" since the Natural Rubber Clauses are not intended for use for shipments of liquid latex.

(b) Clause 4.6 ("insolvency" clause) is in the modified form which we have already noted in connection with the Institute Commodity Trades Clauses (see page 62).

(c) The Deliberate Damage Clause (Clause 4.7 in the Institute Cargo Clauses (B)) is omitted.

Clause 5 — Unseaworthiness and Unfitness Exclusion Clause

5   **5.1**   In no case shall this insurance cover loss damage or expense arising from

    5.1.1   unseaworthiness of vessel or craft or unfitness of vessel or craft for the safe carriage of the subject-matter insured, where the Assured are privy to such unseaworthiness or unfitness, at the time the subject-matter insured is loaded therein

    5.1.2   unfitness of container liftvan or land conveyance for the safe carriage of the subject-matter insured, where loading therein is carried out prior to attachment of this insurance or by the Assured or their servants.

    5.2   Where this insurance has been assigned to the party claiming hereunder who has bought or agreed to buy the subject-matter insured in good faith under a binding contract, exclusion 5.1.1 above shall not apply.

    5.3   The Underwriters waive any breach of the implied warranties of seaworthiness of the ship and fitness of the ship to carry the subject-matter insured to destination.

This clause is in the modified form which we have already noted under the Institute Commodity Trades Clauses. See page 62.

Clauses 6 and 7 — War and Strikes Exclusion Clauses

These are in the same form as in the Institute Cargo Clauses

Clause 8 — Transit Clause

8   **8.1**   This insurance attaches from the time the goods leave the warehouse or place of storage at the port of shipment named herein for the commencement of the transit and continues during the ordinary course of transit until the goods are delivered to a warehouse or place of storage at the port of destination named herein and, provided it is not a manufacturer's warehouse or place of storage, whilst there for a period not exceeding 30 days.

    8.2   If the goods are to be forwarded to a place outside the limits of the said port of destination the insurance continues until the goods are loaded on to a vessel, craft or conveyance or until the expiry of 30 days from midnight of the day on which the discharge overside of the insured goods from the oversea vessel at the said port of destination is completed, whichever shall first occur.

    8.3   *By giving notice to the Underwriters before the insurance ceases the Assured may obtain an extension at a premium to be arranged to cover the goods beyond the limits in 8.1 and 8.2 above.*

    8.4   This insurance shall remain in force (subject to termination as provided for above and to the provisions of Clause 9 below) during delay beyond the control of the Assured, any deviation, forced discharge, reshipment or transhipment and during any variation of the adventure arising from the exercise of a liberty granted to shipowners or charterers under the contract of affreightment.

It will be noted that whereas the attachment of the risk is the same as under Institute Cargo Clauses, namely, from the time the goods leave the warehouse or place of storage of the port of shipment, the provisions of this clause relating to the termination of the risk are slightly more favourable to the assured. In the ordinary way, the risk continues until either

— the goods are delivered to a manufacturer's warehouse or place of storage, or

— the expiry of 30 days at a warehouse or place of storage at the port of destination.

There is a further extension to the benefit of the assured, in that if the goods are to be forwarded beyond the limits of the port of destination named in the policy, the insurance will continue until the goods are loaded onto the forwarding vessel, craft or conveyance, or until the expiry of 30 days after completion of discharge from the ocean steamer at the port of destination. An extension can be obtained by the assured in terms of Clause 8.3 if so desired.

Clauses 8.4, 9 and 10 and 11 to 14

Clauses 8.4, 9 and 10 are in the same form as in the Institute Cargo Clauses, as are Clauses 11 to 14 inclusive.

Clause 15 — Arbitration Clause

15 In the event of a dispute between the Assured and the Underwriters' Surveyors as to the extent of the depreciation to be allowed on damaged rubber, samples shall be drawn by recognised samplers and forwarded together with the Survey Report to the Rubber Trade Association of London whose award shall be final and binding on all parties so far as concerns the extent of depreciation.

The purpose and effect of this clause are self-explanatory. Its inclusion in earlier forms of the Rubber Clauses, as well as in the present form, demonstrates the advantage of the close liaison between the members of the Rubber Trade Association of London and British market underwriters.

Clauses 16 to 20 and Note

Clauses 16 to 20 correspond to Clauses 15 to 19 in the Institute Cargo Clauses. There is also the usual Note at the foot of the form.

H. INSTITUTE FOSFA TRADES CLAUSES (1/7/85)
Agreed with The Federation of Oils, Seeds and Fats Associations

These clauses are available in forms (A) (B) (C). The clauses are an exact ' replica of the Institute Cargo Clauses (A) (B) and (C), except for:

— Clause 4.6: "the insolvency clause", and
— Clause 5: Unseaworthiness and Unfitness Exclusion Clause,

both of which are in the modified form which we have already noted in the Institute Commodity Trades Clauses.

There are also four sets of Supplementary Clauses available for use in the FOSFA trades, likewise dated 1/7/85. They are as follows:

1. Institute FOSFA Supplementary Clauses (1) (for use in conjunction with Institute FOSFA Trades Clauses (B))

It is hereby agreed that this insurance shall also include

1   Loss of or damage to the subject-matter insured, due to breakdown or collapse of proper stow in vessel or craft caused by stress of weather, subject always to the exclusions contained in this insurance.

2   Institute Malicious Damage Clause 1/8/82.

Clause 1 of these Supplementary Clauses reintroduces a cause of loss or damage for which an assured obtained coverage (subject to the Memorandum percentage being attained) under the old Institute Cargo Clauses (W.A.). This is for a species of damage caused by a "peril of the sea", namely, heavy weather — in this clause called "stress of weather". So when goods, properly stowed in the carrying vessel or craft, have sustained loss or damage by the stowage being disturbed by the violent motion of the vessel or craft in heavy weather the underwriters will respond.

"... breakdown or collapse of proper stow"

The use of the word "proper" in this context makes it clear that the assured has to exercise the burden of proving that the collapse of the stow was due to the violent motion of the vessel in a storm, and that such collapse or breakdown of stow would not have occurred in any event due to an improper or inadequate method of stowage.

Clause 2 imports the Institute Malicious Damage Clause. See page 79.

2. Institute FOSFA Supplementary Clauses (2) (for use in conjunction with Institute FOSFA Trades Clauses (C))

It is hereby agreed that this insurance shall also include

1   Total loss of any package lost overboard or dropped whilst loading on to, or unloading from, vessel or craft, subject always to the exclusions contained in this insurance.

2   Washing overboard of Containers, subject always to the exclusions contained in this insurance.

3   Institute Malicious Damage Clause 1/8/82.

The effect of Clauses 1 and 2 is to up-lift the cover granted by the FOSFA Trades Clauses (C) almost to the equivalent of the FOSFA Trades Clauses (B).

Clause 1 — "total loss of any package etc. ...". The words are the same as in Institute Cargo Clauses (B), Clause 1.3.

Clause 2 adds the risk of loss or damage to the goods by reason of the container in which they are stowed being washed overboard. The reference to containers, which does not appear in the corresponding Clause (1.2.2) in the Institute Cargo Clauses (B), recognises that FOSFA goods would not properly be carried on deck, except in containers.

Clause 3 imports the Institute Malicious Damage Clause. See page 79.

3. Institute FOSFA Supplementary Clause (3): Ship Navigation & Management (for use in conjunction with Institute FOSFA Trades Clauses (B) & (C))

In consideration of an additional premium, it is hereby agreed that this insurance covers, subject always to the exclusions contained in this insurance, loss of or damage to the subject-matter insured, whilst on the ship, caused by error, neglect or default of the carrier or his servants in the navigation or management of the ship, for which they are relieved from liability under the contract of carriage.

This clause gives added protection to an assured to cover, on payment of an additional premium, loss or damage caused to the goods whilst on the ship, for which the carrier would be exonerated from liability by virtue of Article IV, Rule 2(a) of the Hague Rules (and likewise the Hague-Visby Rules).

Article IV, Rule 2 of those Rules reads:

"2. Neither the carrier nor the ship shall be responsible for loss or damage arising or resulting from —

(a) Act, neglect or default of the Master, mariners, pilot or the servants of the carrier in the navigation or in the management of the ship:"

Examples are: Want of proper attention to the ship's pumps; negligence in clearing the ship's decks of water; neglect in clearing a waste pipe, or in ascertaining the condition of tanks before filling them, have all been held to be faults in the management of the ship.[51]

However, a failure to take proper care of the cargo would not fall within the Hague Rules exception, nor within the cover provided by this Supplementary Clause.

It is to be noted that the cover is limited to loss or damage which is sustained by the goods whilst they are on board the ship. The reason for this is that both the Hague Rules and the Hague-Visby Rules spell out the rights and responsibilities of the carrier under Article II "in relation to the loading, handling, stowage, carriage, custody, care, and discharge" of the goods, and consequently the immunities granted by Article IV do not apply to responsibilities which the carrier may have to exercise prior to the loading of the goods or after their discharge from the ship.

It will be appreciated that this Supplementary Clause (3) provides a logical extension to the restricted cover accorded by the FOSFA Trades Clauses (B) and (C), since the risks which are insured under those clauses are very much the same as those for which the carrier is exonerated from liability, for example those of fire, "perils, dangers and accidents of the sea or other navigable waters", Act of God, etc. As mentioned in our historical perspective on page 6, this is the area in which the merchant desires the protection of insurance.

---

51. Carver's *Carriage of Goods*, 13th edn. (British Shipping Laws), Sections 192 to 194 and cases there cited.

4. Institute FOSFA Supplementary Clause (4): Grade Clause
(for use in conjunction with Institute FOSFA Trades Clauses)

Held covered at a premium to be arranged in event of omission or error in description of grade, quality &/or other technical characteristics of the insured commodity, as named in the relevant FOSFA contract.

By this clause underwriters agree to hold the assured covered, at a premium to be arranged, in the event of any innocent misdescription of the subject-matter insured, in terms of the relevant FOSFA contract. As noted above in the commentary on Clause 10 of the Institute Cargo Clauses, this concession, previously available under virtually all forms of cargo insurance, was dropped from the standard marine cargo forms issued from 1/1/82 onwards.

I. INSTITUTE FROZEN MEAT CLAUSES (1/1/86)

Three forms are available:

  Institute Frozen Meat Clauses (A)
  Institute Frozen Meat Clauses (A) — 24 Hours Breakdown
  Institute Frozen Meat Clauses (C) and 24 Hours Breakdown

All these Clauses are sub-titled: (Not suitable for chilled, cooled or fresh meat)

Risks Covered

The (A) Clauses cover all risks of loss of or damage to the subject-matter insured except as provided in the Exclusion Clauses 4, 5, 6 and 7.
    The (A) — 24 Hours Breakdown form covers:

1   This insurance covers, except as provided in Clauses 4, 5, 6 and 7 below,
    1.1   all risks of loss of or damage to the subject-matter insured, other than loss or damage resulting from any variation in temperature howsoever caused,
    1.2   loss of or damage to the subject-matter insured resulting from any variation in temperature attributable to
    1.2.1   breakdown of refrigerating machinery resulting in its stoppage for a period of not less than 24 consecutive hours
    1.2.2   fire or explosion
    1.2.3   vessel or craft being stranded grounded sunk or capsized
    1.2.4   overturning or derailment of land conveyance
    1.2.5   collision or contact of vessel craft or conveyance with any external object other than water
    1.2.6   discharge of cargo at a port of distress.

These risks are precisely the same as those covered by the Institute Frozen Food Clauses (A), and similar observations apply. See page 48.

The (C) and 24 Hours Breakdown form covers:

1   This insurance covers, except as provided in Clauses 4, 5, 6 and 7 below,

   1.1 loss of or damage to the subject-matter insured attributable to

   1.1.1   fire or explosion

   1.1.2   vessel or craft being stranded grounded sunk or capsized

   1.1.3   overturning or derailment of land conveyance

   1.1.4   collision or contact of vessel craft or conveyance with any external object other than water

   1.1.5   discharge of cargo at a port of distress

   1.1.6   breakdown of refrigerating machinery resulting in its stoppage for a period of not less than 24 consecutive hours

   1.2 loss of or damage to the subject-matter insured caused by

   1.2.1   general average sacrifice

   1.2.2   jettison.

The risks covered are the same as in the Institute Cargo Clauses (C) but with the addition of loss or damage caused by the breakdown of refrigerating machinery resulting in its stoppage for a period not less than 24 hours.

In all three forms, Clause 2 — the General Average Clause and Clause 3 — "Both to Blame Collision" Clause are in standard form.

Exclusions

In the (A) Clauses, exclusions 4.1, 4.2, 4.3, 4.5 and 4.7 are the same as in the Institute Cargo Clauses (A).

Exclusion 4.4 — the "inherent vice" exclusion — excepts loss, damage or expense resulting from variation in temperature whilst this insurance is in force.

Exclusion 4.6 — the "insolvency" exclusion — is in the modified form which we have noted in connection with the Institute Commodity Trades Clauses. See page 62.

Exclusion 4.8 is unexpected in an All Risks insurance. It reads:

"loss, damage or expense on shore caused directly or indirectly by earthquake, volcanic eruption and/or fire resulting therefrom".

It is to be noted that this exclusion only applies when the goods are on land. Exclusion 4.9 is:

"loss, damage or expense arising from any failure of the assured or their servants to take all reasonable precautions to ensure that the subject-matter insured is kept in refrigerated or, where appropriate, properly insulated and cooled space".

This is the same as we have noted under the Institute Frozen Food Clauses. See page 49.

In the (A) — 24 Hours Breakdown form the exclusions are the same, except that the exception to 4.4 — the "inherent vice" exclusion — is worded "except loss, damage or expense resulting from variation in temperature specifically covered under Clause 1.2 above".

In the (C) and 24 Hours Breakdown form there is an additional exclusion:

> "4.7 deliberate damage to or deliberate destruction of the subject-matter insured or any part thereof by the wrongful act of any person or persons".

This exclusion, as we have already noted, is customary when the insurance is on restricted conditions.

Clause 5 — Unseaworthiness and Unfitness Exclusion Clause

In all three forms, Clause 5 — Unseaworthiness and Unfitness Exclusion Clause — is in the modified form which we have noted in connection with the Institute Commodity Trades Clauses.

Clauses 6 and 7 — War and Strikes Exclusion Clauses

Clauses 6 and 7 — the War and Strikes Exclusion Clauses appear in the standard form.

Clause 8 — Transit Clause

This clause is the same in all three forms:

8 **8.1** This insurance attaches from the time

8.1.1 the goods pass into the cooling and/or freezing chambers of the works at the place named herein, provided that the period in such chambers prior to shipment on board the oversea vessel thall not exceed 60 days unless prompt notice be given to the Underwriters and an additional premium paid for each further period of 30 days or part thereof.

8.1.2 the goods are loaded into the conveyance at the freezing works or cold store at the place named herein for the commencement of the transit.

8.1.3 of loading of the goods into the oversea vessel.

DELETE SECTIONS NOT APPLICABLE

8.2 This insurance continues during the ordinary course of transit to and whilst in

8.2.1 cold store at the destination named herein

or

8.2.2 any other cold store which the Assured elect to use following discharge of the goods from the oversea vessel at the port of discharge either

8.2.2.1 for storage other than in the ordinary course of transit or

8.2.2.2 for allocation or distribution.

8.3 This insurance terminates

8.3.1 *for transit to a destination in the Continent of Europe (including Eire and the United Kingdom), U.S.A. or Canada* on the expiry of 30 days

8.3.2 *for transit to a destination elsewhere* on the expiry of 5 days

after final discharge of the goods from the oversea vessel at the port of discharge.

8.4 Any disposal of the goods other than by storage as in 8.2.1 or 8.2.2 above (except with the prior consent of the Underwriters) or any removal from cold store before the expiry of the relevant period in 8.3.1 or 8.3.2 above shall terminate the insurance on such goods.

8.5 If, after discharge overside from the oversea vessel at the final port of discharge, but prior to termination of this insurance, the goods are to be forwarded to a destination other than that to which they are insured hereunder, this insurance, whilst remaining subject to termination as provided for above, shall not extend beyond the commencement of transit to such other destination.

8.6   This insurance shall remain in force (subject to termination as provided for above and to the provisions of Clause 9 below) during delay beyond the control of the Assured, any deviation, forced discharge, reshipment or transhipment and during any variation of the adventure arising from the exercise of a liberty granted to shipowners or charterers under the contract of affreightment.

It is to be noted that there are three options available to the assured for the commencement of the risk, namely, as provided in Clause 8.1.1, 8.1.2 or 8.1.3. Furthermore, the time when the insurance terminates depends upon whether the transit is to a destination in Europe, the USA or Canada in which event it expires 30 days after final discharge of the goods from the oversea vessel, or elsewhere in the world in which event the insurance terminates five days after final discharge of the goods. However, if the goods are removed from the cold store into which they have been placed after discharge from the ocean steamer, such removal will, by Clause 8.4, bring about a prior termination of the risk.

Clauses 8.5 and 8.6

Clauses 8.5 and 8.6 are in the same terms as Clauses 8.2 and 8.3 of the Institute Cargo Clauses.

Clause 9 — Termination of Contract of Affreightment Clause

This is in similar terms to Clause 9 of Institute Cargo Clauses, except that in the event of prompt notice being given to the underwriters for a continuation of the cover after termination of the contract of affreightment, the period of time for which underwriters will agree to continue the cover (subject to any agreed extension) is limited to 30 days, compared with 60 days under Institute Cargo Clauses.

Clauses 10 to 13

Clauses 10 to 13 are all the same as found in the Institute Cargo Clauses.

Clause 14 — Adjustment Clause

14   Should the subject-matter insured or any part thereof not be shipped any claim in respect thereto shall be adjusted on the basis of its insured value less, where included, freight, duty and all charges not incurred.

The effect of this clause is that in the event of any claim for loss or damage to the goods, or part of them, prior to their shipment on board the ocean steamer, the adjustment will be made on the basis of the proportion of the loss being applied not to the full value insured, but to that figure less any freight, duty or charges which the assured will not be liable to pay because of the loss or damage sustained to the goods.

Clauses 15 to 20, Note and Special Note

Clauses 15 to 20 correspond to Clauses 14 to 19 of the Institute Cargo Clauses. So likewise does the Note regarding prompt notice at the foot of the form. There is also a Special Note which reads:

SPECIAL NOTE:— This insurance does not cover loss damage or expense caused by embargo, or by rejection prohibition or detention by the government of the country of import or their agencies or departments, but does not exclude loss of or damage to the subject-matter insured caused by risks insured hereunder and sustained prior to any such embargo rejection prohibition or detention.

This note, and its effect, are the same as in the 1/1/86 version of the Institute Frozen Food Clauses. See page 51.

J. INSTITUTE TIMBER TRADE FEDERATION CLAUSES
(agreed with the Timber Trade Federation) (1/4/86)

Clause 1 — Risks Clause

1   **Cargo whilst stowed on deck**
   1.1   This insurance covers, except as provided in Clauses 4, 5, 6 and 7 below,
     1.1.1   loss of or damage to the subject-matter insured whilst stowed on deck of the oversea vessel, or any part or item thereof whilst so stowed, reasonably attributable to
     1.1.1.1   fire or explosion
     1.1.1.2   vessel being stranded grounded sunk or capsized
     1.1.1.3   collision or contact of vessel with any external object other than water
     1.1.1.4   discharge of cargo at a port of distress,
     1.1.2   loss of or damage to the subject-matter insured whilst stowed on deck of the oversea vessel, or any part or item thereof whilst so stowed, caused by
     1.1.2.1   general average sacrifice
     1.1.2.2   jettison or washing overboard
     1.1.2.3   theft or non-delivery
     1.1.2.4   malicious act.
   Cargo whilst not stowed on deck
   1.2   This insurance covers all risks of loss of or damage to the subject-matter insured excluding any part or item thereof whilst stowed on deck on the oversea vessel, except as provided in Clauses 4, 5, 6 and 7 below. Subject-matter insured or any part or item thereof stowed in poop, forecastle, deck house, shelter deck, other enclosed space, or in a container, shall be deemed to be subject-matter insured not stowed on deck.

Because of their high volume/weight ratio, timber cargoes are frequently carried on deck and are thus exposed to greater risks than cargo stowed under deck. This is therefore reflected in the terms of the insurance offered by underwriters on timber cargoes, and consequently when a ship has been chartered to carry a full cargo of wood goods, the cargo stowed under deck will be covered against "all risks", while the cargo stowed on deck is covered only against the named perils in Clause 1.1.

Timber stowed under cover or in a container (even though the container is itself stowed on deck) is given the advantage of the all risks cover as if it had been stowed under deck.

The specific perils insured for "on deck" cargo are, on the whole, wider than as provided in the Institute Cargo Clauses (C). Washing overboard, which is a very real hazard with deck cargoes is specifically covered in Clause 1.1.2.2, and so is theft or non-delivery by Clause 1.1.2.3, and any "malicious act". On the other hand, overturning or derailment of land conveyance is omitted from the list of perils insured, as is the risk of lighter or craft (but not, of course, the oversea vessel) being stranded, grounded, sunk, capsized or in collision or contact with any other object.

As already stated, cargo stowed under deck or in covered spaces or in a container is insured on "all risks" conditions.

Clause 2 — The General Average Clause

Clause 3 — "Both to Blame Collision" Clause

These are in standard form.

Clause 4 — The General Exclusions Clause

Other than exclusion 4.6, which is in the modified form which we have noted under the Institute Commodity Trades Clauses, the list of exclusions 4.1 to 4.5 inclusive and 4.7 are in the same form as in the Institute Cargo Clauses (A).

Clause 5 — Unseaworthiness and Unfitness Exclusion Clause

This clause is also in the modified form which we have noted in the Institute Commodity Trades Clauses.

Clauses 6 and 7 — War and Strikes Exclusion Clauses

These are in standard form.

Clause 8 — Transit Clause

8 **8.1** This insurance attaches on or after the loading of the goods insured hereunder on land and/or water conveyances or their floating at the mill, warehouse, factory, yard or premises wheresoever, from which the despatch to the oversea vessel is made, continues during the ordinary course of transit and terminates either

8.1.1 on delivery of the goods by land or water into the mill, warehouse, factory, yard or premises at their final destination, whether at the port of discharge of the oversea vessel or (further sea voyage excepted) elsewhere, and are there made available to the Assured or Receivers

8.1.2 on delivery to any other warehouse or place of storage which the Assured elect to use for storage other than in the ordinary course of transit
or

8.1.3 on the expiry of 60 days after completion of discharge overside of the goods hereby insured from the oversea vessel at the final port of discharge, whichever shall first occur.

8.2 This insurance shall remain in force (subject to termination as provided for above and to the provisions of Clause 9 below) during delay beyond the control of the Assured, any deviation, forced discharge, reshipment or transhipment and during any variation of the adventure arising from the exercise of a liberty granted to shipowners or charterers under the contract of affreightment.

8.3 Each bill of lading to be deemed a separate insurance if required by the Assured at any time.

8.4 The provisions of Clause 8 shall apply notwithstanding that the description of the voyage in the body of the policy may state only the ports and places of shipment and discharge.

Clause 8.1 contains flexible provisions for the attachment of the risk. This may occur on loading the timber into land or water conveyances, wherever this takes place for the despatch to the ocean steamer. It may even be that logs are floated down river from the timber mill where they are prepared, in which event the insurance attaches at the time they are put into the water.

Termination of the risk is in accordance with either of Clauses 8.1.1, 8.1.2 or 8.1.3, whichever first occurs.

There is an interesting provision in Clause 8.3, which has been carried over from the previous version of the Timber Trade Federation Clauses (1/1/62). This is that each separate bill of lading may be deemed a separate insurance, if required by the assured. While this was relevant when the clauses were subject to an attainable franchise (as they were in the 1/1/62 form), it would not appear to be of any value to an assured under the current form, unless the insurance is specifically made subject either to an attainable franchise or to a deductible.

By Clause 8.4, an assured who requires to apply the flexible provisions of Clause 8.1, particularly as regards the attachment of the risk, will not be prejudiced by reason of his describing the voyage as from the port of shipment to the port of discharge. The reason for this concession is that in the timber trade, it frequently happens that the exporter who arranges the insurance will not know from which mills or logging camps the pieces of timber will have started their journey to the port of loading.

The remainder of the clauses, viz. Clause 9 to Clause 19 and the Note at the end are all in the same terms as in Institute Cargo Clauses.

5. OCCASIONAL AND ADDITIONAL CLAUSES

A. INSTITUTE MALICIOUS DAMAGE CLAUSE (1/8/83)

> In consideration of an additional premium, it is hereby agreed that the exclusion "deliberate damage to or deliberate destruction of the subject-matter insured or any part thereof by the wrongful act of any person or persons" is deemed to be deleted and further that this insurance covers loss of or damage to the subject-matter insured caused by malicious acts vandalism or sabotage, subject always to the other exclusions contained in this insurance.

The cover granted by this clause falls into two parts:

(a) The exclusion (by Clause 4.7 in Institute Cargo Clauses (B) and (C)) of "deliberate damage to or deliberate destruction of the subject-matter insured or any part thereof by the wrongful act of any person or persons" is deleted and

(b) positive cover is granted against loss or damage caused by "malicious acts, vandalism or sabotage".

It will be appreciated that the extension of cover granted by this clause will benefit an assured whose goods are covered under restricted conditions but such extension will not be required when the goods are insured under "all risks" conditions.

A malicious act is one performed out of spite or ill-will, or something of the like. By that definition, vandalism and sabotage are merely examples of malicious acts.

Coverage against loss or damage caused by persons acting maliciously used to be provided by the Institute Strikes Clauses, but this is now not the case so far as cargo is concerned. See Part V, on page 200. Instead, the current Institute Strikes Clauses (Cargo) provides cover for loss or damage caused by "any terrorist or any person acting from a political motive", but this is not the same thing at all. Consequently, unless the assured has an "all risks" marine policy, he will need, in addition to the Institute War Clauses (Cargo) and the Institute Strikes Clauses (Cargo) the Institute Malicious Damage Clause to provide himself with all-round cover.

B. INSTITUTE THEFT, PILFERAGE AND NON-DELIVERY CLAUSE (For use only with Institute Clauses) (1/12/83)

> In consideration of an additional premium, it is hereby agreed that this insurance covers loss of or damage to the subject-matter insured caused by theft or pilferage, or by non-delivery of an entire package, subject always to the exclusions contained in this insurance.

Once again, this additional clause will not be required by an assured who has taken out a policy on "all risks" conditions.

It is something of an open question whether three separate risks are covered by this clause, or whether they are merely three different species of the same genus. In *Middows Ltd.* v. *Robertson,*[52] Hilbery J. was invited at

---

52. *Middows Ltd.* v. *Robertson* at first instance, (1940) 67 Ll.L.Rep. 484.

first instance to consider the non-delivery of a full cargo by reason of the carrying ship being diverted by order of the government in time of war. The insurance included a typed clause covering "damage by hook, oil, sweat, heat, fresh water and other cargo (liquid or solid), theft, pilferage and non-delivery". The judge said:

> "These general words 'non-delivery' following enumerated perils insured against cannot be divorced from what has gone before and treated as intended to denominate an entirely new risk. They are limited by the context in which they are found. Such words in such a context are to be construed not as creating a new or further risk but affecting the burden of proof. Where such words occur in such a context the insured need not prove loss by theft or pilferage; it is enough if he proves non-delivery and gives prima facie proof that the goods were not lost in any other way than by theft or pilferage. ... The case I am deciding ... is not a case which on its facts has anything to do with 'non-delivery' when those words are applied in the context in which they occur."

In the opinion of the authors, the context of the words "by theft or pilferage, or by non-delivery of an entire package" do not *by their context*, have to be construed *ejusdem generis*. On the contrary, it is considered that there are really two separate perils insured:
(1) theft or pilferage, and quite separately (2) non-delivery of an entire package. This construction is supported by the comma which appears after the word "pilferage", and by the repetition of the words "or by" before "non-delivery".

"theft or pilferage"

In *Nishina Trading Co.* v. *Chiyoda Fire & Marine Insurance Co.*,[53] shipowners, in the erroneous belief that they had a valid lien on the cargo for arrears of time-charter hire due to them from the time charterers, landed the goods at an intermediate port on the voyage and sold them there. Lord Denning M.R. said:

> "was there a 'theft' of cargo by the master? The word 'theft' is not used here in the strict sense of the criminal law. It does not bring in all the eccentricities of the law of larceny. It means only what an ordinary commercial man would consider to be theft: and before finding theft, the Court should be satisfied that it is an appropriate description of what took place. The Court need not be satisfied beyond reasonable doubt (as in the criminal law) but it should find on balance that there is sufficient to warrant the serious imputation of 'theft'."

It was held by the Court of Appeal that the shipowners' action did not amount to theft.

"Pilferage" is a species of theft performed surreptitiously.

---

53. *Nishina Trading Co.* v. *Chiyoda Fire & Marine Insurance Co.* [1969] 1 Lloyd's Rep. 293, *per* Lord Denning M.R. at p. 298.

"non-delivery of an entire package"

Many cargo assured are under the impression that the inclusion of this risk in their policy entitles them to claim for any loss (of an entire package) which has occurred at any time, and from any cause, during the voyage. This is not so, as the following examples should make clear:

(a) A case of fireworks is short delivered at destination, and the carrier explains that it was seized by the Customs authorities at an intermediate port, as they considered it to be hazardous cargo. This is not a loss by non-delivery; it is a loss by "seizure", which is an excluded peril (Clause 6.2 of Institute Cargo Clauses).

(b) A case of fireworks is short delivered, but this time the carrier explains that the master ordered the case to be thrown overboard, since he considered it to be a danger to the other cargo on board. This is not a loss by non-delivery; it is a loss by jettison, and unless there was wilful misconduct on the part of the assured in shipping the fireworks, or in misdescribing them, there will be a claim under Institute Cargo Clauses without the addition of the Theft, Pilferage and Non-Delivery Clause.

(c) One package is short delivered and, after inquiry, the carrier "regrets that it may have been delivered to another consignee by mistake". This is a non-delivery as regards the bill of lading holder and, subject to his holding the carrier responsible as he is required to do by Clause 16.2 of the Institute Cargo Clauses, he will have a valid claim under the Institute Theft, Pilferage and Non-Delivery Clause.

(d) A case is short delivered and, after inquiry, it appears to have been over-carried to another port, and the ship's agent claims that he does not know what to do with it. In this case, although there has been a "non-delivery" in the ordinary sense of that word, there is no loss to the subject-matter insured, which is perfectly safe and sound. In fact it is the carrier's duty to ship it back at his own expense to the port to which it was consigned and there tender it to the bill of lading holder.

(e) A case is short delivered and, after inquiry, no one can offer any plausible explanation for its disappearance. This is a loss by non-delivery, in circumstances which suggest that the package may have been stolen, although there is insufficient evidence to prove it. This is the case where the cause of the loss is *ejusdem generis* with theft or pilferage, so whatever construction might be required of the words in the clause, the loss will be paid for by the underwriters.

PART III

Marine Hull Forms

1. HISTORICAL PERSPECTIVE

Insurance for merchant adventurers and container operators

Lloyd's S.G. form catered for the merchant adventurer. The same form of policy was available to cover both the ship and the goods which the merchant adventurer — very often the owner or the master of the ship — had purchased or contracted to carry to distant parts of the world. On disposal of the outward cargoes at destination, the merchant adventurer would reckon to have the means, perhaps with something in hand, to purchase a homeward cargo, from the sale of which he would expect to be able to pay off his crew, refit and reprovision his ship and still be able to show a profit for himself and his co-adventurers.

For such an adventure a policy of insurance expressed to apply to a round voyage "out and home" was entirely adequate. Sometimes the voyage was a three-legged one, for example, from Plymouth to West Africa with home-produced produce, thence with a cargo of slaves to Barbados, and from there to the ship's home port with a cargo of sugar and rum.

If, during the course of such a voyage, the ship sustained damage by insured perils, it would not be possible to make an account of the same until she arrived back in her home port. No doubt the master kept a careful note of any expenditure which he had had to incur for any repairs which had to be done at any of the outports, but since he had no means of presenting these bills to the underwriters until his return home, his account could not be presented until he had safely completed the voyage, at which time he would be able to call in shipwrights upon whose competence he could rely to make good any damage which the ship had sustained since leaving her home port many months before.

We have already noted that the "Memorandum" at the foot of Lloyd's form of policy stated that the ship and freight were "warranted free from Average under three per cent, unless general, or the ship be stranded". For the practical reasons which we have noted above, particular average losses occurring during the voyage were necessarily added together in order to ascertain whether the total cost of making good the damage exceeded the warranty percentage or not, and the practice of so doing was approved in the case of *Blackett* v. *Royal Exchange Assurance* in 1832.

With the expansion of commerce, ships began to engage upon regular liner trades, and also ventured further and wider in seeking cargoes. Hence the development of insurances on ship and freight, expressed not for a voyage, but for a period of time — usually twelve months. The question then arose — over what period could particular average losses occurring during the currency of a time policy be aggregated in order to ascertain whether the memorandum percentage had been attained? It was not until *Stewart* v. *Merchants' Marine Insurance Co.* (1885) that this question was answered. The Court of Appeal held that although the policy was for a period of time, the aggregation of losses, for the purpose of ascertaining whether the stipulated percentage had been attained, should be limited, as in the case of a voyage policy, to those which had been sustained in the course of a round voyage. More or less simultaneously, the practice grew up of including a "voyage clause" in policies of insurance for time, whereby (as in the 1903 Time Clauses), "the warranty and conditions as to average under three per cent to be applicable to each voyage as if separately insured", and there followed detailed provisions as to how each voyage should be made up.

In the old days, the process of adjustment was fairly straightforward. There was but one custom of universal application, and that was that one-third was to be deducted from the cost of all repairs (unless the ship was engaged upon her first voyage), so as to protect the underwriter from having to pay any element of betterment or "improvement" in the value of the ship, by reason of replacing old material with new. With the advent of iron hulls, this practice (although, in the meantime, approved by the courts in *Aitchison* v. *Lohre* in 1879) ceased to be equitable, and in consequence underwriters began to insert in their policies of insurance a clause providing: "Average payable without deduction of thirds new for old, whether the average be particular or general."

As to liabilities, it was decided as long ago as 1836, in *De Vaux* v. *Salvador* that an underwriter on Lloyd's form of policy was not liable to indemnify a shipowner for the amount which he had been found liable to pay to another vessel in consequence of collision. As Lord Denman expressed it, "the obligation to pay was neither a necessary nor a proximate effect of perils of the sea, but growing out of an arbitrary provision of the law of nations". Yet within a few years, underwriters found it expedient to include a special clause in their policies, whereby in addition to any other claims which might be paid thereon up to the amount insured, they would indemnify their assured for three-fourths of such liabilities.

In yet another area underwriters were extremely prompt to close a gap exposed by the courts in the cover which they granted under traditional policy forms. In the well-known case of *The "Inchmaree"* (*Hamilton* v. *Thames and*

Mersey Marine Insurance Company) the underwriters agreed that the facts should be put up for consideration as a "test case" which was eventually decided by the House of Lords in 1887. The facts were that a rupture in an air-chamber in a donkey pump occurred through the negligence of engineers in failing to open the valve connecting the water-chamber with the boilers when the pump was put into operation. The House of Lords held that this could not be considered as the consequence of a peril of the sea or any cause *ejusdem generis* therewith. The immediate effect of this decision was the incorporation in policies of insurance of a new clause (thereafter known as the "Inchmaree" Clause) designed to add perils of this nature to those already covered by the traditional form of policy.

One might cite other instances where underwriters have been desirous of supplementing the cover which their policies provide, but instead we have to note that in the twentieth century the trend has been reversed. In particular, since 1969, the relatively generous provisions of the Voyage Clause have been swept away, and in its place, Clause 12 of the Institute Time Clauses Hulls now provides for a deductible franchise to be applied to the aggregate of all claims arising out of each separate accident or occurrence. A number of other irksome provisions were introduced at the same time, many of which persist in the clauses which we will review hereafter.

Perhaps the feeling was, at the time these restrictive clauses were introduced, that shipowners had become too powerful, and that underwriters needed to be protected against rapacious claims. If that was so, the experience of the last fifteen years has shown how wrong this theory was.

The forms of 1/10/83 onwards have begun to correct the imbalance, but to see how far they have done so, we shall need to examine them in detail.

2. INSTITUTE TIME CLAUSES, HULLS (1/10/83)

"This insurance is subject to English law and practice"

When underwriters were revising the Institute Time Clauses, Hulls, culminating in the 1/10/83 clauses, the representatives of the London market were conscious of the possibility that under the legislation of the European Economic Community British insurers could find themselves as defendants in an action before a court in another EEC country, with that judgement being enforceable in the United Kingdom. This, coupled with the fact that the clauses had been drafted in the light of English law and practice and the Marine Insurance Act 1906, led to the inclusion of the above proviso. In addition, a clause was included in the MAR form of policy adopted by Lloyd's and the Companies Marine Policy adopted by the Institute of London Underwriters, making the insurances subject to English jurisdiction.

However, whilst the clauses were drafted against this backcloth, they were also designed with a view to their adoption by the international insurance and shipping communities and it was anticipated that they would be attached to foreign policy forms which would incorporate different jurisdiction clauses. Even in these circumstances it is still considered preferable for the above wording to be retained in the clauses so that the appropriate court has the benefit of the wealth of English law and practice on marine insurance and it has the added advantage of hopefully bringing about consistency of interpretation.

The difference between the proper law of the contract and the correct jurisdiction was illustrated in the case of *The "Al Wahab"*[1] which went as far as the House of Lords. In this case neither the plaintiffs nor the defendant insurers were English and the policy had been issued in Kuwait. However the policy form used was the Lloyd's S.G. form of policy scheduled to the Marine Insurance Act 1906 with the addition of standard Institute Clauses, the whole policy being in the English language. It was accepted by both sides that in Kuwait at the relevant time there was no indigenous law of marine insurance. The House of Lords held:

(1) It was not possible to interpret the policy or to determine what the mutual legal rights and obligations of the parties were except by reference to the Marine Insurance Act 1906 and its substantive provisions; the English rules of conflict of laws applied and the proper law of the contract embodied in the policy was English law.

(2) In the absence of an indigenous law of marine insurance in Kuwait, English law was the only system of private law by reference to which it was possible for a Kuwaiti court to give a sensible and precise meaning to the language that the parties had chosen to use in the policy.

(3) Having no grounds for doubting that justice could be obtained in a Kuwaiti court there was no justification for compelling the defendants to submit to the jurisdiction of the English court.

Clause 1 — Navigation

> 1.1 The Vessel is covered subject to the provisions of this insurance at all times and has leave to sail or navigate with or without pilots, to go on trial trips and to assist and tow vessels or craft in distress, but it is warranted that the Vessel shall not be towed, except as is customary or to the first safe port or place when in need of assistance, or undertake towage or salvage services under a contract previously arranged by the Assured and/or Owners and/or Managers and/or Charterers. This clause 1.1 shall not exclude customary towage in connection with loading and discharging.

The clause makes it clear that the vessel is covered at all times, including while sailing or navigating with or without pilots, undertaking trial trips and rendering assistance to other vessels or craft in distress. However, it is warranted that the vessel shall not be towed, except when in need of assistance, and then only to the first safe port or place. As to what is the first safe port

1. [1983] 2 Lloyd's Rep. 365.

or place, it is submitted that this has to be construed in the light of all the facts, and the "first safe port" may not necessarily be the nearest in mileage terms and should be construed as that port which, on the whole, and in the actual circumstances is the fittest place for receiving the ship in the light of the repair and other facilities required. The clause makes it clear that the warranty does not exclude "customary" towage, for example in or out of a port or dock or in connection with loading and discharging. The clause further warrants that the vessel will not undertake towage or salvage services under a prearranged contract.

> **1.2**   In the event of the Vessel being employed in trading operations which entail cargo loading or discharging at sea from or into another vessel (not being a harbour or inshore craft) no claim shall be recoverable under this insurance for loss of or damage to the Vessel or liability to any other vessel arising from such loading or discharging operations, including whilst approaching, lying alongside and leaving, unless previous notice that the Vessel is to be employed in such operations has been given to the Underwriters and any amended terms of cover and any additional premium required by them have been agreed.

This clause, previously known unofficially as the "Mothership Clause" first appeared in the I.T.C. in 1969. With the development of larger vessels which because of draft restrictions could not obtain entry to many ports, transhipment operations into smaller vessels became increasingly commonplace and underwriters began to experience correspondingly heavier claims resulting from ranging damage, collisions and contacts. There were also many practical problems in the adjustment of claims, the main difficulty being to assess the number of deductibles to be applied, for example, after a lengthy transhipment operation involving several other vessels, intermittently bad weather, with various minor collisions and periods of ranging having been logged.

The clause stipulates that if cover is required for cargo loading or discharging operations at sea from or into another vessel, previous notice must be given to underwriters and any amended terms of cover and any additional premium agreed. In the absence of such prior agreement, not only would any loss or damage sustained by the insured vessel as a result of the cargo operations (including whilst approaching, lying alongside and leaving) not be covered, but any liability to any other vessel arising from such operations would also be excluded. It should be noted that the clause only relates to employment of the vessel in "trading operations" and the clause does not relate to emergency operations following a casualty, for example, jettison or transhipment/lightening of a stranded vessel. The clause is not intended to deal with the more routine and generally safer operations undertaken in port and consequently any claims arising from loading or discharging cargo, as customary, into harbour or inshore craft, even when undertaken at sea, are not excluded by the clause.

In practice, upon receiving prior notification of a cargo operation falling within Clause 1.2, underwriters will frequently suggest that the cover be amended to include one larger deductible, to be applied to the aggregate of all claims arising out of the whole cargo operation, with the payment of an additional premium where considered necessary. It is accordingly essential for any shipowner considering taking up a charter involving cargo operations described in Clause 1.2 to contact his broker to ensure that he is covered for same and also to obtain details of the additional premium payable which will assist him in forecasting the likely profitability of the fixture.

> 1.3 In the event of the Vessel sailing (with or without cargo) with an intention of being (a) broken up, or (b) sold for breaking up, any claim for loss of or damage to the Vessel occurring subsequent to such sailing shall be limited to the market value of the Vessel as scrap at the time when the loss or damage is sustained, unless previous notice has been given to the Underwriters and any amendments to the terms of cover, insured value and premium required by them have been agreed. Nothing in this Clause 1.3 shall affect claims under Clauses 8 and/or 11.

First introduced in October 1983, this clause deals with the 'situation when the vessel sails with the intention of being broken up or sold for breaking up. In such circumstances the clause stipulates that in the absence of prior notice having been given to underwriters and other terms having been agreed, any claim for loss of or damage to the vessel occurring subsequent to such sailing will be limited to the market value of the vessel as scrap at the time when the loss or damage is sustained. The clause expressly has no effect upon claims for collision liability or general average and salvage.

In the opinion of the authors this is one of the least satisfactory clauses in the I.T.C. A shipowner may well take up a charter which will leave the vessel in the area of one of the major scrapping centres. The shipowner may also have at the back of his mind the possibility of selling the vessel for scrap, depending upon several variable factors, such as the levels of scrap prices and freight rates. In such circumstances, when the vessel sails under the charter is she sailing with the intention of being broken up or being sold for breaking up? What is "the market value of the vessel as scrap at the time when the loss or damage is sustained" if a vessel sinks between two major scrapping centres, with widely disparate price levels? Common sense dictates that it should be the centre in the direction of which the vessel was proceeding at the time of the total loss even if at the time of the loss she is closer geographically to another centre. The abrogation of the agreed value when the clause is invoked could place a shipowner in breach of the insurance requirements laid down in his mortgage deed and great care needs to be exercised when undertaking any voyage which could be construed as falling within the terms of this clause.

Clause 2 — Continuation

> 2 CONTINUATION
> Should the Vessel at the expiration of this insurance be at sea or in distress or at a port of refuge or of call, she shall, provided previous notice be given to the Underwriters, be held covered at a pro rata monthly premium to her port of destination.

If at the end of the period of insurance the vessel is still short of her destination, she is held covered at a pro rata monthly premium until she reaches there, provided previous notice is given to underwriters.

Clause 3 — Breach of Warranty

3   **BREACH OF WARRANTY**
Held covered in case of any breach of warranty as to cargo, trade, locality, towage, salvage services or date of sailing, provided notice be given to the Underwriters immediately after receipt of advices and any amended terms of cover and any additional premium required by them be agreed.

Other clauses contain various warranties and this clause provides for the breach of certain specified warranties to be held covered, subject to notice being given to underwriters immediately after receipt of advices and any amended terms and additional premium being agreed. It is important to note that only breaches of certain specified warranties are held covered and if the policy incorporates additional warranties, their breach may not be held covered under this clause.

Clause 4 — Termination

4   **TERMINATION**
This Clause 4 shall prevail notwithstanding any provision whether written typed or printed in this insurance inconsistent therewith.
Unless the Underwriters agree to the contrary in writing, this insurance shall terminate automatically at the time of
4.1   change of the Classification Society of the Vessel, or change, suspension, discontinuance, withdrawal or expiry of her Class therein, provided that if the Vessel is at sea such automatic termination shall be deferred until arrival at her next port. However where such change, suspension, discontinuance or withdrawal of her Class has resulted from loss or damage covered by Clause 6 of this insurance or which would be covered by an insurance of the Vessel subject to current Institute War and Strikes Clauses Hulls-Time such automatic termination shall only operate should the Vessel sail from her next port without the prior approval of the Classification Society,
4.2   any change, voluntary or otherwise, in the ownership or flag, transfer to new management, or charter on a bareboat basis, or requisition for title or use of the Vessel, provided that, if the Vessel has cargo on board and has already sailed from her loading port or is at sea in ballast, such automatic termination shall if required be deferred, whilst the Vessel continues her planned voyage, until arrival at final port of discharge if with cargo or at port of destination if in ballast. However, in the event of requisition for title or use without the prior execution of a written agreement by the Assured, such automatic termination shall occur fifteen days after such requisition whether the Vessel is at sea or in port.
A pro rata daily net return of premium shall be made.

The wording in heavy type emphasises that this is a clause paramount which prevails notwithstanding any contrary provision in the policy. When underwriters are approached with a proposal for insurance, the fact that a vessel is classed and the status of the Classification Society concerned are important considerations. Any change in the vessel's classification status during the period of the insurance is therefore an important matter for the insurers and the clause provides for automatic termination of the insurance cover, in the absence of underwriters' written agreement to the contrary, at the time of the change of Classification Society or any change, suspension, discontinuance, withdrawal or expiry of the vessel's class. The effect of the clause is ameliorated in certain circumstances, namely:

(a) If the event which triggers automatic termination occurs while the vessel is at sea, termination is deferred until arrival at her next port.

(b) If the cause of the alteration in the vessel's classification status is a result of damage covered by Clause 6 of the I.T.C., or the current War and Strikes Clauses, the automatic termination only operates if the vessel sails from her next port without the prior approval of the Classification Society.

It is interesting to note that the amelioration mentioned in (b) is only in respect of loss or damage covered by Clause 6 of the I.T.C., and not all loss or damage covered by the marine policy. Strictly speaking any change in the classification status brought about by damage covered by a supplementary clause, such as the Institute Additional Perils Clauses — Hulls, would result in automatic termination, but the authors would be extremely surprised if underwriters ever took this point. However, to be on the safe side, shipowners would be well advised to notify their underwriters of any such change.

Under the rules of certain Classification Societies there is provision for retrospective cancellation of class and in such circumstances the insurance could be deemed to be terminated automatically from the retrospective date of such suspension.

The second part of the Termination Clause deals with the change of ownership, transfer to new management, change of flag, charter on a bare-boat basis, or requisition for title or use. The insurance terminates automatically at the time of any of these changes, unless underwriters have given their written agreement to the contrary. Once again the effect of the clause is ameliorated in certain circumstances, namely:

(a) If the vessel has commenced a cargo passage or is at sea in ballast, termination can be deferred, while the vessel continues her planned voyage, until arrival at her final port of discharge, or port of destination if in ballast. Such deferment continues only while the vessel is proceeding on her planned voyage so that if following requisition, the vessel is ordered on a different voyage, cover terminates automatically from the time of deviation from the original voyage.

(b) If the requisition was without the prior execution of a written agreement by the assured, the automatic termination is deferred until 15 days after the requisition.

It is only chartering the vessel on a bare-boat basis which is mentioned in the clause and time or voyage charters do not affect the cover.

It should be emphasised that it is any change, voluntary or otherwise, in the specified areas which can invoke automatic termination so that the action of a mortgagee bank, for example, in foreclosing and transferring the management, against the wishes of the assured, would give rise to automatic termination unless underwriters' written agreement to continue cover is obtained.

The American Institute Hull Clauses (2 June 1977) expressly state that the term "new management" refers only to the transfer of the management of the vessel from one firm or corporation to another, and does not apply to internal changes within the offices of the assured. The drafters of the I.T.C. were advised that such clarification was unnecessary and this is why there is no equivalent wording in the I.T.C., although the construction of the term would undoubtedly be the same.

Finally, Clause 4 provides for a pro rata daily net return of premium in the event of automatic termination of the cover.

Clause 5 — Assignment

5   ASSIGNMENT

No assignment of or interest in this insurance or in any moneys which may be or become payable thereunder is to be binding on or recognised by the Underwriters unless a dated notice of such assignment or interest signed by the Assured, and by the assignor in the case of subsequent assignments, is endorsed on the Policy and the Policy with such endorsement is produced before payment of any claim or return of premium thereunder.

Assignment of the policies is dealt with in sections 50–51 of the Marine Insurance Act 1906 as follows:

"50. — (1) A marine policy is assignable unless it contains terms expressly prohibiting assignment. It may be assigned either before or after loss.

(2) Where a marine policy has been assigned so as to pass the beneficial interest in such policy, the assignee of the policy is entitled to sue thereon in his own name; and the defendant is entitled to make any defence arising out of the contract which he would have been entitled to make if the action had been brought in the name of the person by or on behalf of whom the policy was effected.

(3) A marine policy may be assigned by indorsement thereon or in other customary manner.

51. Where the assured has parted with or lost his interest in the subject-matter insured, and has not, before or at the time of so doing, expressly or impliedly agreed to assign the policy, any subsequent assignment of the policy is inoperative:

Provided that nothing in this section affects the assignment of a policy after loss."

Clause 5 does not prohibit assignment but merely lays down the steps which must be undertaken by the assured, and any subsequent assignors, before an assignment will be recognised by underwriters and become binding upon them. This is a reasonable precaution on the part of underwriters and enables them to ascertain that any claims are paid to the correct party. There is one very important limitation to the assured's right of assignment and this arises not out of Clause 5 but Clause 4, the Termination Clause. If the assured sells the vessel he is precluded from assigning the policy to the new owner by reason of the automatic termination of the insurance cover operative under Clause 4 in the event of change of ownership.

Clause 6 — Perils

6   PERILS

6.1   This insurance covers loss of or damage to the subject-matter insured caused by

6.1.1   perils of the seas rivers lakes or other navigable waters

6.1.2   fire, explosion

6.1.3   violent theft by persons from outside the Vessel

6.1.4   jettison

6.1.5   piracy

6.1.6   breakdown of or accident to nuclear installations or reactors

6.1.7   contact with aircraft or similar objects, or objects falling therefrom, land conveyance, dock or harbour equipment or installation

6.1.8   earthquake volcanic eruption or lightning.

6.2   This insurance covers loss of or damage to the subject-matter insured caused by

6.2.1   accidents in loading discharging or shifting cargo or fuel

6.2.2   bursting of boilers breakage of shafts or any latent defect in the machinery or hull

6.2.3   negligence of Master Officers Crew or Pilots

6.2.4   negligence of repairers or charterers provided such repairers or charterers are not an Assured hereunder

6.2.5   barratry of Master Officers or Crew,

provided such loss or damage has not resulted from want of due diligence by the Assured, Owners or Managers

6.3   Master Officers Crew or Pilots not to be considered Owners within the meaning of this Clause 6 should they hold shares in the Vessel.

Incidence of loss under the policies

Before we consider the perils in detail, it may be useful to examine the question of the incidence of loss and the change brought about by the I.T.C. 1/10/83. Under the S.G. policy form with the previous editions of the I.T.C. attached, it was necessary to differentiate between:

(1) A claim under the body of the policy where it was the perils which were covered *per se*, and

(2) the Inchmaree Clause contained in the I.T.C. where it was the loss or damage caused by the enumerated additional perils which was covered.

Some examples may illustrate the position.

If a vessel struck a submerged object two days before a change in policies but did not actually sink until after the next set of policies had incepted, the claim, which arose from a basic peril in the body of the policy (perils of the seas), would have fallen on the first set of policies which were current when the peril operated.

The incidence upon the policies of a claim under the Inchmaree Clause, where the cover is against "loss or damage caused by ...", must then be differentiated. Let us take as an example a claim resulting from the incorrect refitting of a propeller seal ring at a routine drydocking, resulting in corrosion during the next four years, which is only discovered at the next routine drawing of the tailshaft. Here the claim would be apportioned over all four policy years covering the period when the damage occurred (and not when the negligent act took place).

Under the I.T.C. 1/10/83., the clauses now include the perils which used to be found in the body of the S.G. policy, but instead of covering the perils *per se*, the insurance cover is against "loss of or damage to the subject-matter insured caused by", bringing it into line with the basis of cover provided by the Inchmaree Clause. It must be emphasised that this does not affect the positive cover given by the perils, merely the incidence of loss on different policies.

Turning now to the individual perils they are as follows:

"6.1.1   perils of the seas, rivers, lakes or other navigable waters"

With the disappearance of the *ejusdem generis* wording of "and of all other perils ... ", which will be discussed in more detail later, it was decided to extend the wording to include rivers, lakes or other navigable waters.

The Rules for Construction of the Policy (Schedule 1 of the Marine Insurance Act 1906) state:

> 7. The term "perils of the seas" refers only to fortuitous accidents or casualties of the seas. It does not include the ordinary action of the winds and waves.

Although attempts have been made over the years, no one has successfully produced a complete definition of the expression perils of the seas. The word peril denotes that something fortuitous and accidental is envisaged; incursion of sea water into the vessel does not necessarily amount to a loss by perils of the seas. So that when due to the old and leaky condition of a storage hulk, sea water gained entry and damaged the cargo, this was not classed as a loss by perils of the seas. See *Sassoon* v. *Western Assurance Company*.[2] The policy only covers against accidents which may happen, not against events which must happen. Similarly, it does not include the deliberate action of the assured or his agents, for example in scuttling the vessel (*Samuel* v. *Dumas*).[3]

The term does not cover every accident or casualty which may happen to

2. (1912) 12 Asp.M.L.C. 206; 17 Com.Cas. 274.
3. [1924] A.C. 431.

the subject-matter insured on the sea. It must be a peril "of" the sea. So that in *Phillips* v. *Barber*[4] where the insured vessel was blown over by a violent gust of wind while in graving dock, this was held not to be a loss by "perils of the seas" (the court did however find in favour of the assured under the *ejusdem generis* wording). However, providing the elements of fortuity and "of the sea" are present, violence of the weather is not an essential pre-requisite so that if, for example, a vessel strands on the coast in fair weather, or as a result of negligence is involved in a collision with another vessel, the resulting loss would be attributable to "perils of the seas".

"6.1.2 fire, explosion"

Fire was one of the enumerated perils in the S.G. form of policy and "explosions on shipboard, or elsewhere" used to appear in the Inchmaree Clause. Because of the due diligence provision in the Inchmaree Clause it was sometimes necessary to attempt to determine whether a loss was by fire or by explosion and this is frequently a difficult if not impossible exercise. The inclusion of both perils in the same clause, with neither subject to the due diligence proviso, is a logical and practical development. There is no explicit reference in the clauses to extinguishing damage; none is necessary under English law which recognises that any loss incurred to prevent a loss by an insured peril is recoverable as a loss by that peril. What constitutes an explosion has been the subject of a recent judicial decision (see page 37).

"6.1.3 violent theft by persons from outside the Vessel"

The equivalent peril in the S.G. form of policy was "thieves" with the Rules of Construction of Policy (Schedule 1, Marine Insurance Act 1906) providing that the term "does not cover clandestine theft or a theft committed by any one of the ship's company, whether crew or passengers". It has always been an accepted rule that simple theft is something which should be capable of prevention by the master and as such is not a proper subject for insurance under the marine policy. The above words are intended to uphold this principle by stipulating that the theft must be:

(1) violent (in *Fabrique de Produits Chimiques* v. *Large*[5] it was held that violence towards persons was not essential to meet the definition; it was sufficient if the thieves had perpetrated violence towards property during the act of theft; *per* Bailhache J. "as when people go with crowbars and smash in doors and then steal the goods from a warehouse") and

(2) by persons from outside the vessel.

4. (1821) B. & A. 161.
5. (1923) 28 Com.Cas. 248; 16 Asp.M.L.C. 110.

"6.1.4   jettison"

It is generally the cargo which is jettisoned at a time of danger but the vessel may be damaged as a result of such an operation or in extreme circumstances part of the ship's equipment may be jettisoned, in which case this would be recoverable as a general average sacrifice.

"6.1.5   piracy"

Since 1937 piracy had been in the war cover but in the 1983 revision of the clauses it was returned to the marine clauses. The Rules for Construction of Policy (Schedule 1, Marine Insurance Act 1906) provide that the term "pirates" includes passengers who mutiny and rioters who attack the ship from the shore. However this definition is not exhaustive. In the case of *Republic of Bolivia* v. *Indemnity Mutual Marine Assurance Company Limited*,[6] the Court of Appeal held that the word "pirates" meant persons plundering indiscriminately for their own ends, and not persons simply operating, albeit illegally and criminally, against the property of a particular state for a political end. See further commentary in Part V, page 185.

"6.1.6   breakdown of or accident to nuclear installations or reactors"

Fortunately, in view of the potential scale of such disasters, the authors are not aware of any claims under this clause, but the cover is nonetheless necessary in the modern world. In the event of contamination of an insured vessel by radioactive material, following say the accidental emission from a nuclear power station, the clean-up costs would be recoverable as the reasonable cost of repairs. If however the contamination was so severe as to make the vessel unusable the assured would have a claim for a total loss.

"6.1.7   contact with aircraft or similar objects, or objects falling therefrom, and conveyance, dock or harbour equipment or installation"

During the revision leading up to the 1983 clauses attention was focused upon the increasing risk of vessels being damaged by satellites running out of control and/or pieces of aircraft or space debris falling to earth. The wording was accordingly amended to encompass these additional risks. As we have already seen when considering perils of the seas, damage sustained by a vessel toppling over in a graving dock is not recoverable as a loss arising from a peril of the sea. However, in appropriate circumstances, it could be recoverable under this clause as damage caused by contact with a dock installation.

6. (1909) 11 Asp.M.L.C. 218; 14 Com.Cas. 156.

"6.1.8   earthquake volcanic eruption or lightning"

If a vessel were to be covered in volcanic dust following an eruption such as Mount St. Helens, this would constitute damage and the cost of cleaning the vessel would be recoverable under this clause. Apart from this, these perils speak for themselves and no special comment is necessary.

We now come to the second part of Clause 6 which has the same preamble namely that "this insurance covers loss of or damage to the subject-matter insured caused by":

"6.2.1   accidents in loading discharging or shifting cargo or fuel"

This was one of the earliest perils incorporated into the Inchmaree Clause and followed the decision in *Stott (Baltic) Steamers* v. *Marten.*[7] In this case the facts were as follows. Whilst lying in dock the vessel was taking on board a boiler from a floating crane. During the loading operation the boiler fouled the hatch coaming, the floating crane listed away from the vessel, and the crane tackle gave way, as a result of which the boiler fell into the lower hold damaging the ship, the claim on underwriters being for the cost of repairing the damage sustained by the vessel. The court held that an accident which might have happened in exactly the same way if the crane had been fixed on the quay could not be called a peril of the sea, or a peril, loss or misfortune of the same kind as a peril of the sea.

It is important to realise that it is only loss or damage caused by the accidents in the operations of loading, discharging or shifting cargo or fuel which is covered and damage suffered by the vessel as a result of cargo having been loaded into the vessel is not recoverable. An example of a claim which would not be recoverable under this clause is damage to the hull plating from the loading (and carriage) of a corrosive cargo.

"6.2.2   bursting of boilers, breakage of shafts or any latent defect in the machinery or hull"

Incorporated into the 1983 clauses in the same form as it appeared in the Inchmaree Clause, this clause was originally drawn up following the case of *"The Inchmaree"*.

In *The "Inchmaree"* (*Thames and Mersey Marine Insurance Company* v. *Hamilton, Fraser & Co.*)[8] the claim was for the cost of replacing the air chamber of a donkey engine which burst due to a screw-valve, which should have been open, having been accidentally or negligently left closed. The House of Lords held that damage had not been caused by one of the

7. (1914) 19 Com.Cas. 93.
8. (1887) 6 Asp.M.L.C. 200.

enumerated perils, or by a peril of a like kind under the *ejusdem generis* rule. It was impossible to say that the damage sustained was of a character to which a marine adventure is specially susceptible and was therefore recoverable *ejusdem generis* with perils of the seas.

The policy only covers "loss or damage to the subject-matter insured caused by" and it is only the consequential damage which is covered and not the cost of repairing or replacing the latently defective parts. So that in the case of a boiler explosion or a shaft breakage, if there is no evidence that the original accident was caused by an insured peril, only the consequential damage would be recoverable and there would be no claim for the cost of repairing or replacing the damaged boiler or shaft. The construction of this clause was the subject of a long line of law cases and in view of the importance of the clause the main authorities are summarised hereunder.

Oceanic Steamship Company v. *Faber.*[9] Upon drawing the tailshaft for routine Classification Society survey, a fracture was discovered and it was condemned. It was subsequently proved that the fracture arose from a new end having been imperfectly welded on to the shaft some years before, it being accepted that this defect had not been visible at the previous Classification Society survey some two and a half years before and must have then constituted a latent defect. The court held that there had been no damage caused by a latent defect. It was nothing more than a latent defect becoming patent, which was not within the words of the Inchmaree Clause and there was therefore no claim.

Wills & Sons v. *The World Marine Insurance Co.*[10] illustrates the kind of consequential damage which the Inchmaree Clause was designed to cover. A link in the hoisting chain of the bucket ladder of a dredger gave way, resulting in the ladder and buckets falling and damaging the hull and machinery. It was held that the underwriters were liable under the clause for the consequential damage to the hull and machinery even though the latently defective link had been in that condition long before the commencement of the policy.

In *Hutchins Bros.* v. *The Royal Exchange Corporation,*[11] the assured had insured their vessel for a period of twelve months from December 1908 on conditions including the Inchmaree Clause. In 1909 and during the currency of the policies, a defect was discovered in the vessel's stern frame and it was condemned. It was found that the stern frame had contained a latent defect when it had been fitted during the building of the ship in 1906. The Court of first instance found in favour of the underwriters and this judgment was affirmed in the Court of Appeal, *per* Scrutton J.:

> "The only damage is the latent defect itself, which by wear and tear has become patent. But the latent defect did not arise during the currency of the policy; it

9. (1907) 11 Com.Cas. 179; 13 Com.Cas. 28; 10 Asp.M.L.C. 303.
10. *The Times*, 14 March 1911.
11. (1911) 16 Com.Cas. 242; 12 Asp.M.L.C. 21.

existed in 1906; the only change is that a previous latent defect has by wear and tear become patent. It has not been constructively lost during the currency of the policy; it was constructively lost in 1906, if the true facts had been known; what has happened during the currency of the policy is the discovery of the true facts."

As will be seen from the above, the point which had been left open in *Oceanic* v. *Faber*[12] was whether underwriters were liable for the cost of replacing a latently defective shaft which actually broke during the currency of the policy. This point was decided in underwriters' favour in *Scindia Steamship (London) Ltd.* v. *London Assurance*.[13] In this case the facts were quite straightforward. During a routine drawing of the tailshaft as the propeller was being wedged off, the tailshaft broke, owing to a latent defect in the shaft. The defendant underwriters, whilst admitting liability for the consequential damage sustained by the propeller when it fell to the dock floor, denied liability for the cost of replacing the latently defective tailshaft. Branson J. found in favour of the underwriters. He concluded that the clause envisaged a state of affairs in which the main cause produces damage which has an effect upon something else.

> "What I have said already in regard to the breakage of the shaft and the necessity of there being some damage caused by the breakage of the shaft itself, seems to me to apply also to the case of a latent defect. Damage to hull and machinery caused through a latent defect in the machinery is something different from damage involved in a latent defect in the machinery itself."

In *Jackson* v. *Mumford*[14] it was held that a "latent defect in the machinery" did not cover a weakness of design. *Per* Kennedy J.: "the phrase defect in machinery in a business document means a defect of material, in respect either of its original composition or in respect of its after acquired condition".

The extent of cover against latent defect has been widened quite considerably by the decision in *The "Caribbean Sea"*.[15] In this case, which was considering the assured's claim for a total loss following the sinking of the vessel, the court found as a question of fact that the cause of the fatal ingress of sea water was the existence of fatigue cracks in a wedge shaped nozzle between a sea valve and the shell plating. The presence of these cracks was attributed to two factors — the manner in which the ship was designed (viz., the welding of gussets to the nozzle in proximity to another circumferential weld) and the effect upon the nozzle of the ordinary working of the ship. The court also found that these fractures must have been in existence at the inception of the policies current at the time of the total loss.

12. (1907) 11 Com.Cas. 179; 13 Com.Cas. 28.
13. (1937) 10 Asp.M.L.C. 303; 56 Ll.L.Rep. 136.
14. (1902) 8 Com.Cas. 61; 9 Com.Cas. 114; 52 W.R. 342.
15. *Prudent Tankers Ltd. S.A.* v. *Dominion Ass. Co. Ltd.* [1980] 1 Lloyd's Rep. 338.

In considering whether there was a defect in the hull and machinery which directly caused the loss, the judge held that the court is concerned with the actual state of the hull and machinery and not with the historical reason why it has come about that the hull and machinery is in that state. He also held that the condition of the nozzle, which had arisen in part from the ordinary working of the ship, was not ordinary wear and tear and therefore was not excluded under section 55 of the Marine Insurance Act 1906.

Before leaving this clause we should return to the case of *Jackson* v. *Mumford*[16] which also considered what constituted a "shaft" within the meaning of the clause. Kennedy J. held that the breakage of a connecting rod of a main engine was not *ejusdem generis* with the breakage of a shaft.

> "A connecting rod and a shaft are always distinguished in the language of engineers. ... the functions really have a difference and that, while both rod and shaft alike transmit power, the connecting rod and the crankshaft transmit it by strains which are of an essentially different character."

"6.2.3   Negligence of Master Officers Crew or Pilots"

Negligence has been defined as:

> "The omission to do something which a reasonable man, guided by those considerations which ordinarily regulate the conduct of human affairs, would do, or do something which a prudent and reasonable man would not do."[17]

It is only loss of or damage caused by negligence of the master, officers, crew or pilot which is covered, not the cost of effecting work which should have been carried out by the crew. For example, cases are sometimes experienced where due to a negligent chief engineer no routine maintenance and/or cleaning has been carried out for a considerable period. Any physical damage resulting from such neglect would be recoverable but there is no claim for the cost of catching up on the routine maintenance and cleaning which the ship's engineers should have, but failed to carry out. Any deliberate loss or damage resulting from wilful misconduct on the part of the crew may be recoverable under Clause 6.2.5 which will be considered later.

"6.2.4   negligence of repairers or charterers provided such repairers or charterers are not an Assured hereunder"

In giving cover against loss or damage caused by negligence of repairers or charterers, underwriters are conscious of the possibility of obtaining a recovery under their subrogated rights from the negligent party. This would not be possible if the repairers or charterers were named assureds in the policy and the cover is therefore subject to the proviso. To found a claim under

---

16. (1902) 8 Com.Cas. 61; 9 Com.Cas. 114; 52 W.R. 342.
17. *Blyth* v. *Birmingham Waterworks Co. Ltd.* (1856) 11 Ex.784; 4 W.R. 294.

this clause there must be physical loss or damage to the subject-matter insured as a consequence of the repairers' or charterers' negligence. If, for example, a shipowner discovers that a repairer has failed to undertake the replacement of parts for which he was contracted and paid for, there is no claim for the cost of purchasing and fitting the replacement parts, there being no consequential loss or damage as a result of the repairers' negligence.

"6.2.5 Barratry of Master Officers or Crew"

The Rules for Construction of Policy (Schedule 1, Marine Insurance Act 1906) state:

> "The term "barratry" includes every wrongful act wilfully committed by the Master or Crew to the prejudice of the owner, or, as the case may be, the charterer."

This definition is not exhaustive and barratry includes not only every type of fraud and malfeasance deliberately committed by the master or crew for the intention of benefiting themselves at the expense of the shipowners, but every wilful act on the part of the master or crew of illegality, corruption or criminal negligence, whereby the shipowners or the charterers are prejudiced.

"Provided such loss or damage has not resulted from want of due diligence by the Assured, Owners or Managers"

This is a most important proviso which is only applicable to the perils in Clause 6.2 and does not apply to the perils enumerated under Clause 6.1.

Whether due diligence has been observed can only be a question of fact in each case. Typical circumstances where the proviso could be pleaded by underwriters as a defence to a claim might be:

(1) The bursting of a boiler which was found to have been beyond its due date for Classification Society survey at the time of the casualty (in such circumstances Clause 4.1 might also give underwriters a defence).
(2) A succession of crew negligence claims, where the evidence points to the crew employed being of insufficient calibre, perhaps coupled with inadequate management controls checks on the crew's performance by the owners or managers.

"6.3 Master Officers Crew or Pilots not to be considered Owners within the meaning of this Clause 6 should they hold shares in the vessel"

It is not uncommon, particularly with smaller coasting type or fishing vessels, for the master or crew to have shares in the vessel and this clause is to cover this situation by making it clear that in such circumstances they will not be considered as owners within the meaning of the proviso.

In the case of *The "Alastor"*,[18] which turned upon the question of whether the owner was entitled to limit liability under the Merchant Shipping Acts, the Court of Appeal held that if the owner of a yacht decided to carry out his own maintenance and then did the maintenance negligently he would be acting as owner when he made the decision and it was impossible to say that the defendant's negligence in the doing of the maintenance was in his capacity as owner. The Court of Appeal decided that the question as to capacity could be tested by asking: "If he had appointed an engineer, would the owner normally give instructions to the engineer as to what inspection should be made or would he leave it to the engineer?" and the answer was that unless the engineer had shown himself to be negligent, or unless so long a period had elapsed and such circumstances had intervened that an inspection at a particular time was obviously necessary to any reasonable owner, then it was a matter which was to be left to the engineer.

Once it was accepted that an owner could combine the functions of owner and crew member there was no other way of ascertaining the capacity in which he acted than by a comparison with what the position would have been where the ownership and crew membership were separated.

The loss of the ejusdem generis wording

The basic perils in the S.G. policy were followed by the words "against all other perils, losses, and misfortunes, that have or shall come to hurt, detriment, or damage of the said goods and merchandises, and ship, etc., or any part thereof". This wording "includes only perils similar in kind to the perils specifically mentioned in the policy" (Rules for Construction of Policy, Schedule 1, Marine Insurance Act 1906). This is the *ejusdem generis* rule of construction, where specific words are followed and amplified by general words.

In the drafting of the Perils Clause these words have been dropped. There is no doubt that many assureds, who were not conversant with insurance law, found the wording to be misleading. Some commentators have argued that the decided cases in which the *ejusdem generis* wording covered losses which would not have been covered by the standard perils are few in number. As the wording has now disappeared, an analysis of the relevant law cases would not be warranted in this work. The authors however wish to record their passing with the comment that the words were of great comfort to an assured who might not, for reasons outside his control, be able precisely to bring the cause of damage within the named perils.

18. [1981] 1 Lloyd's Rep. 581.

Clause 7 — Pollution Hazard

7   POLLUTION HAZARD

This insurance covers loss of or damage to the Vessel caused by any governmental authority acting under the powers vested in it to prevent or mitigate a pollution hazard, or threat thereof, resulting directly from damage to the Vessel for which the Underwriters are liable under this insurance, provided such act of governmental authority has not resulted from want of due diligence by the Assured, the Owners, or Managers of the Vessel or any of them to prevent or mitigate such hazard or threat. Master, Officers, Crew or Pilots not to be considered Owners within the meaning of this Clause 7 should they hold shares in the Vessel.

Although only introduced into the I.T.C. in 1983 this clause has been in regular use since its introduction in 1973, following major casualties involving pollution and governmental intervention such as the *"Torrey Canyon"* and the *"Amoco Cadiz"*. The clause extends the insurance to cover loss of or damage to the vessel in the following circumstances:

(1) The loss or damage must be caused by a governmental authority when acting to prevent or mitigate real or threatened pollution hazard, and

(2) the pollution hazard must result directly from damage to the vessel covered by the policy.

The clause is subject to a similar proviso as to the want of due diligence as is found in Clause 6.

Clause 8 — 3/4ths Collision Liability

8   3/4THS COLLISION LIABILITY

8.1   The Underwriters agree to indemnify the Assured for three-fourths of any sum or sums paid by the Assured to any other person or persons by reason of the Assured becoming legally liable by way of damages for

8.1.1   loss of or damage to any other vessel or property on any other vessel

8.1.2   delay to or loss of use of any such other vessel or property thereon

8.1.3   general average of, salvage of, or salvage under contract of, any such other vessel or property thereon,

where such payment by the Assured is in consequence of the Vessel hereby insured coming into collision with any other vessel.

8.2   The indemnity provided by this Clause 8 shall be in addition to the indemnity provided by the other terms and conditions of this insurance and shall be subject to the following provisions:

8.2.1   Where the insured Vessel is in collision with another vessel and both vessels are to blame then, unless the liability of one or both vessels becomes limited by law, the indemnity under this Clause 8 shall be calculated on the principle of cross-liabilities as if the respective Owners had been compelled to pay to each other such proportion of each other's damages as may have been properly allowed in ascertaining the balance or sum payable by or to the Assured in consequence of the collision.

8.2.2   In no case shall the Underwriters' total liability under Clauses 8.1 and 8.2 exceed their proportionate part of the three-fourths of the insured value of the Vessel hereby insured in respect of any one collision.

8.3   The Underwriters will also pay three-fourths of the legal costs incurred by the Assured or which the Assured may be compelled to pay in contesting liability or taking proceedings to limit liability, with the prior written consent of the Underwriters.

EXCLUSIONS
8.4   Provided always that this Clause 8 shall in no case extend to any sum which the Assured shall pay
for or in respect of

8.4.1   removal or disposal of obstructions, wrecks, cargoes or any other thing whatsoever

8.4.2   any real or personal property or thing whatsoever except other vessels or property on other
vessels

8.4.3   the cargo or other property on, or the engagements of, the insured Vessel

8.4.4   loss of life, personal injury or illness

8.4.5   pollution or contamination of any real or personal property or thing whatsoever (except other
vessels with which the insured Vessel is in collision or property on such other vessels).

Previously known as the R.D.C. or Running Down Clause. This is a marvellous example of how a clause initially introduced to fill a gap in the insurance cover has been developed and refined over the years to meet changing requirements. Although forms of a Running Down Clause had been in use since the early part of the nineteenth century its inclusion only became common-place following the case of *De Vaux* v. *Salvador*[19] in 1836 which decided that under the ordinary form of policy underwriters were not liable for the balance which the insured vessel had to pay to the other when both were to blame for a collision. The clause has subsequently been refined over the years in the light of the decisions of the courts and in recent years, with the increasing importance and magnitude of the liabilities arising from consequential risks such as pollution, the clause has been recast to differentiate quite clearly between the positive cover and the areas of exclusion, in particular those which are within the ambit of the P. & I. cover.

Two cases which illustrate the development of the clause were as follows:

In *Xenos* v. *Fox*[20] the owners of the insured vessel successfully defended the claim of another ship which had sunk following a collision with the insured vessel. The assured claimed under the Sue and Labour Clause in the policy for the costs incurred in defending the other ship's claim. The claim was rejected by the court which held that the Sue and Labour clause applied only to the ordinary perils covered by the policy and did not extend to those covered by the Collision Clause, which was a supplemental agreement and did not contain any provision relating to costs. Following this decision the clause was amended to include a provision whereby underwriters would meet their due proportion of the costs, provided they had given their prior consent to the proceedings.

A further refinement took place following the case of *The "Balnacraig"* (*The London Steamship Owners' Mutual Insurance Association* v. *The Grampian Steamship Co*).[21] The *"Balnacraig"* was involved in a collision for which both vessels were equally to blame. Due to the fact that the *"Balnacraig"* had sustained the greater damage, under the principle of single liability, which we shall consider later, there was a balance payable to the owners of the *"Balnacraig"* by the other vessel. The owners of the *"Balnacraig"*

19. (1836) 5 L.J.K.B. 134.
20. (1868) 38 L.J.C.P. 351; 17 W.R. 893.
21. (1890) 38 W.R. 651; 6 Asp.M.L.C. 506.

claimed under the Collision Clause in their policy for their liability towards the damage sustained by the other vessel, which had been set-off against the other side's liability, thereby reducing the amount recovered by the "Balnacraig". The claim under the policy failed due to the fact that the assured had not actually paid anything to the owner of the other vessel. Following this decision the clause was extended to import the concept of "cross-liabilities" which we will consider in detail when we look at the actual provision in the present clause.

Turning to the clause in its present form, the salient points are as follows:

The agreement is to indemnify the assured for three-fourths of any sum or sum paid by the assured within the terms of the clause. The reason for coverage being limited to three-fourths is historical, it having been underwriters' original intention when introducing the clause to encourage care on the part of the assured by insisting upon one-fourth being self-insured. In practice, the remaining one-fourth is now invariably covered by entry in a Protection and Indemnity Association.

Payment must be made by the assured to give rise to a claim under the clause although in cases subject to the Third Parties (Rights Against Insurers) Act 1930 there could be circumstances in which a third party could invoke a direct claim against the policy. The payment must arise "by reason of the Assured becoming legally liable by way of damages" and the clause only covers liabilities arising out of tort. So that when a shipowner entered into an agreement for the hire of a tug on terms that he should be liable for all damage to the tug, however caused, the payment made by the shipowner under the agreement, following a collision for which the tug was wholly to blame was held not to be recoverable under the clause (*Furness Withy & Co. Ltd. v. Duder*).[22]

The clause then specifies in 8.1.1 to 8.1.3 the various heads of claim of the other vessel or property thereon, liability for which is covered under the clause, and it is specified that such payment must be in consequence of the vessel insured "coming into collision with any other vessel". What constituted a collision with another "ship or vessel", which used to be the appropriate words in the Collision Clause, has been the subject of several judicial decisions, the leading ones of which were as follows:

An insured vessel collided with a pontoon crane which was permanently moored to a river bank in a naval dockyard. It was held that the pontoon was not a ship or vessel, the primary purpose for which it had been designed and adapted being to float and to lift, and not to navigate. The judge held that whatever other qualities are attached to a ship or vessel, the adaptability for navigation, and its uses for that purpose, is one of the most essential elements for bringing the craft within the definition. (*Merchants' Marine Insurance Co.* v. *North of England Protecting and Indemnity Association.*[23])

22. (1936) 55 Ll.L.Rep. 52.
23. (1926) 32 Com.Cas. 165.

The words can encompass part of a vessel's equipment, so that where a vessel struck the anchor of another vessel this was held to be a collision with the vessel (*Margetts* v. *Ocean Accident and Guarantee Corporation*[24]) but the fouling of nets attached to, but a mile distant from, a fishing vessel was not construed as a collision with another ship or vessel (*Bennett Steamship Co.* v. *Hull Mutual Steamship Protecting and Indemnity Association*[25]).

As to whether contact with a sunken vessel constitutes a collision with another ship or vessel depends upon the facts of each case but some guidance can be obtained from previous cases. In *Chandler* v. *Blogg,*[26] the insured vessel ran into a barge, which was lying half-submerged following a recent collision with another vessel; this was held to be a collision within the terms of the policy. In *Pelton Steamship Co.* v. *North of England Protecting and Indemnity Association*[27] the collision was with a vessel which had been sunk and was lying at the bottom of the sea, but salvage operations were in hand and the salvors had a reasonable expectation of raising her. This was held to be a collision with a ship or vessel within the terms of the Collision Clause. The test to be applied to any vessel which has sunk appears to be that if salvage operations have been abandoned, or were never contemplated, the wreck ceases to be a ship or vessel within the terms of the clause.

However, once there has been a collision with another vessel within the meaning of the clause, the assured is indemnified for all payments by way of damages for the categories of claims specified. So, for example, if insured vessel A is in collision with vessel B, which as a result is forced onto vessel C, any damages paid to vessel C would be recoverable under A's insurance, even though vessel A had not been in physical contact with vessel C.

Clause 8.2. makes it clear that the indemnity for collision liability is in addition to the indemnity provided by the other terms and conditions of the insurance and Clause 8.2.2 limits underwriters' total liability under Clauses 8.1 and 8.2. to three-fourths of the insured value in respect of any one collision. This means that regardless of any other claim, the limit of liability for any claim under Clause 8 will be three-fourths of the insured value (with three-fourths of the costs payable in addition — see Clause 8.3).

Clause 8.2.1 imports the principle of cross-liabilities into the adjustment of claims under the clause. When two vessels are in collision and both are to blame, the respective liabilities are assessed, a set-off then occurs and there is a single payment by the vessel with the balance to pay (*The "Khedive"*[28]). This is known as Single Liability. Under the principle of cross-liabilities, imported into the policy by this clause, the claim upon underwriters is assessed as if each side actually made a payment to the other side of their

24. (1901) 49 W.R. 669; 9 Asp. M.L.C. 217.
25. (1914) 18 Com.Cas. 274.
26. [1898] 1 Q.B. 32; 67 L.J.Q.B. 436; 77 L.T. 524; 8 Asp M.L.C. 349; 3 Com.Cas. 18.
27. (1925) 22 Ll.L.Rep. 510.
28. *Stoomvaart Maatschappij Nederland* v. *P. & O. Steam Navigation Company* (1882) 7 App.Cas. 795; 4 Asp.M.L.C. 567.

respective liability. Some figures may illustrate the practical effect of the adoption of the cross-liabilities method for assessing the claim on the policy.

Vessels A and B are in collision, for which they are equally to blame, their respective losses being as follows:

A is damaged to the extent:
Repairs	£8,000
Demurrage	2,000
	£10,000

B is damaged to the extent of:
Repairs	£5,000
Demurrage	1,000
	£6,000

The actual settlement between the vessels will be as follows:

B is liable for 50% of A's damage and demurrage	£5,000
A is liable for 50% of B's damage and demurrage	3,000
Single liability of B to A	£2,000

If this were the basis of the claim under the respective policies, the position (ignoring policy deductibles) would be as follows:

Vessel A —	P.A. damage	£8,000
	Credit recovery from B	£2,000
		£6,000

Vessel B —	P.A. damage	£5,000
	Three-fourths of single liability payment	£1,500
		£6,500

However, by reason of the cross-liabilities basis of adjustment the actual claims will be calculated as follows:

CLAIM UNDER A's POLICY

	P.A.	3/4ths Collision Liability	Owners
A's Damage	£10,000		
A's Notional Liability to B:			
50% of £6,000	£3,000	2,250	750
Credit:			
Notional recovery from B:	Cr.		
50% of £10,000	£5,000		
	£5,000	£2,250	£750

Claim under A's Policy

Particular Average (nett of notional recovery)	£5,000
3/4ths Collision Liability	£2,250
	£7,250

CLAIM UNDER B's POLICY

		P.A.	3/4ths Collision Liability	Owners
B's Damage:		£6,000		
B's Notional Liability to A:				
50% of £10,000	£5,000		3,750	1,250
Credit:				
Notional recovery from A:		Cr.		
50% of £6,000		3,000		
		£3,000	£3,750	£1,250

Claim under B's Policy

Particular Average (nett of notional recovery)	£3,000
3/4ths Collision Liability	£3,750
	£6,750

There is an important limitation to the application of cross-liabilities, namely, when the liability of one or both vessels is limited by law. The reason for this is said to be that the limitation would distort the figures if cross-liabilities were applied. It should be mentioned in this connection that it is the Scandinavian practice for cross-liabilities to be applied even when one or both of the vessels has limited liability and the Norwegian Plan, for example, makes specific provision for this.

Following a collision the assured will invariably incur legal costs, the main areas of expense being:

(1) Determining and/or contesting liability.
(2) Instituting proceedings to limit liability.
(3) Any proportion of the other side's legal costs recoverable from the assured.
(4) Drawing up the claim of the insured vessel against the other side.
(5) Examining the claim received from the other side.

Although Clause 8.3 strictly only expressly deals with (1), (2) and (3), costs incurred under (5) are recoverable under the clause in practice as costs of defence, three-fourths of which are payable under the policy. Costs incurred in drawing up the claim of the insured vessel against the other side are "costs of recovery" or attempted recovery. They are apportioned between underwriters and the assured based upon their respective entitlement in the amount ranking for recovery. In practice, the apportionment of costs in collision cases is governed by Rule of Practice A8 of the Association of Average Adjusters which provides as follows:

> "APPORTIONMENT OF COSTS IN COLLISION CASES
>
> That when a vessel sustains and does damage by collision, and litigation consequently results for the purpose of testing liability, the technicality of the vessel having been plaintiff or defendant in the litigation shall not necessarily govern the apportionment of the costs of such litigation, which shall be apportioned between claim and counter-claim in proportion to the amount, excluding interest, which has been or would have been allowed in respect of each in the event of the claim or counter-claim being established; provided that when a claim or counter-claim is made solely for the purpose of defence, and is not allowed, the costs apportioned thereto shall be treated as costs of defence."

Under Clause 8.3, underwriters agree to pay three-fourths of the legal costs involved in testing liability or in limiting liability, provided that they were incurred with the prior written consent of underwriters. In practice, in addition to obtaining underwriters' initial consent it is extremely advisable to keep underwriters fully informed and to obtain their agreement to every major step in any collision action.

It is interesting to note that the word "legal" has been inserted before "costs". The intention behind this has not, so far as the authors are aware, been the subject of any commentary elsewhere. It is submitted that it does not limit the recoverable costs to the fees and disbursements of members of the legal profession. Such a strict interpretation would exclude numerous properly claimable items examples of which are: P. and I. Club correspondents' fees; master's travel expenses in connection with attendance at a hearing, etc. A more reasonable test, it is suggested, would be to examine whether the expenses would be accepted in principle by a Registrar or Taxing Master as party and party costs.

The exclusions detailed under Clause 8.4 are those liabilities which are customarily covered by a Protection and Indemnity Association and require no special comment.

Clause 9 — Sistership

9   SISTERSHIP

Should the Vessel hereby insured come into collision with or receive salvage services from another vessel belonging wholly or in part to the same Owners or under the same management, the Assured shall have the same rights under this insurance as they would have were the other vessel entirely the property of Owners not interested in the Vessel hereby insured; but in such cases the liability for the collision or the amount payable for the services rendered shall be referred to a sole arbitrator to be agreed upon between the Underwriters and the Assured.

If two vessels under the same ownership are in collision, there is no tortious liability between the two ships due to the fact that a person cannot bring an action against himself (*Simpson* v. *Thompson*[29]). If both vessels are insured, the shipowner can of course claim for the physical damage under his policies, subject to two policy deductibles, however he cannot recover any proportion of his loss of earnings which would have been recoverable if the colliding vessel had been in different ownership. Similarly, in the case of salvage services to a sister-ship, although the shipowner can claim salvage from the cargo (*Cargo ex "Laertes"*[30]) he is precluded under English law from claiming salvage in respect of the services to the ship and freight.

By this clause the assured is placed in the same position, when the insured vessel is in collision or receives salvage services from a vessel under the same ownership or management, as if the colliding or salving vessel belonged to entirely different owners. The clause also deals with the procedural manner in which liability for the collision or the amount payable for the salvage services is to be assessed. In practice these matters are often referred to an average adjuster for an independent opinion, which may be submitted to the leading underwriters and to the assured for their agreement.

Clause 10 — Notice of Claim and Tenders

10   NOTICE OF CLAIM AND TENDERS

10.1 In the event of accident whereby loss or damage may result in a claim under this insurance, notice shall be given to the Underwriters prior to survey and also, if the Vessel is abroad, to the nearest Lloyd's Agent so that a surveyor may be appointed to represent the Underwriters should they so desire.

10.2 The Underwriters shall be entitled to decide the port to which the Vessel shall proceed for docking or repair (the actual additional expense of the voyage arising from compliance with the Underwriters' requirements being refunded to the Assured) and shall have a right of veto concerning a place of repair or a repairing firm.

10.3 The Underwriters may also take tenders or may require further tenders to be taken for the repair of the Vessel. Where such a tender has been taken and a tender is accepted with the approval of the Underwriters, an allowance shall be made at the rate of 30% per annum on the insured value for time lost between the despatch of the invitations to tender required by Underwriters and the acceptance of a tender to the extent that such time is lost solely as the result of tenders having been taken and provided that the tender is accepted without delay after receipt of the Underwriters' approval.

Due credit shall be given against the allowance as above for any amounts recovered in respect of fuel and stores and wages and maintenance of the Master Officers and Crew or any member thereof, including amounts allowed in general average, and for any amounts recovered from third parties in respect of damages for detention and/or loss of profit and/or running expenses, for the period covered by the tender allowance or any part thereof.

Where a part of the cost of the repair of damage other than a fixed deductible is not recoverable from the Underwriters the allowance shall be reduced by a similar proportion.

10.4 In the event of failure to comply with the conditions of this Clause 10 a deduction of 15% shall be made from the amount of the ascertained claim.

29. (1877) 3 Asp.M.L.C. 567.
30. (1887) 6 Asp.M.L.C. 174.

When an accident which may give rise to a claim under the policy has occurred, it is natural that underwriters will wish to be informed as quickly as possible so that they may make arrangements for an early survey of the damage. This enables them to obtain an early indication of the extent of the damage and the initial survey is also an ideal opportunity to obtain much of the evidence regarding the accident. Clause 10.1 stipulates that when an accident giving rise to a potential claim has occurred, notice should be given to underwriters, or where appropriate to the nearest Lloyd's Agents. Under 10.2 underwriters have the right to decide to which port the vessel shall proceed for the damage drydocking and/or repair and they reserve the right of veto concerning a place of repair or a repairing firm. When underwriters elect to nominate a port of repair they agree to refund to the assured the additional expense of the voyage arising from compliance with their instructions.

Clause 10.3 gives underwriters the right to take tenders or to require further tenders to be taken. When underwriters invoke their rights under this clause an allowance is payable by underwriters at the rate of 30% per annum on the insured value. The conditions of this allowance are:

(1) It is only for the period between the despatch of the invitation to tender required by underwriters and the acceptance of a tender.

(2) The time lost under (1) must result solely as a result of tenders having been taken and the tender must have been accepted without undue delay, following receipt of underwriters' approval. In I.T.C. Hulls 1/10/69 and 1/10/70 there was no provision for any allowance when tenders were required on underwriters' instructions but were taken directly by the assured. Now, in the event that one of the tenders originally taken by the assured proves to be the most reasonable and is accepted with the approval of the underwriters, the allowance will be made.

The period of any allowance under Clause 10.3 may also attract admissions in general average or be subject to a recovery from a third party, and in such circumstances credit has to be given against the allowance for any such recoveries. A final qualification to Clause 10.3 is that when part of the cost of the damage repair (other than a fixed deductible) is not recoverable, the allowance has to be reduced proportionately.

It is very unusual for underwriters to invoke the provisions of Clause 10.3. Although this must to a large extent be due to underwriters' satisfaction in the vast majority of cases with the repair arrangements made by their assured, when one considers that on a typical insured value of U.S.$10,000,000 the daily allowance works out at U.S.$4,110 per day this may well be another important reason.

There is a fixed penalty for non-compliance with the conditions of this clause and this is specified as a 15% deduction from the ascertained claim (the ascertained claim being the net claim after the policy deductible).

Clause 11 — General Average and Salvage

11   **GENERAL AVERAGE AND SALVAGE**

    11.1 This insurance covers the Vessel's proportion of salvage, salvage charges and/or general average, reduced in respect of any under-insurance, but in case of general average sacrifice of the Vessel the Assured may recover in respect of the whole loss without first enforcing their right of contribution from other parties.

    11.2 Adjustment to be according to the law and practice obtaining at the place where the adventure ends, as if the contract of affreightment contained no special terms upon the subject; but where the contract of affreightment so provides the adjustment shall be according to the York-Antwerp Rules.

    11.3 When the Vessel sails in ballast, not under charter, the provisions of the York-Antwerp Rules, 1974 (excluding Rules XX and XXI) shall be applicable, and the voyage for this purpose shall be deemed to continue from the port or place of departure until the arrival of the Vessel at the first port or place thereafter other than a port or place of refuge or a port or place of call for bunkering only. If at any such intermediate port or place there is an abandonment of the adventure originally contemplated the voyage shall thereupon be deemed to be terminated.

    11.4 No claim under this Clause 11 shall in any case be allowed where the loss was not incurred to avoid or in connection with the avoidance of a peril insured against.

Clauses 11.1 and 11.4 are in line with sections 66(4), 66(6) and 66(7) of the Marine Insurance Act 1906 which are as follows:

"(4) Subject to any express provision in the policy, where the assured has incurred a general average expenditure, he may recover from the insurer in respect of the proportion of the loss which falls upon him; and, in the case of a general average sacrifice, he may recover from the insurer in respect of the whole loss without having enforced his right of contribution from the other parties liable to contribute.

(6) In the absence of express stipulation, the insurer is not liable for any general average loss or contribution where the loss was not incurred for the purpose of avoiding, or in connexion with the avoidance of, a peril insured against.

(7) Where ship, freight, and cargo, or any two of those interests, are owned by the same assured, the liability of the insurer in respect of general average losses or contributions is to be determined as if those subjects were owned by different persons."

There is a very interesting situation when there is a proportion of general average expenditure incurred by the shipowners which cannot be recovered from cargo because a subsequent casualty has diminished or extinguished the contributory value, or because the expenditure exceeds the total contributory values. The position under English law is quite clear: subject to the vessel being fully insured the insurers are liable to indemnify the assured against the proportion of his expenditure which remains to be borne by him, after taking into account contributions due from others (or as expressed in section 66(4) of the Marine Insurance Act 1906 "the proportion of the loss which falls upon him"); *Green Star Shipping Co.* v. *The London Assurance.*[31] Under Clause 11.1, however, the coverage is against only *vessel's* proportion of salvage, salvage charges and/or general average, which should be differentiated from the proportion of loss which falls upon the *shipowner*. So far as the authors are aware, there was no intention when redrafting this clause to alter the position under English law but this is one more example of where the deletion of the "English law and practice" proviso (see page 84) could give rise to a gap in the cover.

Under Clause 11.2 hull underwriters agree to the adjustment of general average according to either the York/Antwerp Rules, if so provided for in the contract of affreightment (as is the case in the majority of general averages) or, in the absence of any special terms in the contract of affreightment, according to the law and practice obtaining at the place where the adventure ends.

Clause 11.3 provides for the adjustment of general average in those situations where the vessel is in ballast and not under charter, by providing for the York/Antwerp Rules, 1974 excluding the commission and interest rules. It also contains detailed provisions for defining the general average voyage in such circumstances.

Clause 12 — Deductible

12   DEDUCTIBLE

12.1 No claim arising from a peril insured against shall be payable under this insurance unless the aggregate of all such claims arising out of each separate accident or occurrence (including claims under Clauses 8, 11 and 13) exceeds .... in which case this sum shall be deducted. Nevertheless the expense of sighting the bottom after stranding, if reasonably incurred specially for that purpose, shall be paid even if no damage be found. This Clause 12.1 shall not apply to a claim for total or constructive total loss of the Vessel or, in the event of such a claim, to any associated claim under Clause 13 arising from the same accident or occurrence.

12.2 Claims for damage by heavy weather occurring during a single sea passage between two successive ports shall be treated as being due to one accident. In the case of such heavy weather extending over a period not wholly covered by this insurance the deductible to be applied to the claim recoverable hereunder shall be the proportion of the above deductible that the number of days of such heavy weather falling within the period of this insurance bears to the number of days of heavy weather during the single sea passage.

The expression "heavy weather" in this Clause 12.2 shall be deemed to include contact with floating ice.

12.3 Excluding any interest comprised therein, recoveries against any claim which is subject to the above deductible shall be credited to the Underwriters in full to the extent of the sum by which the aggregate of the claim unreduced by any recoveries exceeds the above deductible.

12.4 Interest comprised in recoveries shall be apportioned between the Assured and the Underwriters, taking into account the sums paid by the Underwriters and the dates when such payments were made, notwithstanding that by the addition of interest the Underwriters may receive a larger sum than they have paid.

---

31. (1933) 36 Com.Cas. 258; 39 Ll.L.Rep. 213; 18 Asp.M.L.C. 225.

Up until the revision of the I.T.C. in 1969, hull insurance had almost invariably been subject to a franchise applicable to each voyage as defined in some detail, the effect of this was that once the franchise had been attained, the claim was recoverable in full. Since 1969 the I.T.C. have incorporated a deductible, the exact figure to be specified, which is applied to "the aggregate of all such claims arising out of each separate accident or occurrence". Due to the multifarious situations which can be encountered when dealing with ships, these words created a problem of interpretation.

At the General Meeting of the Association of Average Adjusters, May 1971, the following resolution was passed:

> "That a Special Committee, including representatives of Underwriters and Shipowners, be appointed to consider the interpretation of the expression 'each separate accident or occurrence' in the Institute Time Clauses, Hulls, with particular regard to progressive damages, and to issue a statement of agreed lines of approach towards such interpretation."

The Committee first considered the interpretation of the relevant part of Clause 12 in the light of papers presented by members of the Committee which tended to show that "accident or occurrence" required a wider interpretation than "accident" alone, and that the word "separate" suggested that in some instances involving more than one accident or occurrence, only one deductible might be applicable when those accidents or occurrences formed a connected set of events.

The Committee appointed a working party consisting of the four average adjusters on the Committee to examine this interpretation with reference to multi-accident situations and to report to the Committee thereon.

The working party reported on 10 January 1972. Thirty cases of multi-accident situations were considered and the working party presented a summary of facts and a short commentary in each case, leading to the question whether one or more deductible should be applied. These cases and commentary, preceded by an analysis of the working party's conclusions, are set out as an Appendix to the Committee's report which is included in the Report of the Association of Average Adjusters' General Meeting, May 1972.

The working party confirmed that the provisional interpretation given to Clause 12 provided a reasonable basis in most of the cases considered for deciding whether one or more deductible should be applied, but observed that in certain instances a strict interpretation of the clause could in practice lead to results which were inequitable. The working party suggested therefore that in these cases a reasonable and practical approach might be preferred to a strict interpretation of the clause.

At its second meeting, the Committee discussed the report of the working party and considered the following questions:

1. Were any of the following factors material in determining how many deductibles should be applied:

(a) The fact that there were different heads of claim, e.g., particular average, general average contribution and 3/4ths collision liability, arising out of the accident or occurrence.

(b) The fact that certain items of claim might be recoverable under different principles if the policy conditions were varied by the attachment of other clauses, i.e., the "Liner" Negligence and Additional Perils Clause.

(c) The fact that in certain instances of progressive damage the claim might be divisible over more than one policy period.

(d) The fact that a repair of part of the damage may have been effected prior to the ascertainment of other damage arising out of the same accident or occurrence.

In the opinion of the Committee none of these factors was in any way relevant to the interpretation of Clause 12.

2. What general line of approach should be adopted to the interpretation of Clause 12? In the opinion of the Committee the interpretation of Clause 12, giving each word its due weight and significance in its context, requires that:

(a) One deductible is to be applied when either:
  (i) there is only one accident or occurrence from which the claims arise, or
  (ii) even though there is more than one accident or occurrence, these accidents or occurrences are not separate but form a connected set of events from which the claims arise.

(b) On the other hand, if one or more of the events from which the claims arise are the result of a new cause, not directly connected with the previous events, i.e., that which would be considered in law a *novus actus interveniens*, then more than one deductible is to be applied to the claims.

3. What weight should be attached to the examples of multi-accident situations considered by the working party and the commentary thereon? The Committee considered that these examples provided guidelines to a reasonable interpretation of the clause in multi-accident situations, although they should not be considered as binding any party to a particular solution. In a number of cases the underwriters' representatives indicated that they did not agree with the comments of the working party. The Committee recognised that in practice the determination of the number of deductibles to be applied will depend upon a close consideration of the facts in each case.

4. What solution could be suggested in respect to the difficulties of interpretation in those instances where a strict interpretation of the clause could in practice lead to results which were inequitable, namely:

(i) Cases of a sequence of events where a strict interpretation suggests the application of only one deductible, but the working party considers that it would be more reasonable to apply more than one deductible.

(ii) Cases of a sequence of events where a strict interpretation suggests the application of more than one deductible, but the working party considered that it would be more reasonable to apply only one deductible.

At the suggestion of the average adjusters on the Committee, consideration was given to the question whether it would be reasonable in such cases for shipowners and underwriters respectively to forgo a strict interpretation of the clause, in the interest of avoiding dispute and simplifying the adjustment of claims. It was appreciated that such a solution would involve some "give and take" on both sides, and that the effect of such an approach would have to be studied with care. In the meantime, the Committee expressed the hope that in such cases effect will be given to the clause in a sense which is both reasonable and practical.

The clause specifies that the aggregate of all claims includes claims for collision liability, general average, salvage and sue and labour charges. No deductible however is to be applied to a claim for a total or constructive total loss, or in the event of such a claim, any expenses claimable under Clause 13 (which includes sue and labour charges).

Stuck rather oddly in the middle of Clause 12.1 is the old Sighting Bottom Clause, which provides that underwriters will pay for the cost of sighting the bottom after a stranding, even if no damage is found, provided that the expense was reasonably incurred specially for that purpose, any claim thereunder being payable without application of the policy deductible.

The difficulty, referred to earlier, of deciding what constitutes a separate accident or occurrence can be particularly problematical in claims for heavy weather or ice damage. Clause 12.2 stipulates that all heavy weather (or ice) occurring during a single sea passage between two successive ports shall be treated as due to one accident. There is also detailed provision for the apportionment of the deductible when a period of heavy weather or ice extends over a period not wholly covered by the insurance. This is perhaps best illustrated by an example.

Vessel encounters floating ice during one passage, over the period 20.12.85. to 10.1.86. The relevant policies attaching for the periods of 12 months commencing 1.1.85. (deductible £6,000) and 1.1.86. (deductible £12,000), respectively.

The number of days of floating ice recorded in the vessel's deck log book amount to five, two of which occurred in 1985 and three in 1986 (there are no specific areas of damage recorded on any of the days in question).

The total cost of repairs amounted to £10,000.

The claim and the application of the Clause 12 deductible will be as follows:

1985 Policy Year

		Claim
Cost of repairs	£10,000	
Of which applying to this policy 2/5ths		£4,000
Less: Policy deductible 2/5ths x £6,000		2,400
		£1,600

1986 Policy Year

Cost of repairs	£10,000	
Of which applying to this policy 3/5ths		£6,000
Less: Policy deductible 3/5ths x £12,000		7,200
		NO CLAIM

The effective deductible unit in the case of heavy weather or ice claims is a single sea passage between two successive ports and the purpose of the call at a port, be it for bunkering only or even as a port of refuge, will terminate that passage insofar as the clause is concerned.

Recoveries

The rights of an insurer upon payment of a claim for a partial loss are laid down in section 79(2) of the Marine Insurance Act 1906 as follows:

"Subject to the foregoing provisions, where the insurer pays for a partial loss, he acquires no title to the subject-matter insured, or such part of it as may remain, but he is thereupon subrogated to all rights and remedies of the assured in and in respect of the subject-matter insured as from the time of the casualty causing the loss, in so far as the assured has been indemnified, according to this Act, by such payment for the loss."

English law, as codified in the above section, proceeds upon the basis that "the assured has been indemnified, according to this Act ... ". With the advent of policy deductibles, the basis of indemnification was substantially altered.

Where, by reason of the application of the policy deductible, the amount paid by the underwriter is less than an indemnity, English practice, in the absence of any policy provision to the contrary, is to divide the amount recovered rateably between the assured and the insurers in proportion to the nett claim paid by the insurers and the policy deductible borne by the assured. Under the American Institute Hull Clauses, 2 June 1977, this principle of subrogation is specifically incorporated into the insurance conditions.

Clause 12.3 however lays down a quite different basis upon which recoveries against any claim which has been subject to a deductible are to be adjusted; the recovery (excluding interest) is credited to underwriters in full until the sum which they have paid is fully reimbursed. It is only after this point is reached that the assured may participate in the sum recovered.

The method of dividing interest comprised in recoveries between underwriters and the assured is laid down in Clause 12.4. The crucial information needed to make such an apportionment is:

(1) The sums ranking for recovery.
(2) The interest recovered thereon, including information as to the period and rates of interest.
(3) The amounts and dates of underwriters' settlements (including any interim payments on account).

Clause 13 — Duty of Assured (Sue and Labour)

13 DUTY OF ASSURED (SUE AND LABOUR)

13.1 In case of any loss or misfortune it is the duty of the Assured and their servants and agents to take such measures as may be reasonable for the purpose of averting or minimising a loss which would be recoverable under this insurance.

13.2 Subject to the provisions below and to Clause 12 the Underwriters will contribute to charges properly and reasonably incurred by the Assured their servants or agents for such measures. General average, salvage charges (except as provided for in Clause 13.5) and collision defence or attack costs are not recoverable under this Clause 13.

13.3 Measures taken by the Assured or the Underwriters with the object of saving, protecting or recovering the subject-matter insured shall not be considered as a waiver or acceptance of abandonment or otherwise prejudice the rights of either party.

13.4 When expenses are incurred pursuant to this Clause 13 the liability under this insurance shall not exceed the proportion of such expenses that the amount insured hereunder bears to the value of the Vessel as stated herein, or to the sound value of the Vessel at the time of the occurrence giving rise to the expenditure if the sound value exceeds that value. Where the Underwriters have admitted a claim for total loss and property insured by this insurance is saved, the foregoing provisions shall not apply unless the expenses of suing and labouring exceed the value of such property saved and then shall apply only to the amount of the expenses which is in excess of such value.

13.5 When a claim for total loss of the Vessel is admitted under this insurance and expenses have been reasonably incurred in saving or attempting to save the Vessel and other property and there are no proceeds, or the expenses exceed the proceeds, then this insurance shall bear its pro rata share of such proportion of the expenses, or of the expenses in excess of the proceeds, as the case may be, as may reasonably be regarded as having been incurred in respect of the Vessel; but if the Vessel is insured for less than its sound value at the time of the occurrence giving rise to the expenditure, the amount recoverable under this clause shall be reduced in proportion to the under- insurance.

13.6 The sum recoverable under this Clause 13 shall be in addition to the loss otherwise recoverable under this insurance but shall in no circumstances exceed the amount insured under this insurance in respect of the Vessel.

Before looking at Clause 13 in detail it will be useful to consider the Sue and Labour Clause as it appeared in the S.G. form of policy.

"and in case of any loss or misfortune it shall be lawful to the assured, their factors, servants and assigns, to sue, labour, and travel for, in and about the defence, safeguards, and recovery of the said goods and merchandises, and ship, &c., or any part thereof, without prejudice to this insurance; to the charges whereof we, the assurers, will contribute each one according to the rate and quantity of his sum herein assured".

Section 78 of the Marine Insurance Act, 1906 states the following:

"(1) Where the policy contains a suing and labouring clause, the engagement thereby entered into is deemed to be supplementary to the contract of insurance, and the assured may recover from the insurer any expenses properly incurred pursuant to the clause, notwithstanding that the insurer may have paid for a total loss, or that the subject-matter may have been warranted free from particular average, either wholly or under a certain percentage.

(2) General average losses and contributions and salvage charges, as defined by this Act, are not recoverable under the suing and labouring clause.

(3) Expenses incurred for the purpose of averting or diminishing any loss not covered by the policy are not recoverable under the suing and labouring clause.

(4) It is the duty of the assured and his agents, in all cases, to take such measures as may be reasonable for the purpose of averting or minimising a loss."

Turning now to Clauses 13.1 and 13.2 they express, rather neatly, in modern language the old Sue and Labour Clause.

"in case of any loss or misfortune"

It is necessary to found a claim under the clause that as the result of the operation of insured perils the subject-matter of the insurance has been brought into such danger that without unusual or extraordinary labour and/or expense a loss will probably fall on the underwriters. This is an essential prerequisite to avoid claims for expenses reasonably and prudently incurred by the assured before any loss or danger had been experienced but without which a loss may well have occurred. Such expenses are part of the cost of owning and operating the insured property and in the absence of an insured peril creating a loss or danger of loss, are outside the ambit of insurance.

"it is the duty of the Assured and their servants and agents to take such measures as may be reasonable"

This imposes a positive duty upon the assured and their agents to take such measures as may be reasonable (and necessary). As to whose expenditure is recoverable under the clause, it should be noted that it is only those expenses which are incurred by the assured their servants or agents. The case of *Uzielli* v. *Boston Marine Insurance Company*[32] illustrated one limitation of these words. In this case A, an underwriter had reinsured with B, who in turn had reinsured with C. A, having paid the original assured for a total loss, himself incurred expenses in salving the vessel, which he recovered from B. B, however could not recover those expenses from C because A was not the "factor, servant or assign" (as the wording then was) of B.

32. (1884) 5 Asp.M.L.C. 405.

"for the purpose of averting or minimising a loss which would be recoverable under this insurance"

These words do no more than restate the position under English law. In considering whether the measures undertaken were for the purpose of averting or minimising a loss which would be recoverable under the insurance two aspects have to be considered. The first is that the peril must be one that is covered by the policy. The second is that there must have been the danger of a loss which would have been covered by the policy so that if the only danger had been of a partial loss under a policy which covered total loss only, there would be no claim for any sue and labour expenses incurred (*Great Indian Peninsula Railway Company* v. *Saunders*[33] and *Booth* v. *Gair*[34]).

"Subject to the provisions below and to Clause 12"

The provisions below are those dealing with reduction of the claim for sue and labour charges in the event of under-insurance (which is in derogation of English law) together with provisions dealing with the adjustment of the expenses in the event of a total loss. The reference to Clause 12 is due to the fact that claims under Clause 13 are subject to the policy deductible unless, as provided in Clause 12, the claim under Clause 13 is associated with a claim for a total or constructive total loss of the vessel.

"General average, salvage charges (except as provided for in Clause 13.5) and collision defence or attack costs are not recoverable under this Clause 13"

As we have already seen the Marine Insurance Act 1906 provides (section 78(2)) that general average losses and contributions and salvage charges are not recoverable under the Suing and Labouring Clause. The exclusion of salvage charges is based upon the leading case of *Aitchison* v. *Lohre* [35] which held that a distinction had to be drawn between salvage proper, which gave the salvors a lien on the property, and salvors working under special contract to the assured or the assured's agents. As we have already seen, the case of *Xenos* v. *Fox*[36] decided that the Sue and Labour Clause did not extend to the Running Down Clause. Clause 13 accordingly provides that collision costs, which fall for consideration under Clause 8, are not recoverable under the Duty of Assured Clause.

Clause 13.3 is a redrafting of the Waiver Clause in the S.G. form of policy and makes it clear that if the assured or the underwriters undertake any measures with the object of saving, protecting or recovering the insured

33. (1862) 6 L.T. 297; 10 W.R. 520.
34. (1863) 9 L.T. 286; 12 W.R. 106.
35. (1879) 4 Asp.M.L.C. 168.
36. (1868) 17 W.R. 893.

property such measures shall not be construed as a waiver or acceptance of abandonment or be allowed to prejudice the rights of either party *inter se.* Whereas English law, as codified in the Marine Insurance Act 1906 makes provision for reduction in the measure of indemnity for general average contributions and salvage charges in the event of under-insurance, there is no similar provision for sue and labour charges. Clause 13.4 puts sue and labour charges on to a similar basis, the measure of indemnity being assessed by comparing the amount insured under the policy with either the insured value, or the sound value of the vessel at the time of the occurrence giving rise to the expenditure, if that value is higher than the insured value. The effect of the clause is ameliorated where a claim for total loss has been admitted under the policy, when it is only the excess of the expenses over and above the proceeds, which is subjected to reduction to take account of any under-insurance.

Clause 13.5 deals with the situation when a claim for total loss has been admitted under the policy and the assured has incurred expenses in saving or attempting to save the vessel and other property and there are no proceeds, or the expenses exceed the proceeds. A simple example can perhaps best illustrate the type of expenditure contemplated by this clause.

Suppose a vessel with cargo on board is badly stranded. Having found that due to the gravity of the position none of the available tugs is willing to undertake the refloating of the vessel on a "No-Cure No-Pay" basis, the shipowner is forced to enter into a contract for the hire of a tug on a daily basis. He is therefore committed to paying the cost of hiring the tug regardless of success. If the ship and cargo are successfully salved there is no problem as the cost of hiring the tug is included with the subsequent expenditure as general average. But what happens when the tug services prove abortive; either nothing is saved or the cost of hiring the tug exceeds the proceeds of the property salved. Where does the shipowner recover the cost of hiring the tug? It is quite properly general average expenditure but cannot be recovered under that heading; the contributory values are nil and there is no liability upon hull underwriters after they have paid for a total loss. It is not salvage, being a charge incurred under contract, nor is it sue and labour expenditure, having been incurred to benefit both the ship and cargo and not solely the insured property. In such circumstances hull underwriters have always accepted that they should be liable for the proportion of the expenditure attaching to the ship but, in practice the difficulty has been to determine what that proportion should be. The clause quite sensibly leaves the position open by providing that the hull policy shall bear its proportion of the expenses as may reasonably be regarded as having been incurred in respect of the vessel. This then leaves it for the average adjuster to investigate the facts of the particular case and make an equitable division.

Finally, Clause 13.5 provides for the reduction of any claim thereunder in the event of under-insurance. Clause 13.6 stipulates that any claim under

Clause 13 is payable over and above any other loss recoverable under the policy, subject to the limit of the amount insured.

Clause 14 — New for Old

14 NEW FOR OLD
Claims payable without deduction new for old.

A contract of marine insurance is a contract of indemnity and when old parts of the vessel which have been lost or damaged through the operation of insured perils are replaced by new parts there is an element of betterment. However the practical difficulties of calculating the appropriate deduction to be made in respect of what is frequently only a notional betterment is simply not warranted and for many years hull insurances have provided for claims to be payable without being subject to "new for old" deductions.

Clause 15 — Bottom Treatment

15 BOTTOM TREATMENT
In no case shall a claim be allowed in respect of scraping gritblasting and/or other surface preparation or painting of the Vessel's bottom except that
15.1 gritblasting and/or other surface preparation of new bottom plates ashore and supplying and applying any "shop" primer thereto,
15.2 gritblasting and/or other surface preparation of:

the butts or area of plating immediately adjacent to any renewed or refitted plating damaged during the course of welding and/or repairs,

areas of plating damaged during the course of fairing, either in place or ashore,
15.3 supplying and applying the first coat of primer/anti-corrosive to those particular areas mentioned in 15.1 and 15.2 above,
shall be allowed as part of the reasonable cost of repairs in respect of bottom plating damaged by an insured peril.

The clause which appeared in the I.T.C. up until the 1983 revision was as follows: "no claim shall in any case be allowed in respect of scraping or painting the Vessel's bottom".

The above clause had remained unchanged for close on a century and it was increasingly felt that it had become outdated due to the dramatic advance in the qualities and expected life of bottom coatings and the changes in the surface preparation required. At the Annual General Meeting of the Association of Average Adjusters in May 1978 a resolution was approved appointing a special committee which would include representatives of shipowners and underwriters to consider the treatment of modern bottom coatings damaged by an insured peril in the context of Clause 14. Following the report of this special committee a new Rule of Practice (D8) of the Association of Average Adjusters was drawn up and this is now incorporated in the I.T.C. as Clause 15. The clause is of necessity of a fairly technical nature and the adjustment of any claims thereunder is generally left to the average adjuster and his technical consultant. For any readers who wish to have any more background information on this clause reference should be made to the Association of Average Adjusters' report of the General Meeting held on 10 May 1979 which includes the report of the Special Committee on the treatment of modern bottom coatings.

Clause 16 — Wages and Maintenance

16   WAGES AND MAINTENANCE

No claim shall be allowed, other than in general average, for wages and maintenance of the Master, Officers and Crew, or any member thereof, except when incurred solely for the necessary removal of the Vessel from one port to another for the repair of damage covered by the Underwriters, or for trial trips for such repairs, and then only for such wages and maintenance as are incurred whilst the Vessel is under way.

The wages and maintenance of crew may under certain circumstances be allowed in general average, in which event ship's proportion may form a claim under Clause 11 of the I.T.C. As to whether there is any liability under English law for wages and maintenance of the crew as part of a claim for particular average is highly questionable but over the years the practice had grown up for appropriate allowances to be made in particular average for either the whole or part crew on removal passages and whilst engaged on such practices as docking and undocking the vessel and acting as shipkeepers during average repairs. This practice had been so long-standing that shipowners had become accustomed to receive such allowances for wages and maintenance of crew as a part of their indemnity. Hull underwriters had long been of the view that the wages and maintenance were not a proper item to be included in a particular average claim: they contended that in the absence of the operation of an insured peril and the damage resulting therefrom the shipowners would still have been liable for the wages and maintenance of the crew. In 1969 a clause was introduced excluding claims for the wages and maintenance of the crew other than in general average or other limited circumstances. Looking at the present wording in detail:

"No claim shall be allowed, other than in general average, for wages and maintenance of the Master, Officers and crew..."

The exclusion only relates to the wages and maintenance and would not preclude a claim for overtime and/or special payments made to the crew in appropriate circumstances, for example, assisting on damage repairs, tank cleaning etc. The terms "wages and maintenance" and "crew" were considered by the Advisory Committee of the Association of Average Adjusters which set out the following recommendations as to the reasonable interpretation of the clause with the object of achieving uniformity of interpretation in practice.

"1. Wages and Maintenance

(a) Wages

The term 'wages' comprises the gross amount of all those payments made by the Shipowners to the members of the crew on a monthly, weekly or other periodic basis including leave pay, overseas allowance etc., and the employers' contribution to State and other Insurance and/or Pension Schemes which relate to those payments, and also payments of overtime to the crew in pursuance of their normal watchkeeping and/or other duties which may loosely be termed regular overtime.

However, when a vessel is in need of repair, whether at sea or in port, and the members of the crew are called upon to assist in those repairs, any payment for such services additional to wages as described above does not fall within the definition of the word because it is not earned on a regular periodic basis. This applies whether the payment is due under the terms of the contract of employment or whether it is a special payment made to the crew for additional services, the quantum of which is determined without reference to the crew basic wage or overtime structure.

(b) Maintenance

The term 'maintenance' comprises the cost of provisions, laundry etc., for the crew, together with the cost of providing accommodation on shore in certain circumstances.

2. Crew

The term 'crew' comprises those members of the ship's complement of sea-going rank engaged under articles and/or entered in the Master's portage bill or harbour wage account."

"Except when incurred solely for the necessary removal of the vessel from one port to another for repair of damage covered by the underwriters"

It should be noted that the limitation to the exclusion only applies when the wages and maintenance have been incurred solely for the necessary removal of the vessel for damage repairs. So that if the removal was for both average and owners' repairs, no wages and maintenance are in practice paid by underwriters under this clause.

"or for trial trips for such repairs"

If following say a main engine damage, which forms a claim under the policy, the vessel goes out for a trial trip the wages and maintenance of the crew for the period whilst under way on trials will be claimable.

"and then only for such wages and maintenance as are incurred whilst the vessel is under way"

An allowance can only be made for the period whilst the vessel is actually under way, so that any period spent at anchor outside a port for example would be excluded.

Clause 17 — Agency Commission

17   AGENCY COMMISSION

In no case shall any sum be allowed under this insurance either by way of remuneration of the Assured for time and trouble taken to obtain and supply information or documents or in respect of the commission or charges of any manager, agent, managing or agency company or the like, appointed by or on behalf of the Assured to perform such services.

The authors think that underwriters would be the first to admit that this is undoubtedly the worst piece of drafting in the I.T.C. Although the exclusion expressly relates only to "time and trouble taken to obtain and supply information or documents", and by implication should not exclude any claim for time and trouble taken in say arranging for salvage services or repairs, in practice underwriters have made it clear that their intention was to exclude all claims for remuneration by the assured, their managers or agents for time and trouble incurred on any aspect of a claim. In practice, underwriters will now only accept those expenses which fall within the terms of the Association of Average Adjusters Rule of Practice A3 which reads as follows.

"That, in practice, neither commission (excepting bank commission) nor any charge by way of agency or remuneration for trouble is allowed to the shipowner in average, except in respect of services rendered on behalf of cargo when such services are not involved in the contract of affreightment."

Finally it should be mentioned that the clause does not exclude the fees and charges of an agent at a port of call, which can still be recoverable under certain circumstances with the other port charges as part of the cost of repairs.

Clause 18 — Unrepaired Damage

18   UNREPAIRED DAMAGE

18.1 The measure of indemnity in respect of claims for unrepaired damage shall be the reasonable depreciation in the market value of the Vessel at the time this insurance terminates arising from such unrepaired damage, but not exceeding the reasonable cost of repairs.

18.2 In no case shall the Underwriters be liable for unrepaired damage in the event of a subsequent total loss (whether or not covered under this insurance or any extension thereof) sustained during the period covered by this insurance or any extension thereof.

18.3 The Underwriters shall not be liable in respect of unrepaired damage for more than the insured value at the time this insurance terminates.

Before looking at the above clause it would be as well to consider English law on this subject. The Marine Insurance Act 1906, section 69(3) states:

"Where the ship has not been repaired, and has not been sold in her damaged state during the risk, the assured is entitled to be indemnified for the reasonable depreciation arising from the unrepaired damage, but not exceeding the reasonable cost of repairing such damage"

It will be noted at once that the subsection is not exhaustive, since it excludes the case where the vessel has been sold in damaged condition during the currency of the policies, which will be referred to shortly.

The subsection was subject to judicial interpretation in *Irvin* v. *Hine*.[37] In interpreting the subsection, there were two main questions:

(a) What was the reasonable cost of repairs?

In determining this, Devlin J. held that the cost is to be taken at the time when repairs would, in the particular circumstances of the case, have been effected, and not at the time of the loss.

(b) What was the reasonable depreciation?

Having found that the sound value of the trawler was £3,000 and with the proceeds of sale having been agreed at £685 the question then became one of law; for the purpose of the Act was the reasonable depreciation:

(1) The sound value less proceeds, that is £3,000 less £685 = £2,315, or
(2) The proportion of the insured value which the figure produced in the last calculation bore to the actual sound value, that is £2,315/3,000ths of the insured value, £9,000 = £6,945, or
(3) The insured value less proceeds, that is £9,000 less £685 = £8,315.

The learned judge held that the reasonable depreciation was not to be arrived at by the first of these calculations, and further than that he did not go, since the result produced by either of the alternatives exceeded the sum which he had previously found to be the reasonable cost of repairing the damage.

Although *Irvin* v. *Hine*[37] was the first, and indeed the only case in which the English courts have been called upon to give effect to section 69(3) of the Marine Insurance Act, it was not the first case in which the subsection had been the subject of judicial pronouncement. This is due to the fact that in an earlier case, *Elcock* v. *Thompson*[38] the words of section 69(3) were referred to by Morris J. as affording him guidance in a fire insurance case. In that case the learned judge held that where in a fire insurance policy, provision was made for "reasonable depreciation", this was taking into account any agreed valuation in the policy. It was perhaps unfortunate that the

37. (1950) 83 Ll.L.Rep. 162; [1949] 2 All E.R. 1089.
38. [1949] 2 All E.R. 381; 82 Ll.L.Rep. 892.

attention of Devlin J. in *Irvin* v.*Hine*[37] was not called to the case of *Elcock* v. *Thompson*,[38] which had been heard very shortly before. Perhaps if the previous case had been mentioned by counsel, Devlin J's judgment might have been framed rather differently.

If the law rested there, it is submitted that it would be unreasonable to extract any certain rule from these two cases, since in *Irvin* v. *Hine*[37] it was not necessary to establish the principle in order to reach the correct decision, and in *Elcock* v. *Thompson*[38] the statement of principle was not, strictly speaking, in point in a non-marine case.

The matter does not rest there, for subsequently in 1954, the District Court of New York considered the matter in *Compania Maritima Astra S.A.* v. *Archdale*.[39] Whilst it is true that American decisions do not bind the English courts nevertheless they are of considerable persuasive authority and particularly in a case such as this when the American law is founded on English law. In applying section 69(3) of the Marine Insurance Act, Rabin J. considered both *Elcock* v. *Thompson*[38] and *Irvin* v. *Hine*[37] and held that the formula to apply to determine the reasonable depreciation was the proportion of the insured value that the difference between the sound and damaged values bore to the sound value. The figure arrived at using this formula proved to be higher than the estimated cost of repairs and accordingly judgment was given for this lesser sum.

As mentioned previously, there is one situation which is not covered by the Marine Insurance Act, namely, where the ship has been sold in damaged condition during the currency of the policy. This case is governed by the well known decision in *Pitman* v. *The Universal Marine Insurance Company*.[40] In this case the learned judge held that the correct mode of ascertaining the proportion of loss to be made good by the underwriters is to compare the value of the sound ship at port of distress with her value there when damaged, and to apply this proportion to her real value at the commencement of the risk if the policy be opened, or to her agreed value, if, as in the case under consideration the policy be valued.

It is therefore submitted that in both cases, that is whether the ship has been sold during the currency of the risk or not, the principle of indemnity under English law remains the same. The assured is entitled to recover the proportion of the insured or insurable value, as the case may be, as the difference between the sound and damaged values bears to the sound value, but always with the proviso that where the shipowner could have repaired the damage for a lesser sum the liability of underwriters shall not exceed the estimated cost of repairs.

Clause 18 makes a radical alteration in the basis for assessing claims for unrepaired damage. Clause 18.1 lays down the measure of indemnity in

39. 1954 A.M.C. 1674; [1954] 2 Lloyd's Rep. 95.
40. (1882) 30 W.R. 900; 4 Asp.M.L.C. 544.

respect of claims for unrepaired damage, namely, "the reasonable depreciation in the market value of the vessel at the time this insurance terminates
arising from such unrepaired damage, but not exceeding the reasonable cost
of repairs". As will be seen, there is no reference to the insured value in the
clause and the indemnity is based upon the depreciation in the market value.
The depreciation is to be assessed at the time when the insurance terminates
and this is in line with section 69(3) of the Marine Insurance Act 1906 which
deals with those cases where the vessel has not been sold in her damaged
state during the risk. Similarly, where the vessel is sold during the risk the
insurance would terminate automatically in accordance with Clause 4 of the
I.T.C. and this would then be the relevant date under the clause for assessing the reasonable depreciation in the market value of the vessel. In fact,
providing there were no other factors affecting the sale price obtained, a
comparison of the actual price realised with a valuers' estimate as to the
value of the vessel if she had been in sound condition, would be *prima facie*
evidence of the depreciation arising from the unrepaired damage. In line
with English law the measure of indemnity for unrepaired damage is limited
to the estimated reasonable cost of repairs if this figure is less than the
depreciation in the market value of the vessel.

Clause 18.2 is a restatement of the position under English law as codified
by section 77(2) of the Marine Insurance Act 1906, which provides as
follows:

> "Where, under the same policy, a partial loss, which has not been repaired or
> otherwise made good, is followed by a total loss, the assured can only recover in
> respect of the total loss"

The reason for these provisions is that in the event of a subsequent total loss
any unrepaired damage becomes merged in the total loss and the assured
has lost nothing by reason of the unrepaired damage. Two important points
should be noted regarding any subsequent total loss:

(1) It does not matter whether the total loss is covered under the policy.
    See *British & Foreign Marine Insurance Company* v. *Wilson Shipping
    Company Limited*[41] where the vessel was insured, as customary, under
    separate policies against marine and war risks, respectively. Having
    sustained some damage which was left unrepaired and gave rise to a
    potential claim under the marine policy she was subsequently a total loss
    as the result of being torpedoed by a submarine (a risk covered under the
    war policy). The unrepaired partial loss was deemed to have been
    merged in the subsequent total loss and could not be recovered under
    the Marine Policy.

(2) The subsequent total loss must have occurred during the period
    covered by the insurance, or any extension thereof, as for example

41. (1919) 4 Ll.L.Rep. 371; 26 Com.Cas. 13.

under Clause 2. So that a total loss during the currency of a subsequent policy would not affect any claim(s) for unrepaired damage under previous policies.

Under Clause 18.3 underwriters set an overall limit for their liability in respect of unrepaired damage, which is set at the insured value at the time when the insurance terminates.

Clause 19 — Constructive Total Loss

19   CONSTRUCTIVE TOTAL LOSS

19.1 In ascertaining whether the Vessel is a constructive total loss, the insured value shall be taken as the repaired value and nothing in respect of the damaged or break-up value of the Vessel or wreck shall be taken into account.

19.2 No claim for constructive total loss based upon the cost of recovery and/or repair of the Vessel shall be recoverable hereunder unless such cost would exceed the insured value. In making this determination, only the cost relating to a single accident or sequence of damages arising from the same accident shall be taken into account.

The relevant sections of section 60 of the Marine Insurance Act 1906 are as follows:

"60. Constructive Total Loss defined

(1) Subject to any express provision in the policy, there is a constructive total loss where the subject-matter insured is reasonably abandoned on account of its actual total loss appearing to be unavoidable, or because it could not be preserved from actual total loss without an expenditure which would exceed its value when the expenditure had been incurred.

(2) In particular, there is a constructive total loss —

(ii) In the case of damage to a ship, where she is so damaged by a peril insured against, that the cost of repairing the damage would exceed the value of the ship when repaired.

In estimating the cost of repairs, no deduction is to be made in respect of general average contributions to those repairs payable by other interests, but account is to be taken of the expense of future salvage operations and of any future general average contributions to which the ship would be liable if repaired;"

As will be seen, section 60 is subject to any express provision in the policy and Clause 19.1 does contain the express provision that the insured value shall be taken as the repaired value. This means quite simply that it is the insured value which forms the point of reference when determining whether the vessel is a constructive total loss and against which the estimated cost of repairing the damage must be compared. Under English law there has been considerable controversy over the years as to whether the value of the wreck should be included in the cost of repairs but this matter is put beyond doubt by the second section of Clause 19.1 which stipulates that nothing in respect of the damaged or breakup value of the vessel or wreck shall be taken into account in the computation. The clause only deals with the basis of calculating the figures and does not affect the question who may be entitled to exercise proprietary rights in the wreck.

The first part of Clause 19.2 is a clearly worded restatement of the position that arises out of the stipulations contained in Clause 19.1, when read in conjunction with the provisions of the Marine Insurance Act 1906. The simple test is whether the cost of recovery and/or repair of the vessel exceeds the insured value. If it does, the assured has the choice of either claiming for a constructive total loss or, alternatively, the assured may exercise his option of repairing the vessel and claiming for a 100 per cent partial loss. The latter course would be to the advantage of an assured who wished to retain the vessel.

The second part of Clause 19.2 deals with another point which is a grey area under English law, by stipulating that in assessing the cost of recovery and/or repair only the cost relating to a single accident or sequence of damages arising from the same accident may be taken into account.

Clause 20 — Freight Waiver

20   FREIGHT WAIVER
In the event of total or constructive total loss no claim to be made by the Underwriters for freight whether notice of abandonment has been given or not.

Section 63(2) of the Marine Insurance Act, 1906 provides as follows:

"Upon the abandonment of a ship, the insurer thereof is entitled to any freight in course of being earned, and which is earned by her subsequent to the casualty causing the loss, less the expenses of earning it incurred after the casualty; and, where the ship is carrying the owner's goods, the insurer is entitled to a reasonable remuneration for the carriage of them subsequent to the casualty causing the loss."

Under Clause 20 underwriters give up their rights to any freight in the course of being earned when the vessel is a total or constructive total loss, so that it remains the property of the shipowner.

Clause 21 — Disbursements Warranty

21   DISBURSEMENTS WARRANTY
21.1 Additional insurances as follows are permitted:
21.1.1 *Disbursements, Managers' Commissions, Profits or Excess or Increased Value of Hull and Machinery.* A sum not exceeding 25% of the value stated herein.
21.1.2 *Freight, Chartered Freight or Anticipated Freight, insured for time.* A sum not exceeding 25% of the value as stated herein less any sum insured, however described, under 21.1.1.
21.1.3 *Freight or Hire, under contracts for voyage.* A sum not exceeding the gross freight or hire for the current cargo passage and next succeeding cargo passage (such insurance to include, if required, a preliminary and an intermediate ballast passage) plus the charges of insurance. In

the case of a voyage charter where payment is made on a time basis, the sum permitted for insurance shall be calculated on the estimated duration of the voyage, subject to the limitation of two cargo passages as laid down herein. Any sum insured under 21.1.2 to be taken into account and only the excess thereof may be insured, which excess shall be reduced as the freight or hire is advanced or earned by the gross amount so advanced or earned.

21.1.4   *Anticipated Freight if the Vessel sails in ballast and not under Charter.* A sum not exceeding the anticipated gross freight on next cargo passage, such sum to be reasonably estimated on the basis of the current rate of freight at time of insurance plus the charges of insurance. Any sum insured under 21.1.2 to be taken into account and only the excess thereof may be insured.

21.1.5   *Time Charter Hire or Charter Hire for Series of Voyages.* A sum not exceeding 50% of the gross hire which is to be earned under the charter in a period not exceeding 18 months. Any sum insured under 21.1.2 to be taken into account and only the excess thereof may be insured, which excess shall be reduced as the hire is advanced or earned under the charter by 50% of the gross amount so advanced or earned but the sum insured need not be reduced while the total of the sums insured under 21.1.2 and 21.1.5 does not exceed 50% of the gross hire still to be earned under the charter. An insurance under this Section may begin on the signing of the charter.

21.1.6   *Premiums.* A sum not exceeding the actual premiums of all interests insured for a period not exceeding 12 months (excluding premiums insured under the foregoing sections but including, if required, the premium or estimated calls on any Club or War etc. Risk insurance) reducing pro rata monthly.

21.1.7   *Returns of Premium.* A sum not exceeding the actual returns which are allowable under any insurance but which would not be recoverable thereunder in the event of a total loss of the Vessel whether by insured perils or otherwise.

21.1.8   *Insurance irrespective of amount against:* Any risks excluded by Clauses 23, 24, 25 and 26 below.

21.2   Warranted that no insurance on any interests enumerated in the foregoing 21.1.1 to 21.1.7 in excess of the amounts permitted therein and no other insurance which includes total loss of the Vessel P.P.I., F.I.A., or subject to any other like term, is or shall be effected to operate during the currency of this insurance by or for account of the Assured, Owners, Managers or Mortgagees. Provided always that a breach of this warranty shall not afford the Underwriters any defence to a claim by a Mortgagee who has accepted this insurance without knowledge of such breach.

Originally introduced following the case of *The "Gunford"* (*Thames and Mersey Marine Insurance Company* v. *"Gunford" Ship Company*).[42] In this case the vessel was insured on a valuation which was in excess of the insurable value, and the freight was insured under a valued policy for a sum in excess of the gross amount at risk. In addition, the shipowners had effected a valued policy on disbursements. In examining the list of payments which were alleged by the assured to be the subject-matter of the disbursements policy, the court found that they were items which were already covered by either the freight or the ship policies. It was accordingly held that the disbursements policy constituted an over-insurance by double insurance and the assured was not entitled to any sum in excess of the indemnity permitted by law. One of the Law Lords took the opportunity to condemn disbursements policies which are duplications of insurances on freight as "a gamble, discountenanced by sound principle and not enforceable by law".

Apart from the element of gambling, there are sound underwriting reasons for prohibiting excessive insurances on disbursements. In assessing the rate of premium, the underwriter is basing his calculations in part upon the assumption that the insured value represents the full value of the

42. (1911) 16 Com.Cas. 270; 12 Asp.M.L.C. 49.

subject-matter insured. In the absence of any restriction upon the amount of additional insurances allowed, it would be possible for an assured to cover his vessel on full conditions for a valuation which he judged sufficient to cover most partial losses and he could then arrange additional cover on "total loss only" conditions at a lower rate of premium in order to bring the cover up to the full value required. Such an insurance programme would result in the first insurance becoming a first loss policy and would distort the premium/loss ratio figures.

It was for the above reasons that the Disbursements Clause was introduced with a view to limiting the amount of such ancillary insurances which can be effected.

The clause commences by listing the additional insurances which are permitted. Little comment is necessary upon the types of additional insurance listed which are self-explanatory. It should be noted that the limits under several sub-clauses are related to the sums insured under certain previous sub-clauses. As an example, the limit for freight, chartered freight or anticipated freight, insured for time (under Clause 21.1.2) must be calculated taking into account any sum insured under Clause 21.1.1. In practice the assured has the choice, subject to the rules of insurable interest, of apportioning the 25 per cent additional insurances allowed between the different types of insurances as set out in the clause as he sees fit and to suit his individual circumstances.

Clause 21.2 contains the express warranty against any insurances in excess of the amounts permitted in Clauses 21.1.1 to 21.1.7 and any other insurance which includes total loss of the vessel PPI (policy proof of interest), FIA (full interest admitted) or subject to any other like term. It is only PPI insurances which include total loss of the vessel which are caught by the express warranty so that any other PPI policies would not be in breach of the warranty.

To protect the position of an innocent mortgagee who has accepted the hull insurance in ignorance of a breach of the warranty, underwriters waive the right to set up this defence against claim by such a mortgagee within the meaning of the proviso.

Clause 22 — Returns for Lay-Up and Cancellation

22 RETURNS FOR LAY-UP AND CANCELLATION

22.1 To return as follows:

22.1.1 Pro rata monthly net for each uncommenced month if this insurance be cancelled by agreement.

22.1.2 For each period of 30 consecutive days the Vessel may be laid up in a port or in a lay-up area provided such port or lay-up area is approved by the Underwriters (with special liberties as hereinafter allowed)

(a).....................per cent net not under repair

(b).....................per cent net under repair.

If the Vessel is under repair during part only of a period for which a return is claimable, the return shall be calculated pro rata to the number of days under (a) and (b) respectively.

22.2 PROVIDED ALWAYS THAT

22.2.1   a total loss of the Vessel, whether by insured perils or otherwise, has not occurred during the period covered by this insurance or any extension thereof

22.2.2   in no case shall a return be allowed when the Vessel is lying in exposed or unprotected waters, or in a port or lay-up area not approved by the Underwriters but, provided the Underwriters agree that such non-approved lay-up area is deemed to be within the vicinity of the approved port or lay-up area, days during which the Vessel is laid up in such non-approved lay-up area may be added to days in the approved port or lay-up area to calculate a period of 30 consecutive days and a return shall be allowed for the proportion of such period during which the Vessel is actually laid up in the approved port or lay-up area

22.2.3   loading or discharging operations or the presence of cargo on board shall not debar returns but no return shall be allowed for any period during which the Vessel is being used for the storage of cargo or for lightering purposes

22.2.4   in the event of any amendment of the annual rate, the above rates of return shall be adjusted accordingly

22.2.5   in the event of any return recoverable under this Clause 22 being based on 30 consecutive days which fall on successive insurances effected for the same Assured, this insurance shall only be liable for an amount calculated at pro rata of the period rates 22.1.2(a) and/or (b) above for the number of days which come within the period of this insurance and to which a return is actually applicable. Such overlapping period shall run, at the option of the Assured, either from the first day on which the Vessel is laid up or the first day of a period of 30 consecutive days as provided under 22.1.2(a) or (b), or 22.2.2 above.

As stated in the heading of the clause, it provides for returns of premium in two circumstances:

(1) If the insurance is cancelled by agreement a return is due of the pro rata monthly net premium for each uncommenced month.

(2) If the vessel is laid up in a port or in a lay-up area approved by underwriters a return of premium is due for each period of 30 consecutive days, at the specified rates which have to be entered into the clause, different rates applying depending on whether the vessel is under repair or otherwise. For those periods ranking for a return of premium when the vessel is under repair for only part of the period, the return of premium is calculated in proportion to the number of days under each category.

The returns are subject to the following provisos:

(a) If a total loss of the vessel occurs during the period of the policy (or any extension thereto) no return of premium is due. This is the case regardless of whether the total loss resulted from insured perils or otherwise.

(b) As we have already seen, returns are only payable whilst the vessel is laid up if she is in a port or lay-up area which has been approved by underwriters. Clause 22.2.2, re-emphasises this fact by stating that in no case shall a return be allowed when the vessel is lying in exposed or unprotected waters but underwriters do give the concession that provided such non-approved lay-up area is within the vicinity of the approved port or lay-up area, the period spent in the non-approved lay-up area may be added to the period spent in the approved lay-up area to calculate a minimum ranking period of 30 consecutive days, but the return of premium is of course only due for the proportion of such a period during which the vessel is actually laid up in the approved port or lay-up area.

(c) Clause 22.2.3 makes it clear that loading or discharging operations or the presence of cargo on board will not prejudice returns of premium, where appropriate, but when the vessel is being used for the storage of cargo or for lightering purposes no return will be allowed for any period spent on such operations.

(d) If the annual rate of premium is adjusted it is only equitable that the rates of return should be adjusted accordingly and this is provided for by Clause 22.2.4.

(e) A return of premium may be due based on 30 consecutive days which fall on successive policies and in these circumstances Clause 22.2.5, sets out the basis for the calculation, giving the assured the option to decide the date from which the overlapping period shall run. This option can of course be of considerable benefit to the assured when there is a difference in the rate of return due under the different policies.

Clause 22 stipulates for the return of premium in two specified circumstances but it should be realised that under English law there can be other grounds for a return of premium. These are set out in section 84 of the Marine Insurance Act 1906 as follows:

"(1) Where the consideration for the payment of the premium totally fails, and there has been no fraud or illegality on the part of the assured or his agents, the premium is thereupon returnable to the assured.

(2) Where the consideration for the payment of the premium is apportionable and there is a total failure of any apportionable part of the consideration, a proportionate part of the premium is, under the like conditions, thereupon returnable to the assured.

(3) In particular —

(a) Where the policy is void, or is avoided by the insurer as from the commencement of the risk, the premium is returnable, provided that there has been no fraud or illegality on the part of the assured; but if the risk is not apportionable, and has once attached, the premium is not returnable;

(b) Where the subject-matter insured, or part thereof, has never been imperilled, the premium, or, as the case may be, a proportionate part thereof, is returnable;

Provided that where the subject-matter has been insured "lost or not lost" and has arrived in safety at the time when the contract is concluded, the premium is not returnable unless, at such time, the insurer knew of the safe arrival.

(c) Where the assured has no insurable interest throughout the currency of the risk, the premium is returnable, provided that this rule does not apply to a policy effected by way of gaming or wagering;

(*d*) Where the assured has a defeasible interest which is terminated during the currency of the risk, the premium is not returnable;

(*e*) Where the assured has over-insured under an unvalued policy, a proportionate part of the premium is returnable;

(*f*) Subject to the foregoing provisions, where the assured has over-insured by double insurance, a proportionate part of the several premiums is returnable;

Provided that, if the policies are effected at different times, and any earlier policy has at any time borne the entire risk, or if a claim has been paid on the policy in respect of the full sum insured thereby, no premium is returnable in respect of that policy, and when the double insurance is effected knowingly by the assured no premium is returnable."

Clauses 23, 24, 25 — War, Strikes and Malicious Acts Exclusions

The following clauses shall be paramount and shall override anything contained in this insurance inconsistent therewith.

23 WAR EXCLUSION

In no case shall this insurance cover loss damage liability or expense caused by

23.1 war civil war revolution rebellion insurrection, or civil strife arising therefrom, or any hostile act by or against a belligerent power

23.2 capture seizure arrest restraint or detainment (barratry and piracy excepted), and the consequences thereof or any attempt thereat

23.3 derelict mines torpedoes bombs or other derelict weapons of war.

24 STRIKES EXCLUSION

In no case shall this insurance cover loss damage liability or expense caused by

24.1 strikers, locked-out workmen, or persons taking part in labour disturbances, riots or civil commotions

24.2 any terrorist or any person acting from a political motive.

25 MALICIOUS ACTS EXCLUSION

In no case shall this insurance cover loss damage liability or expense arising from

25.1 the detonation of an explosive

25.2 any weapon of war

and caused by any person acting maliciously or from a political motive.

These clauses are expressed to be paramount and to override anything contained in the policy inconsistent therewith. They replace the old F.C. & S (Free of Capture and Seizure) Warranty, which we shall consider when we look at the positive cover afforded by the War and Strikes Risks forms (Part V). Consequently only a limited amount of comment is required on the exclusions.

As we have already seen when examining the perils covered by Clause 6, in the redrafting of the I.T.C. the opportunity was taken to transfer piracy from the war to the marine cover. Both piracy and barratry can result in the "seizure or arrest restraint or detainment of the vessel", for example seizure of the vessel by pirates or the impounding of the vessel by customs authorities following smuggling by the crew. It is for this reason that the exclusion of claims caused by capture, seizure, arrest, restraint or detainment is expressed to be "barratry and piracy excepted".

For some years the debate continued as to whether claims resulting from derelict mines etc., which could arise decades after the cessation of hostilities, should more properly fall upon the marine policies, as being no more than a "peril of the seas" rather than the war policies. The matter is now placed beyond doubt by Clause 23.3 which excludes such claims from the marine policies.

Before the Malicious Acts Exclusion (Clause 25) can apply, it is necessary to establish not only that the claim arises from the detonation of an explosion or any weapon of war but also that it was caused by a person acting maliciously or from a political motive. A claim resulting from the accidental explosion of a cargo of explosives would not be affected by the exclusion and would still be covered under Clause 6.1.

Clause 26 — Nuclear Exclusion

26 NUCLEAR EXCLUSION
   In no case shall this insurance cover loss damage liability or expense arising from any weapon of war employing atomic or nuclear fission and/or fusion or other like reaction or radioactive force or matter.

This is the customary nuclear war exclusion universally found in insurance policies.

3. INSTITUTE TIME CLAUSES — HULLS — RESTRICTED CONDITIONS

Not all shipowners require insurance on full conditions; the saving in premium obtained by opting for restricted conditions may be the governing factor; for older vessels the ship-owner may have no choice if underwriters are not willing to offer insurance on full conditions.

We will now consider the different types of restricted conditions available. To avoid unnecessary duplication, mention will only be made of the differences between each set of clauses and the I.T.C. Hulls 1/10/83, which have already been reviewed in detail (See Part III).

Institute Time Clauses — Hulls — Total Loss, General Average and 3/4ths Collision Liability (Including Salvage, Salvage Charges and Sue and Labour) (1/10/83)

This insurance is subject to English law and practice

1   NAVIGATION
   1.1   The Vessel is covered subject to the provisions of this insurance at all times and has leave to sail or navigate with or without pilots, to go on trial trips and to assist and tow vessels or craft in distress, but it is warranted that the Vessel shall not be towed, except as is customary or to the first safe port or place when in need of assistance, or undertake towage or salvage services under a contract previously arranged by the Assured and/or Owners and/or Managers and/or Charterers. This Clause 1.1 shall not exclude customary towage in connection with loading and discharging.

1.2 In the event of the Vessel being employed in trading operations which entail cargo loading or discharging at sea from or into another vessel (not being a harbour or inshore craft) no claim shall be recoverable under this insurance for loss of or damage to the Vessel or liability to any other vessel arising from such loading or discharging operations, including whilst approaching, lying alongside and leaving, unless previous notice that the Vessel is to be employed in such operations has been given to the Underwriters and any amended terms of cover and any additional premium required by them have been agreed.

1.3 In the event of the Vessel sailing (with or without cargo) with an intention of being (a) broken up, or (b) sold for breaking up, any claim for loss of or damage to the Vessel occurring subsequent to such sailing shall be limited to the market value of the Vessel as scrap at the time when the loss or damage is sustained, unless previous notice has been given to the Underwriters and any amendments to the terms of cover, insured value and premium required by them have been agreed. Nothing in this Clause 1.3 shall affect claims under Clauses 8 and/or 11.

2 CONTINUATION

Should the Vessel at the expiration of this insurance be at sea or in distress or at a port of refuge or of call, she shall, provided previous notice be given to the Underwriters, be held covered at a pro rata monthly premium to her port of destination.

3 BREACH OF WARRANTY

Held covered in case of any breach of warranty as to cargo, trade, locality, towage, salvage services or date of sailing, provided notice be given to the Underwriters immediately after receipt of advices and any amended terms of cover and any additional premium required by them be agreed.

4 TERMINATION

This Clause 4 shall prevail notwithstanding any provision whether written typed or printed in this insurance inconsistent therewith.

Unless the Underwriters agree to the contrary in writing, this insurance shall terminate automatically at the time of

4.1 change of the Classification Society of the Vessel, or change, suspension, discontinuance, withdrawal or expiry of her Class therein, provided that if the Vessel is at sea such automatic termination shall be deferred until arrival at her next port. However where such change, suspension, discontinuance or withdrawal of her Class has resulted from loss or damage which would be covered by an insurance of the Vessel subject to current Institute Time Clauses Hulls or Institute War and Strikes Clauses Hulls-Time such automatic termination shall only operate should the Vessel sail from her next port without the prior approval of the Classification Society,

4.2 any change, voluntary or otherwise, in the ownership or flag, transfer to new management, or charter on a bareboat basis, or requisition for title or use of the Vessel, provided that, if the Vessel has cargo on board and has already sailed from her loading port or is at sea in ballast, such automatic termination shall if required be deferred, whilst the Vessel continues her planned voyage, until arrival at final port of discharge if with cargo or at port of destination if in ballast. However, in the event of requisition for title or use without the prior execution of a written agreement by the Assured, such automatic termination shall occur fifteen days after such requisition whether the Vessel is at sea or in port.

A pro rata daily net return of premium shall be made.

5 ASSIGNMENT

No assignment of or interest in this insurance or in any moneys which may be or become payable thereunder is to be binding on or recognised by the Underwriters unless a dated notice of such assignment or interest signed by the Assured, and by the assignor in the case of subsequent assignment, is endorsed on the Policy and the Policy with such endorsement is produced before payment of any claim or return of premium thereunder.

6 PERILS

6.1 This insurance covers total loss (actual or constructive) of the subject-matter insured caused by

6.1.1 perils of the seas rivers lakes or other navigable waters

6.1.2 fire, explosion

6.1.3 violent theft by persons from outside the Vessel

6.1.4 jettison

6.1.5 piracy

6.1.6 breakdown of or accident to nuclear installations or reactors

6.1.7 contact with aircraft or similar objects, or objects falling therefrom, land conveyance, dock or harbour equipment or installation

6.1.8   earthquake volcanic eruption or lightning.

6.2   This insurance covers total loss (actual or constructive) of the subject-matter insured caused by

6.2.1   accidents in loading discharging or shifting cargo or fuel

6.2.2   bursting of boilers breakage of shafts or any latent defect in the machinery or hull

6.2.3   negligence of Master Officers Crew or Pilots

6.2.4   negligence of repairers or charterers provided such repairers or charterers are not an Assured hereunder

6.2.5   barratry of Master Officers or Crew,

provided such loss or damage has not resulted from want of due diligence by the Assured, Owners or Managers.

6.3   Master Officers Crew or Pilots not to be considered Owners within the meaning of this Clause 6 should they hold shares in the Vessel.

7   POLLUTION HAZARD

This insurance covers total loss (actual or constructive) of the Vessel caused by any governmental authority acting under the powers vested in it to prevent or mitigate a pollution hazard, or threat thereof, resulting directly from damage to the Vessel caused by a peril covered by this insurance, provided such act of governmental authority has not resulted from want of due diligence by the Assured, the Owners, or Managers of the Vessel or any of them to prevent or mitigate such hazard or threat. Master, Officers, Crew or Pilots not to be considered Owners within the meaning of this Clause 7 should they hold shares in the Vessel.

8   3/4THS COLLISION LIABILITY

8.1   The Underwriters agree to indemnify the Assured for three-fourths of any sum or sums paid by the Assured to any other person or persons by reason of the Assured becoming legally liable by way of damages for

8.1.1   loss of or damage to any other vessel or property on any other vessel

8.1.2   delay to or loss of use of any such other vessel or property thereon

8.1.3   general average of, salvage of, or salvage under contract of, any such other vessel or property thereon,

where such payment by the Assured is in consequence of the Vessel hereby insured coming into collision with any other vessel.

8.2   The indemnity provided by this Clause 8 shall be in addition to the indemnity provided by the other terms and conditions of this insurance and shall be subject to the following provisions:

8.2.1   Where the insured Vessel is in collision with another vessel and both vessels are to blame then, unless the liability of one or both vessels becomes limited by law, the indemnity under this Clause 8 shall be calculated on the principle of cross-liabilities as if the respective Owners had been compelled to pay to each other such proportion of each other's damages as may have been properly allowed in ascertaining the balance or sum payable by or to the Assured in consequence of the collision.

8.2.2   In no case shall the Underwriters' total liability under Clauses 8.1 and 8.2 exceed their proportionate part of three-fourths of the insured value of the Vessel hereby insured in respect of any one collision.

8.3   The Underwriters will also pay three-fourths of the legal costs incurred by the Assured or which the Assured may be compelled to pay in contesting liability or taking proceedings to limit liability, with the prior written consent of the Underwriters.

EXCLUSIONS

8.4   Provided always that this Clause 8 shall in no case extend to any sum which the Assured shall pay for or in respect of

8.4.1   removal or disposal of obstructions, wrecks, cargoes or any other thing whatsoever

8.4.2   any real or personal property or thing whatsoever except other vessels or property on other vessels

8.4.3   the cargo or other property on, or the engagements of, the insured Vessel

8.4.4   loss of life, personal injury or illness

8.4.5   pollution or contamination of any real or personal property or thing whatsoever (except other vessels with which the insured Vessel is in collision or property on such other vessels).

9   SISTERSHIP

Should the Vessel hereby insured come into collision with or receive salvage services from another vessel belonging wholly or in part to the same Owners or under the same management, the Assured shall have the same rights under this insurance as they would have were the other vessel entirely the property of

Owners not interested in the Vessel hereby insured; but in such cases the liability for the collision or the amount payable for the services rendered shall be referred to a sole arbitrator to be agreed upon between the Underwriters and the Assured.

10   NOTICE OF CLAIM

In the event of accident whereby loss or damage may result in a claim under this insurance, notice shall be given to the Underwriters prior to survey and also, if the Vessel is abroad, to the nearest Lloyd's Agent so that a surveyor may be appointed to represent the Underwriters should they so desire.

11   GENERAL AVERAGE AND SALVAGE

11.1   This insurance covers the Vessel's proportion of salvage, salvage charges and/or general average, reduced in respect of any under-insurance.

11.2   **This insurance does not cover partial loss of and/or damage to the Vessel except for any proportion of general average loss or damage which may be recoverable under Clause 11.1 above.**

11.3   Adjustment to be according to the law and practice obtaining at the place where the adventure ends, as if the contract of affreightment contained no special terms upon the subject; but where the contract of affreightment so provides the adjustment shall be according to the York-Antwerp Rules.

11.4   When the Vessel sails in ballast, not under charter, the provisions of the York-Antwerp Rules, 1974 (excluding Rules XX and XXI) shall be applicable, and the voyage for this purpose shall be deemed to continue from the port or place of departure until the arrival of the Vessel at the first port or place thereafter other than a port or place of refuge or a port or place of call for bunkering only. If at any such intermediate port or place there is an abandonment of the adventure originally contemplated the voyage shall thereupon be deemed to be terminated.

11.5   No claim under this Clause 11 shall in any case be allowed where the loss was not incurred to avoid or in connection with the avoidance of a peril insured against.

12   DEDUCTIBLE

12.1   No claim arising from a peril insured against shall be payable under this insurance unless the aggregate of all such claims arising out of each separate accident or occurrence (including claims under Clauses 8 and 13) exceeds...................................in which case this sum shall be deducted. This Clause 12.1 shall not apply to a claim for total or constructive total loss of the Vessel or, in the event of such a claim, to any associated claim under Clause 13 arising from the same accident or occurrence.

12.2   Excluding any interest comprised therein, recoveries against any claim which is subject to the above deductible shall be credited to the Underwriters in full to the extent of the sum by which the aggregate of the claim unreduced by any recoveries exceeds the above deductible.

12.3   Interest comprised in recoveries shall be apportioned between the Assured and the Underwriters, taking into account the sums paid by the Underwriters and the dates when such payments were made, notwithstanding that by the addition of interest the Underwriters may receive a larger sum than they have paid.

13   DUTY OF ASSURED (SUE AND LABOUR)

13.1   In case of any loss or misfortune it is the duty of the Assured and their servants and agents to take such measures as may be reasonable for the purpose of averting or minimising a loss which would be recoverable under this insurance.

13.2   Subject to the provisions below and to Clause 12 the Underwriters will contribute to charges properly and reasonably incurred by the Assured their servants or agents for such measures. General average, salvage charges (except as provided for in Clause 13.5) and collision defence or attack costs are not recoverable under this Clause 13.

13.3   Measures taken by the Assured or the Underwriters with the object of saving, protecting or recovering the subject-matter insured shall not be considered as a waiver or acceptance of abandonment or otherwise prejudice the rights of either party.

13.4   When expenses are incurred pursuant to this Clause 13 the liability under this insurance shall not exceed the proportion of such expenses that the amount insured hereunder bears to the value of the Vessel as stated herein, or to the sound value of the Vessel at the time of the occurrence giving rise to the expenditure if the sound value exceeds that value. Where the Underwriters have admitted a claim for total loss and property insured by this insurance is saved, the foregoing provisions shall not apply unless the expenses of suing and labouring exceed the value of such property saved and then shall apply only to the amount of the expenses which is in excess of such value.

13.5   When a claim for total loss of the Vessel is admitted under this insurance and expenses have been reasonably incurred in saving or attempting to save the Vessel and other property and there are no proceeds, or the expenses exceed the proceeds, then this insurance shall bear its pro rata share of such proportion of the expenses, or of the expenses in excess of the proceeds, as the case may be, as may reasonably be regarded as having been incurred in respect of the Vessel; but if the Vessel be insured for less than its sound value at the time of the occurrence giving rise to the expenditure, the amount recoverable under this clause shall be reduced in proportion to the under-insurance.

13.6 The sum recoverable under this Clause 13 shall be in addition to the loss otherwise recoverable under this insurance but shall in no circumstances exceed the amount insured under this insurance in respect of the Vessel.

14 NEW FOR OLD

General average payable without deduction new for old.

15 AGENCY COMMISSION

In no case shall any sum be allowed under this insurance either by way of remuneration of the Assured for time and trouble taken to obtain and supply information or documents or in respect of the commission or charges of any manager, agent, managing or agency company or the like, appointed by or on behalf of the Assured to perform such services.

16 CONSTRUCTIVE TOTAL LOSS

16.1 In ascertaining whether the Vessel is a constructive total loss, the insured value shall be taken as the repaired value and nothing in respect of the damaged or break-up value of the Vessel or wreck shall be taken into account.

16.2 No claim for constructive total loss based upon the cost of recovery and/or repair of the Vessel shall be recoverable hereunder unless such cost would exceed the insured value. In making this determination, only the cost relating to a single accident or sequence of damages arising from the same accident shall be taken into account.

17 FREIGHT WAIVER

In the event of total or constructive total loss no claim to be made by the Underwriters for freight whether notice of abandonment has been given or not.

18 DISBURSEMENTS WARRANTY

18.1 Additional insurances as follows are permitted:

18.1.1 *Disbursements, Managers' Commissions, Profits or Excess or Increased Value of Hull and Machinery.* A sum not exceeding 25% of the value stated herein.

18.1.2 *Freight, Chartered Freight or Anticipated Freight, insured for time.* A sum not exceeding 25% of the value as stated herein less any sum insured, however described, under 18.1.1.

18.1.3 *Freight or Hire, under contracts for voyage.* A sum not exceeding the gross freight or hire for the current cargo passage and next succeeding cargo passage (such insurance to include, if required, a preliminary and an intermediate ballast passage) plus the charges of insurance. In the case of a voyage charter where payment is made on a time basis, the sum permitted for insurance shall be calculated on the estimated duration of the voyage, subject to the limitation of two cargo passages as laid down herein. Any sum insured under 18.1.2 to be taken into account and only the excess thereof may be insured, which excess shall be reduced as the freight or hire is advanced or earned by the gross amount so advanced or earned.

18.1.4 *Anticipated Freight if the Vessel sails in ballast and not under Charter.* A sum not exceeding the anticipated gross freight on next cargo passage, such sum to be reasonably estimated on the basis of the current rate of freight at time of insurance plus the charges of insurance. Any sum insured under 18.1.2 to be taken into account and only the excess thereof may be insured.

18.1.5 *Time Charter Hire or Charter Hire for Series of Voyages.* A sum not exceeding 50% of the gross hire which is to be earned under the charter in a period not exceeding 18 months. Any sum insured under 18.1.2 to be taken into account and only the excess thereof may be insured, which excess shall be reduced as the hire is advanced or earned under the charter by 50% of the gross amount so advanced or earned but the sum insured need not be reduced while the total of the sums insured under 18.1.2 and 18.1.5 does not exceed 50% of the gross hire still to be earned under the charter. An insurance under this Section may begin on the signing of the charter.

18.1.6 *Premiums.* A sum not exceeding the actual premiums of all interests insured for a period not exceeding 12 months (excluding premiums insured under the foregoing sections but including, if required, the premium or estimated calls on any Club or War etc. Risk insurance) reducing pro rata monthly.

18.1.7 *Returns of Premium.* A sum not exceeding the actual returns which are allowable under any insurance but which would not be recoverable thereunder in the event of a total loss of the Vessel whether by insured perils or otherwise.

18.1.8 *Insurance irrespective of amount against*:

Any risks excluded by Clauses 20, 21, 22 and 23 below.

18.2 Warranted that no insurance on any interests enumerated in the foregoing 18.1.1 to 18.1.7 in excess of the amounts permitted therein and no other insurance which includes total loss of the Vessel P.P.I., F.I.A., or subject to any other like term, is or shall be effected to operate during the currency of this insurance by or for account of the Assured, Owners, Managers or Mortgagees. Provided always that a breach of this warranty shall not afford the Underwriters any defence to a claim by a Mortgagee who has accepted this insurance without knowledge of such breach.

19 RETURNS FOR LAY-UP AND CANCELLATION

19.1 To return as follows:

19.1.1 Pro rata monthly net for each uncommenced month if this insurance be cancelled by agreement.

19.1.2 For each period of 30 consecutive days the Vessel may be laid up in a port or in a lay-up area provided such port or lay-up area is approved by the Underwriters (with special liberties hereinafter allowed)

(a)...............................per cent net not under repair

(b)...............................per cent net under repair.

If the Vessel is under repair during part only of a period for which a return is claimable, the return shall be calculated pro rata to the number of days under (a) and (b) respectively.

19.2 PROVIDED ALWAYS THAT

19.2.1 a total loss of the Vessel, whether by insured perils or otherwise, has not occurred during the period covered by this insurance or any extension thereof

19.2.2 in no case shall a return be allowed when the Vessel is lying in exposed or unprotected waters, or in a port or lay-up area not approved by the Underwriters but, provided the Underwriters agree that such non-approved lay-up area is deemed to be within the vicinity of the approved port or lay-up area, days during which the Vessel is laid up in such non-approved lay-up area may be added to days in the approved port or lay-up area to calculate a period of 30 consecutive days and a return shall be allowed for the proportion of such period during which the Vessel is actually laid up in the approved port or lay-up area

19.2.3 loading or discharging operations or the presence of cargo on board shall not debar returns but no return shall be allowed for any period during which the Vessel is being used for the storage of cargo or for lightering purposes

19.2.4 in the event of any amendment of the annual rate, the above rates of return shall be adjusted accordingly

19.2.5 in the event of any return recoverable under this Clause 19 being based on 30 consecutive days which fall on successive insurances effected for the same Assured, this insurance shall only be liable for an amount calculated at pro rata of the period rates 19.1.2(a) and/or (b) above for the number of days which come within the period of this insurance and to which a return is actually applicable. Such overlapping period shall run, at the option of the Assured, either from the first day on which the Vessel is laid up or the first day of a period of 30 consecutive days as provided under 19.1.2(a) or (b) or 19.2.2 above.

The following clauses shall be paramount and shall override anything contained in this insurance inconsistent therewith.

20 WAR EXCLUSION

In no case shall this insurance cover loss damage liability or expense caused by

20.1 war civil war revolution rebellion insurrection, or civil strife arising therefrom, or any hostile act by or against a belligerent power

20.2 capture seizure arrest restraint or detainment (barratry and piracy excepted), and the consequences thereof or any attempt thereat

20.3 derelict mines torpedoes bombs or other derelict weapons of war.

21 STRIKES EXCLUSION

In no case shall this insurance cover loss damage liability or expense caused by

21.1 strikers, locked-out workmen, or persons taking part in labour disturbances, riots or civil commotions

21.2 any terrorist or any person acting from a political motive.

22 **MALICIOUS ACTS EXCLUSION**
In no case shall this insurance cover loss damage liability or expense arising from
22.1 the detonation of an explosive
22.2 any weapon of war
and caused by any person acting maliciously or from a political motive.

23 **NUCLEAR EXCLUSION**
In no case shall this insurance cover loss damage liability or expense arising from any weapon of war employing atomic or nuclear fission and/or fusion or other like reaction or radioactive force or matter.

6. Perils

While the perils insured against are the same as those listed in the I.T.C. Hulls 1/10/83, the cover is expressed to be against only "total loss (actual or constructive) of the subject-matter insured caused by".

10. Notice of claim

Due to the fact that partial losses are not covered, the detailed provisions regarding tenders etc. contained in the I.T.C. Hulls 1/10/83 are not required and only clause 10.1 is incorporated.

11. General average and salvage

Clause 11.1 gives positive cover against vessel's proportion of salvage, salvage charges and/or general average (reduced in respect of any under-insurance) but Clause 11.2 emphasises that the policy does not cover partial loss of and/or damage to the vessel, except for any proportion of general average loss or damage which may be recoverable under Clause 11.1. The practical effect of these clauses is that the assured is covered for any proportion of salvage, salvage charges and/or general average attaching to the vessel, including ship's proportion of any general average sacrifice of the ship, subject to reduction in respect of any under-insurance. This alters the position under English law which is codified by section 66(4) of the Marine Insurance Act 1906 which provides as follows:

> "Subject to any express provision in the policy, where the assured has incurred a general average expenditure, he may recover from the insurer in respect of the proportion of the loss which falls upon him; and in the case of a general average sacrifice he may recover from the insurer in respect of the whole loss without having enforced his right of contribution from the other parties liable to contribute."

12. Deductible

The first section of Clause 12.1 is identical to the equivalent clause in the I.T.C. Hulls 1/10/83. In view of the fact that the deductible does not apply to a claim for total or constructive total loss of the vessel, or any associated claim under Clause 13, the deductible is only applicable to the aggregate of any claims for general average, salvage, salvage charges, 3/4ths collision liability and/or Sue and Labour charges arising out of each separate accident or occurrence. Because the policy does not cover partial losses there is no Sighting Bottom Clause. Similarly the provision in Clause 12.2 of the I.T.C. Hulls 1/10/83 defining what constitutes an accident in the case of heavy weather or ice damage is not necessary and is omitted, resulting in the renumbering of the following two subclauses dealing with recoveries.

14. New for old

As the vessel's proportion of any general average loss or damage is the only partial loss covered by the policy, the new for old clause relates solely to general average.

15. Bottom treatment; 16. Wages and maintenance; 18. Unrepaired damage

These clauses, which appear in the I.T.C. Hulls 1/10/83, and relate to partial losses are omitted.

Institute Time Clauses — Hulls Total Loss Only
(Including Salvage, Salvage Charges and Sue and Labour) 1/10/83

This insurance is subject to English law and practice

1   **NAVIGATION**

    1.1   The Vessel is covered subject to the provisions of this insurance at all times and has leave to sail or navigate with or without pilots, to go on trial trips and to assist and tow vessels or craft in distress, but it is warranted that the Vessel shall not be towed, except as is customary or to the first safe port or place when in need of assistance, or undertake towage or salvage services under a contract previously arranged by the Assured and/or Owners and/or Managers and/or Charterers. This Clause 1.1 shall not exclude customary towage in connection with loading and discharging.

    1.2   In the event of the vessel being employed in trading operations which entail cargo loading or discharging at sea from or into another vessel (not being a harbour or inshore craft) no claim shall be recoverable under this insurance for loss of or damage to the Vessel from such loading or discharging operations, including whilst approaching, lying alongside and leaving, unless previous notice that the Vessel is to be employed in such operations has been given to the Underwriters and any amended terms of cover and any additional premium required by them have been agreed.

    1.3   In the event of the Vessel sailing (with or without cargo) with an intention of being (a) broken up, or (b) sold for breaking up, any claim for loss of or damage to the Vessel occurring subsequent to such sailing shall be limited to the market value of the Vessel as scrap at the time when the loss or damage is sustained, unless previous notice has been given to the Underwriters and any amendments to the terms of cover, insured value and premium required by them have been agreed. Nothing in this Clause 1.3 shall affect claims under clause 9.

2   **CONTINUATION**

Should the Vessel at the expiration of this insurance be at sea or in distress or at a port of refuge or of call, she shall, provided previous notice be given to the Underwriters, be held covered at a pro rata monthly premium to her port of destination.

3   **BREACH OF WARRANTY**

Held covered in case of any breach of warranty as to cargo, trade, locality, towage, salvage services or date of sailing, provided notice be given to the Underwriters immediately after receipt of advices and any ammended terms of cover and any additional premium required by them be agreed.

4 TERMINATION

This Clause 4 shall prevail notwithstanding any provision whether written typed or printed in this insurance inconsistent therewith.

Unless the Underwriters agree to the contrary in writing, this insurance shall terminate automatically at the time of

4.1 change of the Classification Society of the Vessel, or change, suspension, discontinuance, withdrawal or expiry of her Class therein, provided that if the Vessel is at sea such automatic termination shall be deferred until arrival at her next port. However where such change, suspension, discontinuance or withdrawal of her Class has resulted from loss or damage which would be covered by an insurance of the Vessel subject to current Institute Time Clauses Hulls or Institute War and Strikes Clauses Hulls-Time such automatic termination shall only operate should the Vessel sail from her next port without the prior approval of the Classification Society,

4.2 any change, voluntary or otherwise, in the ownership or flag, transfer to new management, or charter on a bareboat basis, or requisition for title or use of the Vessel, provided that, if the Vessel has cargo on board and has already sailed from her loading port or is at sea in ballast, such automatic termination shall if required be deferred, whilst the Vessel continues her planned voyage, until arrival at final port of discharge if with cargo or at port of destination if in ballast. However, in the event of requisition for title or use without the prior execution of a written agreement by the Assured, such automatic termination shall occur fifteen days after such requisition whether the Vessel is at sea or in port.

A pro rata daily net return of premium shall be made.

5 ASSIGNMENT

No assignment of or interest in this insurance or in any moneys which may be or become payable thereunder is to be binding on or recognised by the Underwriters unless a dated notice of such assignment or interest signed by the Assured, and by the assignor in the case of subsequent assignment, is endorsed on the Policy and the Policy with such endorsement is produced before payment of any claim or return of premium thereunder.

6 PERILS

6.1 This insurance covers total loss (actual or constructive) of the subject-matter insured caused by

6.1.1 perils of the seas rivers lakes or other navigable waters

6.1.2 fire, explosion

6.1.3 violent theft by persons from outside the Vessel

6.1.4 jettison

6.1.5 piracy

6.1.6 breakdown of or accident to nuclear installations or reactors

6.1.7 contact with aircraft or similar objects, or objects falling therefrom, land conveyance, dock or harbour equipment or installation

6.1.8 earthquake volcanic eruption or lightning.

6.2 This insurance covers total loss (actual or constructive) of the subject-matter insured caused by

6.2.1 accidents in loading discharging or shifting cargo or fuel

6.2.2 bursting of boilers breakage of shafts or any latent defect in the machinery or hull

6.2.3 negligence of Master Officers Crew or Pilots

6.2.4 negligence of repairers or charterers provided such repairers or charterers are not an Assured hereunder

6.2.5 barratry of Master Officers or Crew,

provided such loss or damage has not resulted from want of due diligence by the Assured, Owners or Managers.

6.3 Master Officers Crew or Pilots not to be considered Owners within the meaning of this Clause 6 should they hold shares in the Vessel.

7 POLLUTION HAZARD

This insurance covers total loss (actual or constructive) of the Vessel caused by any governmental authority acting under the powers vested in it to prevent or mitigate a pollution hazard, or threat thereof, resulting directly from damage to the Vessel caused by a peril covered by this insurance, provided such act of governmental authority has not resulted from want of due diligence by the Assured, the Owners, or Managers of the Vessel or any of them to prevent or mitigate such hazard or threat. Master, Officers, Crew or Pilots not to be considered Owners within the meaning of this Clause 7 should they hold shares in the Vessel.

8   NOTICE OF CLAIM

8.1   In the event of accident whereby loss or damage may result in a claim under this insurance, notice shall be given to the Underwriters prior to survey and also, if the Vessel is abroad, to the nearest Lloyd's Agent so that a surveyor may be appointed to represent the Underwriters should they so desire.

9   SALVAGE

9.1   This insurance covers the Vessel's proportion of salvage and salvage charges, reduced in respect of any under-insurance.

9.2   No claim under this Clause 9 shall in any case be allowed where the loss was not incurred to avoid or in connection with the avoidance of a peril insured against.

10   SISTERSHIP

Should the Vessel hereby insured receive salvage services from another vessel belonging wholly or in part to the same Owners or under the same management, the Assured shall have the same rights under this insurance as they would have were the other vessel entirely the property of Owners not interested in the Vessel hereby insured; but in such cases the amount payable for the services rendered shall be referred to a sole arbitrator to be agreed upon between the Underwriters and the Assured.

11   DUTY OF ASSURED (SUE AND LABOUR)

11.1   In case of any loss or misfortune it is the duty of the Assured and their servants and agents to take such measures as may be reasonable for the purpose of averting or minimising a loss which would be recoverable under this insurance.

11.2   Subject to the provisions below the Underwriters will contribute to charges properly and reasonably incurred by the Assured their servants or agents for such measures. General average, salvage charges and collision defence or attack costs are not recoverable under this Clause 11.

11.3   Measures taken by the Assured or the Underwriters with the object of saving, protecting or recovering the subject-matter insured shall not be considered as a waiver or acceptance of abandonment or otherwise prejudice the rights of either party.

11.4   When expenses are incurred pursuant to this Clause 11 the liability under this insurance shall not exceed the proportion of such expenses that the amount insured hereunder bears to the value of the Vessel as stated herein, or to the sound value of the Vessel at the time of the occurrence giving rise to the expenditure if the sound value exceeds that value. Where the Underwriters have admitted a claim for total loss and property insured by this insurance is saved, the foregoing provisions shall not apply unless the expenses of suing and labouring exceed the value of such property saved and then shall apply only to the amount of the expenses which is in excess of such value.

11.5   When a claim for total loss of the Vessel is admitted under this insurance and expenses have been reasonably incurred in saving or attempting to save the Vessel and other property and there are no proceeds, or the expenses exceed the proceeds, then this insurance shall bear its pro rata share of such proportion of the expenses, or of the expenses in excess of the proceeds, as the case may be, as may reasonably be regarded as having been incurred in respect of the Vessel; but if the Vessel be insured for less than its sound value at the time of the occurrence giving rise to the expenditure, the amount recoverable under this clause shall be reduced in proportion to the under-insurance.

11.6   The sum recoverable under this Clause 11 shall be in addition to the loss otherwise recoverable under this insurance but shall in no circumstances exceed the amount insured under this insurance in respect of the Vessel.

12   CONSTRUCTIVE TOTAL LOSS

12.1   In ascertaining whether the Vessel is a constructive total loss, the insured value shall be taken as the repaired value and nothing in respect of the damaged or break-up value of the Vessel or wreck shall be taken into account.

12.2   No claim for constructive total loss based upon the cost of recovery and/or repair of the Vessel shall be recoverable hereunder unless such cost would exceed the insured value. In making this determination, only the cost relating to a single accident or sequence of damages arising from the same accident shall be taken into account.

13   FREIGHT WAIVER

In the event of total or constructive total loss no claim to be made by the Underwriters for freight whether notice of abandonment has been given or not.

14   DISBURSEMENTS WARRANTY

14.1   Additional insurances as follows are permitted:

14.1.1   *Disbursements, Managers' Commissions, Profits or Excess or Increased Value of Hull and Machinery.* A sum not exceeding 25% of the value stated herein.

14.1.2   *Freight, Chartered Freight or Anticipated Freight, insured for time.* A sum not exceeding 25% of the value as stated herein less any sum insured, however described, under 14.1.1.

14.1.3   *Freight or Hire, under contracts for voyage.* A sum not exceeding the gross freight or hire for the current cargo passage and next succeeding cargo passage (such insurance to include, if required, a preliminary and an intermediate ballast passage) plus the charges of insurance. In the case of a voyage charter where payment is made on a time basis, the sum permitted for insurance shall be calculated on the estimated duration of the voyage, subject to the limitation of two cargo passages as laid down herein. Any sum insured under 14.1.2 to be taken into account and only the excess thereof may be insured, which excess shall be reduced as the freight or hire is advanced or earned by the gross amount so advanced or earned.

14.1.4   *Anticipated Freight if the Vessel sails in ballast and not under Charter.* A sum not exceeding the anticipated gross freight on next cargo passage, such sum to be reasonably estimated on the basis of the current rate of freight at time of insurance plus the charges of insurance. Any sum insured under 14.1.2 to be taken into account and only the excess thereof may be insured.

14.1.5   *Time Charter Hire or Charter Hire for Series of Voyages.* A sum not exceeding 50% of the gross hire which is to be earned under the charter in a period not exceeding 18 months. Any sum insured under 14.1.2 to be taken into account and only the excess thereof may be insured, which excess shall be reduced as the hire is advanced or earned under the charter by 50% of the gross amount so advanced or earned but the sum insured need not be reduced while the total of the sums insured under 14.1.2 and 14.1.5 does not exceed 50% of the gross hire still to be earned under the charter. An insurance under this Section may begin on the signing of the charter.

14.1.6   *Premiums.* A sum not exceeding the actual premiums of all interests insured for a period not exceeding 12 months (excluding premiums insured under the foregoing sections but including, if required, the premium or estimated calls on any Club or War etc. Risk insurance) reducing pro rata monthly.

14.1.7   *Returns of Premium.* A sum not exceeding the actual returns which are allowable under any insurance but which would not be recoverable thereunder in the event of a total loss of the Vessel whether by insured perils or otherwise.

14.1.8   *Insurance irrespective of amount against*: Any risks excluded by Clauses 16, 17, 18 and 19 below.

14.2 Warranted that no insurance on any interests enumerated in the foregoing 14.1.1 to 14.1.7 in excess of the amounts permitted therein and no other insurance which includes total loss of the Vessel P.P.I., F.I.A., or subject to any other like term, is or shall be effected to operate during the currency of this insurance by or for account of the Assured, Owners, Managers or Mortgagees. Provided always that a breach of this warranty shall not afford the Underwriters any defence to a claim by a Mortgagee who has accepted this insurance without knowledge of such breach.

15 RETURNS FOR LAY-UP AND CANCELLATION

15.1 To return as follows:

15.1.1   Pro rata monthly net for each uncommenced month if this insurance be cancelled by agreement.

15.1.2   For each period of 30 consecutive days the Vessel may be laid up in a port or in a lay-up area provided such port or lay-up area is approved by the Underwriters (with special liberties as hereinafter allowed)

(a)..................................per cent net not under repair

(b)..................................per cent net under repair.

If the Vessel is under repair during part only of a period for which a return is claimable, the return shall be calculated pro rata to the number of days under (a) and (b) respectively.

15.2 PROVIDED ALWAYS THAT

15.2.1   a total loss of the Vessel, whether by insured perils or otherwise, has not occurred during the period covered by this insurance or any extension thereof

15.2.2   in no case shall a return be allowed when the Vessel is lying in exposed or unprotected waters, or in a port or lay-up area not approved by the Underwriters but, provided the Underwriters agree that such non-approved lay-up area is deemed to be within the vicinity of the approved port or lay-up area, days during which the Vessel is laid up in such non-approved lay-up area may be added to days in the approved port or lay-up area to calculate a period of 30 consecutive days and a return shall be allowed for the proportion of such period during which the Vessel is actually laid up in the aproved port or lay-up area

15.2.3   loading or discharging operations or the presence of cargo on board shall not debar returns but no return shall be allowed for any period during which the Vessel is being used for the storage of cargo or for lightering purposes

15.2.4   in the event of any amendment of the annual rate, the above rates of return shall be adjusted accordingly

15.2.5   in the event of any return recoverable under this Clause 15 being based on 30 consecutive days which fall on successive insurances effected for the same Assured, this insurance shall only be liable for an amount calculated at pro rata of the period rates 15.1.2(a) and/or (b) above for the number of days which come within the period of this insurance and to which a return is actually applicable. Such overlapping period shall run, at the option of the Assured, either from the first day on which the Vessel is laid up or the first day of a period of 30 consecutive days as provided under 15.1.2(a) or (b), or 15.2.2 above.

The following clauses shall be paramount and shall override anything contained in this insurance inconsistent therewith.

16   WAR EXCLUSION

In no case shall this insurance cover loss damage liability or expense caused by

  16.1 war civil war revolution rebellion insurrection, or civil strife arising therefrom, or any hostile act by or against a belligerent power

  16.2 capture seizure arrest restraint or detainment (barratry and piracy excepted), and the consequences thereof or any attempt thereat

  16.3 derelict mines torpedoes bombs or other derelict weapons of war.

17   STRIKES EXCLUSION

In no case shall this insurance cover loss damage liability or expense caused by

  17.1 strikers, locked-out workmen, or persons taking part in labour disturbances, riots or civil commotions

  17.2 any terrorist or any person acting from a political motive.

18   MALICIOUS ACTS EXCLUSION

In no case shall this insurance cover loss damage liability or expense arising from

  18.1 the detonation of an explosive

  18.2 any weapon of war

and caused by any person acting maliciously or from a political motive.

19   NUCLEAR EXCLUSION

In no case shall this insurance cover loss damage liability or expense arising from any weapon of war employing atomic or nuclear fission and/or fusion or other like reaction or radioactive force or matter.

Once again mention will only be made of the differences between the above clauses and the I.T.C. Hulls 1/10/83 which have already been reviewed in detail (see Part III).

6. Perils

While the perils insured against are the same as those listed in the I.T.C. Hulls 1/10/83, the cover is expressed to be against only "total loss (actual or constructive) of the subject-matter insured caused by".

8. Notice of claim

Due to the fact that partial losses are not covered, the detailed provisions regarding tenders etc. contained in the I.T.C. Hulls 1/10/83 are not required and only Clause 10.1 is incorporated.

9. Salvage

Clause 9.1 provides positive cover against the vessel's proportion of salvage and salvage charges, reduced in respect of any under-insurance. Under section 65(1) of the Marine Insurance Act 1906, salvage charges incurred in preventing a loss by perils insured against may be recovered as a loss by those perils, and Clause 9.2 reiterates the position by stating the obverse, namely, that where salvage has been incurred in the avoidance of a loss resulting from an uninsured peril, there will be no claim under the policy for the salvage charges incurred. These clauses do not cover vessel's proportion of general average and there is therefore absolutely no cover against partial loss of and/or damage to the vessel.

Collision liability

Collision liabilities are not covered under these clauses.

Deductible

Claims under these clauses are not subject to any policy deductible.

14. New for old; 15. Bottom treatment; 16. Wages and maintenance; 17. Agency commission; 18. Unrepaired damage

These clauses, which appear in the I.T.C. Hulls 1/10/83 and relate to partial losses, are omitted.

4. INSTITUTE VOYAGE CLAUSES — HULLS

Whereas in the early days of insurance virtually all policies effected were for a round voyage, the reverse is now the case and the vast majority of insurances are effected on a time basis. For the minority of cases where an insurance is required for a voyage, two sets of main clauses are available. To avoid unnecessary duplication mention will only be made of the differences between each set of clauses and the I.T.C. Hulls 1/10/83 which have already been reviewed in detail (See Part III).

Institute Voyage Clauses — Hulls (1/10/83)

This insurance is subject to English law and practice
1   NAVIGATION
    1.1   The Vessel is covered subject to the provisions of this insurance at all times and has leave to sail or navigate with or without pilots, to go on trial trips and to assist and tow vessels or craft in distress, but it is warranted that the Vessel shall not be towed, except as is customary or to the first safe

port or place when in need of assistance, or undertake towage or salvage services under a contract previously arranged by the Assured and/or Owners and/or Managers and/or Charterers. This Clause 1.1 shall not exclude customary towage in connection with loading and discharging.

1.2 In the event of the Vessel being employed in trading operations which entail cargo loading or discharging at sea from or into another vessel (not being a harbour or inshore craft) no claim shall be recoverable under this insurance for loss of or damage to the Vessel or liability to any other vessel arising from such loading or discharging operations, including whilst approaching, lying alongside and leaving, unless previous notice that the Vessel is to be employed in such operations has been given to the Underwriters and any amended terms of cover and any additional premium required by them have been agreed.

2 CHANGE OF VOYAGE

Held covered in case of deviation or change of voyage or any breach of warranty as to towage or salvage services, provided notice be given to the Underwriters immediately after receipt of advices and any amended terms of cover and any additional premium required by them be agreed.

3 ASSIGNMENT

No assignment of or interest in this insurance or in any moneys which may be or become payable thereunder is to be binding on or recognised by the Underwriters unless a dated notice of such assignment or interest signed by the Assured, and by the assignor in the case of subsequent assignment, is endorsed on the Policy and the Policy with such endorsement is produced before payment of any claim or return of premium thereunder.

4 PERILS

4.1 This insurance covers loss of or damage to the subject-matter insured caused by

4.1.1   perils of the seas rivers lakes or other navigable waters

4.1.2   fire, explosion

4.1.3   violent theft by persons from outside the Vessel

4.1.4   jettison

4.1.5   piracy

4.1.6   breakdown of or accident to nuclear installations or reactors

4.1.7   contact with aircraft or similar objects, or objects falling therefrom, land conveyance, dock or harbour equipment or installation

4.1.8   earthquake volcanic eruption or lightning.

4.2 This insurance covers loss of or damage to the subject-matter insured caused by

4.2.1   accidents in loading discharging or shifting cargo or fuel

4.2.2   bursting of boilers breakage of shafts or any latent defect in the machinery or hull

4.2.3   negligence of Master Officers Crew or Pilots

4.2.4   negligence of repairers or charterers provided such repairers or charterers are not an Assured hereunder

4.2.5   barratry of Master Officers or Crew,

provided such loss or damage has not resulted from want of due diligence by the Assured, Owners or Managers.

4.3 Master Officers Crew or Pilots not to be considered Owners within the meaning of this Clause 4 should they hold shares in the Vessel.

5 POLLUTION HAZARD

This insurance covers loss of or damage to the Vessel caused by any governmental authority acting under the powers vested in it to prevent or mitigate a pollution hazard, or threat thereof, resulting directly from damage to the Vessel for which the Underwriters are liable under this insurance, provided such act of governmental authority has not resulted from want of due diligence by the Assured, the Owners, or Managers of the Vessel or any of them to prevent or mitigate such hazard or threat. Master, Officers, Crew or Pilots not to be considered Owners within the meaning of this Clause 5 should they hold shares in the Vessel.

6 3/4THS COLLISION LIABILITY

6.1 The Underwriters agree to indemnify the Assured for three-fourths of any sum or sums paid by the Assured to any other person or persons by reason of the Assured becoming legally liable by way of damages for

6.1.1   loss of or damage to any other vessel or property on any other vessel

6.1.2   delay to or loss of use of any such other vessel or property thereon

6.1.3   general average of, salvage of, or salvage under contract of, any such other vessel or property thereon, where such payment by the Assured is in consequence of the Vessel hereby insured coming into collision with any other vessel.

6.2   The indemnity provided by this Clause 6 shall be in addition to the indemnity provided by the other terms and conditions of this insurance and shall be subject to the following provisions:

6.2.1   Where the insured Vessel is in collision with another vessel and both vessels are to blame then, unless the liability of one or both vessels becomes limited by law, the indemnity under this Clause 6 shall be calculated on the principle of cross-liabilities as if the respective Owners had been compelled to pay to each other such proportion of each other's damages as may have been properly allowed in ascertaining the balance or sum payable by or to the Assured in consequence of the collision.

6.2.2   In no case shall the Underwriters' total liability under Clauses 6.1 and 6.2 exceed their proportionate part of three-fourths of the insured value of the Vessel hereby insured in respect of any one collision.

6.3   The Underwriters will also pay three-fourths of the legal costs incurred by the Assured or which the Assured may be compelled to pay in contesting liability or taking proceedings to limit liability, with the prior written consent of the Underwriters.

EXCLUSIONS

6.4   Provided always that this Clause 6 shall in no case extend to any sum which the Assured shall pay for or in respect of

6.4.1   removal or disposal of obstructions, wrecks, cargoes or any other thing whatsoever

6.4.2   any real or personal property or thing whatsoever except other vessels or property on other vessels

6.4.3   the cargo or other property on, or the engagements of, the insured Vessel

6.4.4   loss of life, personal injury or illness

6.4.5   pollution or contamination of any real or personal property or thing whatsoever (except other vessels with which the insured Vessel is in collision or property on such other vessels).

7   SISTERSHIP

Should the Vessel hereby insured come into collision with or receive salvage services from another vessel belonging wholly or in part to the same Owners or under the same management, the Assured shall have the same rights under this insurance as they would have were the other vessel entirely the property of Owners not interested in the Vessel hereby insured; but in such cases the liability for the collision or the amount payable for the services rendered shall be referred to a sole arbitrator to be agreed upon between the Underwriters and the Assured.

8   NOTICE OF CLAIM AND TENDERS

8.1   In the event of accident whereby loss or damage may result in a claim under this insurance, notice shall be given to the Underwriters prior to survey and also, if the Vessel is abroad, to the nearest Lloyd's Agent so that a surveyor may be appointed to represent the Underwriters should they so desire.

8.2   The Underwriters shall be entitled to decide the port to which the Vessel shall proceed for docking or repair (the actual additional expense of the voyage arising from compliance with the Underwriters' requirements being refunded to the Assured) and shall have a right of veto concerning a place of repair or a repairing firm.

8.3   The Underwriters may also take tenders or may require further tenders to be taken for the repair of the Vessel. Where such a tender has been taken and a tender is accepted with the approval of the Underwriters, an allowance shall be made at the rate of 30% per annum on the insured value for time lost between the despatch of the invitations to tender required by Underwriters and the acceptance of a tender to the extent that such time is lost solely as the result of tenders having been taken and provided that the tender is accepted without delay after receipt of the Underwriters' approval.

Due credit shall be given against the allowance as above for any amounts recovered in respect of fuel and stores and wages and maintenance of the Master Officers and Crew or any member thereof, including amounts allowed in general average, and for any amounts recovered from third parties in respect of damages for detention and/or loss of profit and/or running expenses, for the period covered by the tender allowance or any part thereof.

Where a part of the cost of the repair of damage other than a fixed deductible is not recoverable from the Underwriters the allowance shall be reduced by a similar proportion.

8.4   In the event of failure to comply with the conditions of this Clause 8 a deduction of 15% shall be made from the amount of the ascertained claim.

9 GENERAL AVERAGE AND SALVAGE

9.1 This insurance covers the Vessel's proportion of salvage, salvage charges and/or general average, reduced in respect of any under-insurance, but in case of general average sacrifice of the Vessel the Assured may recover in respect of the whole loss without first enforcing their right of contribution from other parties.

9.2 Adjustment to be according to the law and practice obtaining at the place where the adventure ends, as if the contract of affreightment contained no special terms upon the subject; but where the contract of affreightment so provides the adjustment shall be according to the York-Antwerp Rules.

9.3 When the Vessel sails in ballast, not under charter, the provisions of the York-Antwerp Rules, 1974 (excluding rules XX and XXI) shall be applicable, and the voyage for this purpose shall be deemed to continue from the port or place of departure until the arrival of the Vessel at the first port or place thereafter other than a port or place of refuge or a port or place of call for bunkering only. If at any such intermediate port or place there is an abandonment of the adventure originally contemplated the voyage shall thereupon be deemed to be terminated.

9.4 No claim under this Clause 9 shall in any case be allowed where the loss was not incurred to avoid or in connection with the avoidance of a peril insured against.

10 DEDUCTIBLE

10.1 No claim arising from a peril insured against shall be payable under this insurance unless the aggregate of all such claims arising out of each separate accident or occurrence (including claims under Clauses 6, 9 and 11) exceeds .... in which case this sum shall be deducted. Nevertheless the expense of sighting the bottom after stranding, if reasonably incurred specially for that purpose, shall be paid even if no damage be found. This Clause 10.1 shall not apply to a claim for total or constructive total loss of the Vessel, or in the event of such a claim, to any associated claim under Clause 11 arising from the same accident or occurrence.

10.2 Claims for damage by heavy weather occurring during a single sea passage between two successive ports shall be treated as being due to one accident. In the case of such heavy weather extending over a period not wholly covered by this insurance the deductible to be applied to the claim recoverable hereunder shall be the proportion of the above deductible that the number of days of such heavy weather falling within the period of this insurance bears to the number of days of heavy weather during the single sea passage. The expression "heavy weather" in this Clause 10.2 shall be deemed to include contact with floating ice.

10.3 Excluding any interest comprised therein, recoveries against any claim which is subject to the above deductible shall be credited to the Underwriters in full to the extent of the sum by which the aggregate of the claim unreduced by any recoveries exceeds the above deductible.

10.4 Interest comprised in recoveries shall be apportioned between the Assured and the Underwriters, taking into account the sums paid by the Underwriters and the dates when such payments were made, notwithstanding that by the addition of interest the Underwriters may receive a larger sum than they have paid.

11 DUTY OF ASSURED (SUE AND LABOUR)

11.1 In case of any loss or misfortune it is the duty of the Assured and their servants and agents to take such measures as may be reasonable for the purpose of averting or minimising a loss which would be recoverable under this insurance.

11.2 Subject to the provisions below and to Clause 10 the Underwriters will contribute to charges properly and reasonably incurred by the Assured their servants or agents for such measures. General average, salvage charges (except as provided for in clause 11.5) and collision defence or attack costs are not recoverable under this Clause 11.

11.3 Measures taken by the Assured or the Underwriters with the object of saving, protecting or recovering the subject-matter insured shall not be considered as a waiver or acceptance of abandonment or otherwise prejudice the rights of either party.

11.4 When expenses are incurred pursuant to this Clause 11 the liability under this insurance shall not exceed the proportion of such expenses that the amount insured hereunder bears to the value of the Vessel as stated herein, or to the sound value of the Vessel at the time of the occurrence giving rise to the expenditure if the sound value exceeds that value. Where the Underwriters have admitted a claim for total loss and property insured by this insurance is saved, the foregoing provisions shall not apply unless the expenses of suing and labouring exceed the value of such property saved and then shall apply only to the amount of the expenses which is in excess of such value.

11.5 When a claim for total loss of the Vessel is admitted under this insurance and expenses have been reasonably incurred in saving or attempting to save the Vessel and other property and there are no proceeds, or the expenses exceed the proceeds, then this insurance shall bear its pro rata share of such proportion of the expenses, or of the expenses in excess of the proceeds, as the case may be, as may reasonably be regarded as having been incurred in respect of the Vessel; but if the Vessel be insured for less than its sound value at the time of the occurrence giving rise to the expenditure, the amount recoverable under this clause shall be reduced in proportion to the under-insurance.

11.6 The sum recoverable under this Clause 11 shall be in addition to the loss otherwise recoverable under this insurance but shall in no circumstances exceed the amount insured under this insurance in respect of the Vessel.

12   NEW FOR OLD

Claims payable without deduction new for old.

13   BOTTOM TREATMENT

In no case shall a claim be allowed in respect of scraping gritblasting and/or other surface preparation or painting of the Vessel's bottom except that

13.1 gritblasting and/or other surface preparation of new bottom plates ashore and supplying and applying any "shop" primer thereto,

13.2 gritblasting and/or other surface preparation of:

the butts or area of plating immediately adjacent to any renewed or refitted plating damaged during the course of welding and/or repairs,

areas of plating damaged during the course of fairing, either in place or ashore,

13.3 supplying and applying the first coat of primer/anti-corrosive to those particular areas mentioned in 13.1 and 13.2 above,

shall be allowed as part of the reasonable cost of repairs in respect of bottom plating damaged by an insured peril.

14   WAGES AND MAINTENANCE

No claim shall be allowed, other than in general average, for wages and maintenance of the Master, Officers and Crew, or any member thereof, except when incurred solely for the necessary removal of the Vessel from one port to another for the repair of damage covered by the Underwriters, or for trial trips for such repairs, and then only for such wages and maintenance as are incurred whilst the Vessel is under way.

15   AGENCY COMMISSION

In no case shall any sum be allowed under this insurance either by way of remuneration of the Assured for time and trouble taken to obtain and supply information or documents or in respect of the commission or charges of any manager, agent, managing or agency company or the like, appointed by or on behalf of the Assured to perform such services.

16   UNREPAIRED DAMAGE

16.1 The measure of indemnity in respect of claims for unrepaired damage shall be the reasonable depreciation in the market value of the Vessel at the time this insurance terminates arising from such unrepaired damage, but not exceeding the reasonable cost of repairs.

16.2 In no case shall the Underwriters be liable for unrepaired damage in the event of a subsequent total loss (whether or not covered under this insurance) sustained during the period covered by this insurance or any extension thereof.

16.3 The Underwriters shall not be liable in respect of unrepaired damage for more than the insured value at the time this insurance terminates.

17   CONSTRUCTIVE TOTAL LOSS

17.1 In ascertaining whether the Vessel is a constructive total loss, the insured value shall be taken as the repaired value and nothing in respect of the damaged or break-up value of the Vessel or wreck shall be taken into account.

17.2 No claim for constructive total loss based upon the cost of recovery and/or repair of the Vessel shall be recoverable hereunder unless such cost would exceed the insured value. In making this determination, only the cost relating to a single accident or sequence of damages arising from the same accident shall be taken into account.

18   FREIGHT WAIVER

In the event of total or constructive total loss no claim to be made by the Underwriters for freight whether notice of abandonment has been given or not.

19 DISBURSEMENTS WARRANTY

19.1 Additional insurances as follows are permitted:

19.1.1 *Disbursements, Managers' Commissions, Profits or Excess or Increased Value of Hull and Machinery.* A sum not exceeding 25% of the value stated herein.

19.1.2 *Freight, Chartered Freight or Anticipated Freight, insured for time.* A sum not exceeding 25% of the value as stated herein less any sum insured, however described, under 19.1.1.

19.1.3 *Freight or Hire, under contracts for voyage.* A sum not exceeding the gross freight or hire for the current cargo passage and next succeeding cargo passage (such insurance to include, if required, a preliminary and an intermediate ballast passage) plus the charges of insurance. In the case of a voyage charter where payment is made on a time basis, the sum permitted for insurance shall be calculated on the estimated duration of the voyage, subject to the limitation of two cargo passages as laid down herein. Any sum insured under 19.1.2 to be taken into account and only the excess thereof may be insured, which excess shall be reduced as the freight or hire is advanced or earned by the gross amount so advanced or earned.

19.1.4 *Anticipated Freight if the Vessel sails in ballast and not under Charter.* A sum not exceeding the anticipated gross freight on next cargo passage, such sum to be reasonably estimated on the basis of the current rate of freight at time of insurance plus the charges of insurance. Any sum insured under 19.1.2 to be taken into account and only the excess thereof may be insured.

19.1.5 *Time Charter Hire or Charter Hire for Series of Voyages.* A sum not exceeding 50% of the gross hire which is to be earned under the charter in a period not exceeding 18 months. Any sum insured under 19.1.2 to be taken into account and only the excess thereof may be insured, which excess shall be reduced as the hire is advanced or earned under the charter by 50% of the gross amount so advanced or earned but the sum insured need not be reduced while the total of the sums insured under 19.1.2 and 19.1.5 does not exceed 50% of the gross hire still to be earned under the charter. An insurance under this Section may begin on the signing of the charter.

19.1.6 *Premiums.* A sum not exceeding the actual premiums of all interests insured for a period not exceeding 12 months (excluding premiums insured under the foregoing sections but including, if required, the premium or estimated calls on any Club or War etc. Risk insurance) reducing pro rata monthly.

19.1.7 *Returns of Premium.* A sum not exceeding the actual returns which are allowable under any insurance but which would not be recoverable thereunder in the event of a total loss of the Vessel whether by insured perils or otherwise.

19.1.8 *Insurance irrespective of amount against*: Any risks excluded by Clauses 20, 21, 22 and 23 below.

19.2 Warranted that no insurance on any interests enumerated in the foregoing 19.1.1 to 19.1.7 in excess of the amounts permitted therein and no other insurance which includes total loss of the Vessel P.P.I., F.I.A., or subject to any other like term, is or shall be effected to operate during the currency of this insurance by or for account of the Assured, Owners, Managers or Mortgagees. Provided always that a breach of this warranty shall not afford the Underwriters any defence to a claim by a Mortgagee who has accepted this insurance without knowledge of such breach.

The following clauses shall be paramount and shall override anything contained in this insurance inconsistent therewith.

20 WAR EXCLUSION

In no case shall this insurance cover loss damage liability or expense caused by

20.1 war civil war revolution rebellion insurrection, or civil strife arising therefrom, or any hostile act by or against a belligerent power

20.2 capture seizure arrest restraint or detainment (barratry and piracy excepted), and the consequences thereof or any attempt thereat

20.3 derelict mines torpedoes bombs or other derelict weapons of war.

21 STRIKES EXCLUSION

In no case shall this insurance cover loss damage liability or expense caused by

21.1 strikers, locked-out workmen, or persons taking part in labour disturbances, riots or civil commotions

21.2 any terrorist or any person acting from a political motive.

22 MALICIOUS ACTS EXCLUSION

In no case shall this insurance cover loss damage liability or expense arising from

22.1 the detonation of an explosive

22.2 any weapon of war

and caused by any person acting maliciously or from a political motive.

23   NUCLEAR EXCLUSION

In no case shall this insurance cover loss damage liability or expense arising from any weapon of war employing atomic or nuclear fission and/or fusion or other like reaction or radioactive force or matter.

1. Navigation

Clause 1.3 of the I.T.C. Hulls 1/10/83, which deals with the situation when the vessel sails on a scrapping voyage, does not appear in the voyage clauses. Such a general provision is not required in a voyage insurance because the nature of the voyage is one of the material facts which must be disclosed before the contract is concluded (Marine Insurance Act 1906, section 18). The underwriter in a voyage insurance would therefore have ample opportunity to impose any special conditions considered necessary at the time of the initial negotiations for the placing of the risk.

2. Change of voyage

This clause replaces the Continuation Clause in the I.T.C. Hulls 1/10/83 which would not be relevant to a voyage insurance. The voyage is dealt with in sections 42–49 inclusive of the Marine Insurance Act 1906 which provide as follows:

Implied condition as to commencement of risk

42. — (1) Where the subject-matter is insured by a voyage policy "at and from" or "from" a particular place, it is not necessary that the ship should be at that place when the contract is concluded, but there is an implied condition that the adventure shall be commenced within a reasonable time, and that if the adventure be not so commenced the insurer may avoid the contract.

(2) The implied condition may be negatived by showing that the delay was caused by circumstances known to the insurer before the contract was concluded, or by showing that he waived the condition.

Alteration of port of departure

43. Where the place of departure is specified by the policy, and the ship instead of sailing from that place sails from any other place, the risk does not attach.

Sailing for different destination

44. Where the destination is specified in the policy, and the ship, instead of sailing for that destination, sails for any other destination, the risk does not attach.

Change of voyage

45. — (1) Where, after the commencement of the risk, the destination of the ship is voluntarily changed from the destination contemplated by the policy, there is said to be a change of voyage.

(2) Unless the policy otherwise provides, where there is a change of voyage, the insurer is discharged from liability as from the time of change, that is to say, as from the time when the determination to change it is manifested; and it is immaterial that the ship may not in fact have left the course of voyage contemplated by the policy when the loss occurs.

Deviation

46. — (1) Where a ship, without lawful excuse, deviates from the voyage contemplated by the policy, the insurer is discharged from liability as from the time of deviation, and it is immaterial that the ship may have regained her route before any loss occurs.

(2) There is a deviaton from the voyage contemplated by the policy —

    (*a*) Where the course of the voyage is specifically designated by the policy, and that course is departed from; or

    (*b*) Where the course of the voyage is not specifically designated by the policy, but the usual and customary course is departed from.

(3) The intention to deviate is immaterial; there must be a deviation in fact to discharge the insurer from his liability under the contract.

Several ports of discharge

47. — (1) Where several ports of discharge are specified by the policy, the ship may proceed to all or any of them, but, in the absence of any usage or sufficient cause to the contrary, she must proceed to them, or such of them as she goes to, in the order designated by the policy. If she does not there is a deviation.

(2) Where the policy is to "ports of discharge," within a given area, which are not named, the ship must, in the absence of any usage or sufficient cause to the contrary, proceed to them, or such of them as she goes to, in their geographical order. If she does not there is a deviation.

Delay in voyage

48. In the case of a voyage policy, the adventure insured must be prosecuted throughout its course with reasonable dispatch, and, if without lawful excuse it is not so prosecuted, the insurer is discharged from liability as from the time when the delay became unreasonable.

Excuses for deviation or delay

49. — (1) Deviation or delay in prosecuting the voyage contemplated by the policy is excused —

    (*a*) Where authorised by any special term in the policy; or

    (*b*) Where caused by circumstances beyond the control of the master and his employer; or

    (*c*) Where reasonably necessary in order to comply with an express or implied warranty; or

    (*d*) Where reasonably necessary for the safety of the ship or subject-matter insured; or

(e) For the purpose of saving human life, or aiding a ship in distress where human life may be in danger; or

(f) Where reasonably necessary for the purpose of obtaining medical or surgical aid for any person on board the ship; or

(g) Where caused by the barratrous conduct of the master or crew, if barratry be one of the perils insured against.

(2) When the cause excusing the deviation or delay ceases to operate, the ship must resume her course, and prosecute her voyage, with reasonable dispatch.

The change of voyage clause ameliorates the position under English law very substantially and holds the assured covered in cases of deviation or change of voyage or any breach of warranty as to towage or salvage services. This is subject to the proviso that the assured gives notice to underwriters immediately he becomes aware of the facts and that any amended terms of cover and additional premium are agreed.

The Institute Voyage Clauses do not include Clauses 3 and 4 of the I.T.C. Hulls 1/10/83 which are not relevant to a voyage insurance.

The remainder of the clauses in the Institute Voyage Clauses are identical, apart from their renumbering, to the equivalent clauses in the I.T.C. Hulls 1/10/83.

Institute Voyage Clauses — Hulls — Total Loss, General Average and 3/4ths Collision Liability (Including Salvage, Salvage Charges and Sue and Labour) 1/10/83

The differences between these clauses and the Institute Voyage Clauses Hulls are identical to those between the respective sets of Time Clauses which are considered on pages 152 to 154.

The clauses are as follows:

This insurance is subject to English law and practice

1   NAVIGATION

    1.1   The Vessel is covered subject to the provisions of this insurance at all times and has leave to sail or navigate with or without pilots, to go on trial trips and to assist and tow vessels or craft in distress, but it is warranted that the Vessel shall not be towed, except as is customary or to the first safe port or place when in need of assistance, or undertake towage or salvage services under a contract previously arranged by the Assured and/or Owners and/or Managers and/or Charterers. This Clause 1.1 shall not exclude customary towage in connection with loading and discharging.

    1.2   In the event of the Vessel being employed in trading operations which entail cargo loading or discharging at sea from or into another vessel (not being a harbour or inshore craft) no claim shall be recoverable under this insurance for loss of or damage to the Vessel or liability to any other vessel arising from such loading or discharging operations, including whilst approaching, lying alongside and leaving, unless previous notice that the Vessel is to be employed in such operations has been given to the Underwriters and any amended terms of cover and any additional premium required by them have been agreed.

2   CHANGE OF VOYAGE

    Held covered in case of deviation or change of voyage or any breach of warranty as to towage or salvage services, provided notice be given to the Underwriters immediately after receipt of advices and any amended terms of cover and any additional premium required by them be agreed.

3 ASSIGNMENT

No assignment of or interest in this insurance or in any moneys which may be or become payable thereunder is to be binding on or recognised by the Underwriters unless a dated notice of such assignment or interest signed by the Assured, and by the assignor in the case of subsequent assignment, is endorsed on the Policy and the Policy with such endorsement is produced before payment of any claim or return of premium thereunder.

4 PERILS

4.1 This insurance covers total loss (actual or constructive) of the subject-matter insured caused by

4.1.1 perils of the seas rivers lakes or other navigable waters

4.1.2 fire, explosion

4.1.3 violent theft by persons from outside the Vessel

4.1.4 jettison

4.1.5 piracy

4.1.6 breakdown of or accident to nuclear installations or reactors

4.1.7 contact with aircraft or similar objects, or objects falling therefrom, land conveyance, dock or harbour equipment or installation

4.1.8 earthquake volcanic eruption or lightning.

4.2 This insurance covers total loss (actual or constructive) of the subject-matter insured caused by

4.2.1 accidents in loading discharging or shifting cargo or fuel

4.2.2 bursting of boilers breakage of shafts or any latent defect in the machinery or hull

4.2.3 negligence of Master Officers Crew or Pilots

4.2.4 negligence of repairers or charterers provided such repairers or charterers are not an Assured hereunder

4.2.5 barratry of Master Officers or Crew,

provided such loss or damage has not resulted from want of due diligence by the Assured, Owners or Managers.

4.3 Master Officers Crew or Pilots not to be considered Owners within the meaning of this Clause 4 should they hold shares in the Vessel.

5 POLLUTION HAZARD

This insurance covers total loss (actual or constructive) of the Vessel caused by any governmental authority acting under the powers vested in it to prevent or mitigate a pollution hazard, or threat thereof, resulting directly from damage to the Vessel caused by a peril covered by this insurance, provided such act of governmental authority has not resulted from want of due diligence by the Assured, the Owners, or Managers of the Vessel or any of them to prevent or mitigate such hazard or threat. Master, Officers, Crew or Pilots not to be considered Owners within the meaning of this Clause 5 should they hold shares in the Vessel.

6 3/4THS COLLISION LIABILITY

6.1 The Underwriters agree to indemnify the Assured for three-fourths of any sum or sums paid by the Assured to any other person or persons by reason of the Assured becoming legally liable by way of damages for

6.1.1 loss of or damage to any other vessel or property on any other vessel

6.1.2 delay to or loss of use of any such other vessel or property thereon

6.1.3 general average of, salvage of, or salvage under contract of, any such other vessel or property thereon,

where such payment by the Assured is in consequence of the Vessel hereby insured coming into collision with any other vessel.

6.2 The indemnity provided by this Clause 6 shall be in addition to the indemnity provided by the other terms and conditions of this insurance and shall be subject to the following provisions:

6.2.1 › Where the insured Vessel is in collision with another vessel and both vessels are to blame then, unless the liability of one or both vessels becomes limited by law, the indemnity under this Clause 6 shall be calculated on the principle of cross-liabilities as if the respective Owners had been compelled to pay to each other such proportion of each other's damages as may have been properly allowed in ascertaining the balance or sum payable by or to the Assured in consequence of the collision.

6.2.2 In no case shall the Underwriters' total liability under Clauses 6.1 and 6.2 exceed their proportionate part of three-fourths of the insured value of the Vessel hereby insured in respect of any one collision.

6.3 The Underwriters will also pay three-fourths of the legal costs incurred by the Assured or which the Assured may be compelled to pay in contesting liability or taking proceedings to limit liability, with the prior written consent of the Underwriters.

EXCLUSIONS

6.4 Provided always that this Clause 6 shall in no case extend to any sum which the Assured shall pay for or in respect of

6.4.1 removal or disposal of obstructions, wrecks, cargoes or any other thing whatsoever

6.4.2 any real or personal property or thing whatsoever except other vessels or property on other vessels

6.4.3 the cargo or other property on, or the engagements of, the insured Vessel

6.4.4 loss of life, personal injury or illness

6.4.5 pollution or contamination of any real or personal property or thing whatsoever (except other vessels with which the insured Vessel is in collision or property on such other vessels).

7 SISTERSHIP

Should the Vessel hereby insured come into collision with or receive salvage services from another vessel belonging wholly or in part to the same Owners or under the same management, the Assured shall have the same rights under this insurance as they would have were the other vessel entirely the property of Owners not interested in the Vessel hereby insured; but in such cases the liability for the collision or the amount payable for the services rendered shall be referred to a sole arbitrator to be agreed upon between the Underwriters and the Assured.

8 NOTICE OF CLAIM

In the event of accident whereby loss or damage may result in a claim under this insurance, notice shall be given to the Underwriters prior to survey and also, if the Vessel is abroad, to the nearest Lloyd's Agent so that a surveyor may be appointed to represent the Underwriters should they so desire.

9 GENERAL AVERAGE AND SALVAGE

9.1 This insurance covers the Vessel's proportion of salvage, salvage charges and/or general average, reduced in respect of any under-insurance.

9.2 **This insurance does not cover partial loss of and/or damage to the Vessel, except for any proportion of general average loss or damage which may be recoverable under Clause 9.1 above.**

9.3 Adjustment to be according to the law and practice obtaining at the place where the adventure ends, as if the contract of affreightment contained no special terms upon the subject; but where the contract of affreightment so provides the adjustment shall be according to the York-Antwerp Rules.

9.4 When the Vessel sails in ballast, not under charter, the provisions of the York-Antwerp Rules, 1974 (excluding rules XX and XXI) shall be applicable, and the voyage for this purpose shall be deemed to continue from the port or place of departure until the arrival of the Vessel at the first port or place thereafter other than a port or place of refuge or a port or place of call for bunkering only. If at any such intermediate port or place there is an abandonment of the adventure originally contemplated the voyage shall thereupon be deemed to be terminated.

9.5 No claim under this Clause 9 shall in any case be allowed where the loss was not incurred to avoid or in connection with the avoidance of a peril insured against.

10 DEDUCTIBLE

10.1 No claim arising from a peril insured against shall be payable under this insurance unless the aggregate of all such claims arising out of each separate accident or occurrence (including claims under Clauses 6 and 11) exceeds .... in which case this sum shall be deducted. This Clause 10.1 shall not apply to a claim for total or constructive total loss of the Vessel, or in the event of such a claim, to any associated claim under Clause 11 arising from the same accident or occurrence.

10.2 Excluding any interest comprised therein, recoveries against any claim which is subject to the above deductible shall be credited to the Underwriters in full to the extent of the sum by which the aggregate of the claim unreduced by any recoveries exceeds the above deductible.

10.3 Interest comprised in recoveries shall be apportioned between the Assured and the Underwriters, taking into account the sums paid by the Underwriters and the dates when such payments were made, notwithstanding that by the addition of interest the Underwriters may receive a larger sum than they have paid.

11 DUTY OF ASSURED (SUE AND LABOUR)

11.1 In case of any loss or misfortune it is the duty of the Assured and their servants and agents to take such measures as may be reasonable for the purpose of averting or minimising a loss which would be recoverable under this insurance.

11.2 Subject to the provisions below and to Clause 10 the Underwriters will contribute to charges properly and reasonably incurred by the Assured their servants or agents for such measures. General average, salvage charges (except as provided for in clause 11.5) and collision defence or attack costs are not recoverable under this Clause 11.

11.3 Measures taken by the Assured or the Underwriters with the object of saving, protecting or recovering the subject-matter insured shall not be considered as a waiver or acceptance of abandonment or otherwise prejudice the rights of either party.

11.4 When expenses are incurred pursuant to this Clause 11 the liability under this insurance shall not exceed the proportion of such expenses that the amount insured hereunder bears to the value of the Vessel as stated herein, or to the sound value of the Vessel at the time of the occurrence giving rise to the expenditure if the sound value exceeds that value. Where the Underwriters have admitted a claim for total loss and property insured by this insurance is saved, the foregoing provisions shall not apply unless the expenses of suing and labouring exceed the value of such property saved and then shall apply only to the amount of the expenses which is in excess of such value.

11.5 When a claim for total loss of the Vessel is admitted under this insurance and expenses have been reasonably incurred in saving or attempting to save the Vessel and other property and there are no proceeds, or the expenses exceed the proceeds, then this insurance shall bear its pro rata share of such proportion of the expenses, or of the expenses in excess of the proceeds, as the case may be, as may reasonably be regarded as having been incurred in respect of the Vessel; but if the Vessel be insured for less than its sound value at the time of the occurrence giving rise to the expenditure, the amount recoverable under this clause shall be reduced in proportion to the under-insurance.

11.6 The sum recoverable under this Clause 11 shall be in addition to the loss otherwise recoverable under this insurance but shall in no circumstances exceed the amount insured under this insurance in respect of the Vessel.

12 NEW FOR OLD

General average payable without deduction new for old.

13 AGENCY COMMISSION

In no case shall any sum be allowed under this insurance either by way of remuneration of the Assured for time and trouble taken to obtain and supply information or documents or in respect of the commission or charges of any manager, agent, managing or agency company or the like, appointed by or on behalf of the Assured to perform such services.

14 CONSTRUCTIVE TOTAL LOSS

14.1 In ascertaining whether the Vessel is a constructive total loss, the insured value shall be taken as the repaired value and nothing in respect of the damaged or break-up value of the Vessel or wreck shall be taken into account.

14.2 No claim for constructive total loss based upon the cost of recovery and/or repair of the Vessel shall be recoverable hereunder unless such cost would exceed the insured value. In making this determination, only the cost relating to a single accident or sequence of damages arising from the same accident shall be taken into account.

15 FREIGHT WAIVER

In the event of total or constructive total loss no claim to be made by the Underwriters for freight whether notice of abandonment has been given or not.

16 DISBURSEMENTS WARRANTY

16.1 Additional insurances as follows are permitted:

16.1.1 *Disbursements, Managers' Commissions, Profits or Excess or Increased Value of Hull and Machinery.* A sum not exceeding 25% of the value stated herein.

16.1.2 *Freight, Chartered Freight or Anticipated Freight, insured for time.* A sum not exceeding 25% of the value as stated herein less any sum insured, however described, under 16.1.1.

16.1.3 *Freight or Hire, under contracts for voyage.* A sum not exceeding the gross freight or hire for the current cargo passage and next succeeding cargo passage (such insurance to include, if required, a preliminary and an intermediate ballast passage) plus the charges of insurance. In the case of a voyage charter where payment is made on a time basis, the sum permitted for insurance shall be calculated on the estimated duration of the voyage, subject to the limitation of two cargo passages as laid down herein. Any sum insured under 16.1.2 to be taken into account and only the excess thereof may be insured, which excess shall be reduced as the freight or hire is advanced or earned by the gross amount so advanced or earned.

16.1.4   *Anticipated Freight if the Vessel sails in ballast and not under Charter.* A sum not exceeding the anticipated gross freight on next cargo passage, such sum to be reasonably estimated on the basis of the current rate of freight at time of insurance plus the charges of insurance. Any sum insured under 16.1.2 to be taken into account and only the excess thereof may be insured.

16.1.5   *Time Charter Hire or Charter Hire for Series of Voyages.* A sum not exceeding 50% of the gross hire which is to be earned under the charter in a period not exceeding 18 months. Any sum insured under 16.1.2 to be taken into aocount and only the excess thereof may be insured, which excess shall be reduced as the hire is advanced or earned under the charter by 50% of the gross amount so advanced or earned but the sum insured need not be reduced while the total of the sums insured under 16.1.2 and 16.1.5 does not exceed 50% of the gross hire still to be earned under the charter. An insurance under this Section may begin on the signing of the charter.

16.1.6   *Premiums.* A sum not exceeding the actual premiums of all interests insured for a period not exceeding 12 months (excluding premiums insured under the foregoing sections but including, if required, the premium or estimated calls on any Club or War etc. Risk insurance) reducing pro rata monthly.

16.1.7   *Returns of Premium.* A sum not exceeding the actual returns which are allowable under any insurance but which would not be recoverable thereunder in the event of a total loss of the Vessel whether by insured perils or otherwise.

16.1.8   *Insurance irrespective of amount against*:
Any risks excluded by Clauses 17, 18, 19 and 20 below.

16.2   Warranted that no insurance on any interests enumerated in the foregoing 16.1.1 to 16.1.7 in excess of the amounts permitted therein and no other insurance which includes total loss of the Vessel P.P.I., F.I.A., or subject to any other like term, is or shall be effected to operate during the currency of this insurance by or for account of the Assured, Owners, Managers or Mortgagees. Provided always that a breach of this warranty shall not afford the Underwriters any defence to a claim by a Mortgagee who has accepted this insurance without knowledge of such breach.

The following clauses shall be paramount and shall override anything contained in this insurance inconsistent therewith.

17   WAR EXCLUSION
In no case shall this insurance cover loss damage liability or expense caused by
17.1   war civil war revolution rebellion insurrection, or civil strife arising therefrom, or any hostile act by or against a belligerent power
17.2   capture seizure arrest restraint or detainment (barratry and piracy excepted), and the consequences thereof or any attempt thereat
17.3   derelict mines torpedoes bombs or other derelict weapons of war.

18   STRIKES EXCLUSION
In no case shall this insurance cover loss damage liability or expense caused by
18.1   strikers, locked-out workmen, or persons taking part in labour disturbances, riots or civil commotions
18.2   any terrorist or any person acting from a political motive.

19   MALICIOUS ACTS EXCLUSION
In no case shall this insurance cover loss damage liability or expense arising from
19.1   the detonation of an explosive
19.2   any weapon of war
and caused by any person acting maliciously or from a political motive.

20   NUCLEAR EXCLUSION
In no case shall this insurance cover loss damage liability or expense arising from any weapon of war employing atomic or nuclear fission and/or fusion or other like reaction or radioactive force or matter.

PART IV

Additional Insurances for Shipowners

1. HISTORICAL PERSPECTIVE

One of the oldest precepts in marine insurance, which one may think is perfectly logical, is that the subjects of the insurance will be covered for the value which they have at the commencement of the risk. In the early days, at Edward Lloyd's coffee house, the underwriter might require some proof that the value which he was being called upon to insure was realistic, and what better proof could the shipowner disclose than the bills for the amounts which he had paid for the ship, its fitting-out, and the moneys which he had disbursed in anticipation of the projected adventure.

Section 16(1) of the Marine Insurance Act 1906 restates this old rule:

"Subject to any express provision or valuation in the policy, the insurable value of the subject-matter insured must be ascertained as follows:—

(1) In insurance on ship, the insurable value is the value at the commencement of the risk, of the ship, including her outfit, provisions and stores for the officers and crew, money advanced for seamen's wages, and other disbursements (if any) incurred to make the ship fit for the voyage or adventure contemplated by the policy, plus the charges of insurance upon the whole:"

Upon this principle, that there is an insurable interest for the outlays made upon the commencement of the voyage, and upon which the ship-owner expects to make a profit, it will be seen that if, during the voyage, the shipowner has to disburse additional sums by way of refitting the ship, engaging new members of the crew and taking further provisions, these outlays will also become proper subjects for insurance.

Hence the need to take out additional insurances by way of "disbursements", or, if the ship should have an enhanced value by reason of her being engaged for a special trade, upon her "increased value".

Towards the middle of the nineteenth century, it became customary to agree with the underwriters the value of the ship for the purpose of insurance, and this solved a lot of problems, in particular the amount to be settled by the underwriters in the event of a total loss. Even so, the amount of the valuation might not be adequate to indemnify the shipowner who had made substantial outlays during the course of the voyage, and consequently the shipowner was glad to have the facility of effecting further insurance, when necessary, by way of disbursements or increased value.

As to the current practice, please read on.

2. EXCESS LIABILITIES

As we have already seen when considering the main clauses, claims for salvage, general average and sue and labour charges are subject to reduction in respect of any under-insurance and cover for collision liability is limited to three-fourths of the insured value. It is therefore common practice for shipowners to take out supplementary insurances on "excess liabilities" to enable them, in the event of the vessel being under-valued in the hull policy, to obtain further coverage for the excess of any specified contributions or liabilities over and above the amounts recoverable under the hull policy.

In *Holman & Sons* v. *Merchants' Marine Insurance Company*[1] a vessel was insured under a hull policy on a valuation of £39,000. In addition, the shipowners had taken out a further policy on increased value of hull and machinery for £1,855, the risks insured including "any liability which may attach to the shipowner in consequence of the hull and machinery being valued for contribution to general average and salvage charges at more than the insured valuation" (in the hull policy). Due to the fact that the vessel was under-insured under the hull policy the shipowner was unable to recover under that policy for the full amount of the ship's contribution to salvage and general average. It was contended on behalf of the assured that they were entitled to recover the short-fall in full, up to the whole sum insured under the increased value and excess liabilities policy. It was held that the assured could only recover such proportion of the sum insured against excess liabilities as the £1,855 bore to the total excess valuation for salvage and the total excess contributory value respectively.

Some simple figures will illustrate the correct method of assessing the claim under an excess liabilities policy.

Salved Value	£10,000	on which salvage of	£2,000	is paid
Insured value in hull policy	£10,000			
Deduct — Damage	2,000			
	£8,000	pays —	£1,600	
Excess value	£2,000	pays	£400	

1. (1919) 14 Asp.M.L.C. 433; 24 Com.Cas. 102; 35 T.L.R. 138.

Sum insured on Excess Liabilities £1,800 pays

$$\frac{£1,800}{2,000} \times £400 =$$
£360

The current clauses are:

A. Institute Time Clauses — Hulls — Excess Liabilities (1/10/83)

This insurance is subject to English law and practice

1   1.1   This insurance covers only:

     1.1.1   **General Average, Salvage and Salvage Charges** not recoverable in full under the insurances on hull and machinery by reason of the difference between the insured value of the Vessel as stated therein (or any reduced value arising from the deduction therefrom in process of adjustment of any claim which law or practice or the terms of the insurances covering hull and machinery may have required) and the value of the Vessel adopted for the purpose of contribution to general average, salvage or salvage charges, the liability under this insurance being for such proportion of the amount not recoverable as the amount insured hereunder bears to the said difference or to the total sum insured against excess liabilities if it exceed such difference.

     1.1.2   **Sue and Labour Charges** not recoverable in full under the insurances on hull and machinery by reason of the difference between the insured value of the Vessel as stated therein and the value of the Vessel adopted for the purpose of ascertaining the amount recoverable under the insurances on hull and machinery, the liability under this insurance being for such proportion of the amount not recoverable as the amount insured hereunder bears to the said difference or to the total sum insured against excess liabilities if it exceed such difference.

     1.1.3   **Collision Liability (three-fourths)** not recoverable in full under the Institute 3/4ths Collision Liability and Sistership Clauses in the insurances on hull and machinery by reason of such three-fourths liability exceeding three-fourths of the insured value of the Vessel as stated therein, in which case the amount recoverable under this insurance shall be such proportion of the difference so arising as the amount insured hereunder bears to the total sum insured against excess liabilities.

   1.2   The Underwriters' liability under 1.1.1, 1.1.2 and 1.1.3 separately, in respect of any one claim, shall not exceed the amount insured hereunder.

2   **RETURNS**

To return pro rata monthly net for each uncommenced month if this insurance be cancelled by agreement.

The following clauses shall be paramount and shall override anything contained in this insurance inconsistent therewith.

3   **WAR EXCLUSION**

In no case shall this insurance cover loss damage liability or expense caused by

   3.1   war civil war revolution rebellion insurrection, or civil strife arising therefrom, or any hostile act by or against a belligerent power

   3.2   capture seizure arrest restraint or detainment (barratry and piracy excepted), and the consequences thereof or any attempt thereat

   3.3   derelict mines torpedoes bombs or other derelict weapons of war.

4   **STRIKES EXCLUSION**

In no case shall this insurance cover loss damage liability or expense caused by

   4.1   strikers, locked-out workmen, or persons taking part in labour disturbances, riots or civil commotions

   4.2   any terrorist or any person acting from a political motive.

5   **MALICIOUS ACTS EXCLUSION**

In no case shall this insurance cover loss damage liability or expense arising from

5.1   the detonation of an explosive
5.2   any weapon of war
and caused by any person acting maliciously or from a political motive.

6   **NUCLEAR EXCLUSION**
In no case shall this insurance cover loss damage liability or expense arising from any weapon of war employing atomic or nuclear fission and/or fusion or other like reaction or radioactive force or matter.

The rather complicated wording in Clause 1.1 gives effect to the principle laid down in *Holman* v. *Merchants' Marine Insurance Company.* (see page 160). Parts of the wording require special mention:

*"(or any reduced value arising from the deduction therefrom in process
of adjustment of any claim which law or practice or the terms of
the insurances covering hull and machinery may have required)"*

If the vessel's hull policy is subject to English law and practice the basis of calculating the liability is laid down in the Association of Average Adjusters Rule of Practice B33 which provides as follows:

"**B33**   *UNDERWRITER'S LIABILITY*
If the ship or cargo be insured for more than its contributory value, the underwriter pays what is assessed on the contributory value. But where insured for less than the contributory value, the underwriter pays on the insured value; and when there has been a particular average for damage which forms a deduction from the contributory value of the ship that must be deducted from the insured value to find upon what the underwriter contributes.
This rule does not apply to foreign adjustments, when the basis of contribution is something other than the net value of the thing insured.
That in practice, in applying the above rule for the purpose of ascertaining the liability of underwriters for contribution to general average and salvage charges, deduction shall be made from the insured value of all losses and charges for which underwriters are liable and which have been deducted in arriving at the contributory value.
In adjusting the liability of underwriters on freight for general average contribution and salvage charges, effect shall be given to Section 73 of the Marine Insurance Act, 1906, by comparing the gross and not the net amount of freight at risk with the insured value in the case of a valued policy or the insurable value in the case of an unvalued policy."

The reason for deducting from the insured value all losses and charges for which underwriters are liable and which have been deducted in arriving at the contributory value is to ensure that both figures used in the comparison have been prepared on the same basis.

"... recoverable as the amount insured hereunder bears to the said difference <u>or to the total sum insured against excess liabilities if it exceed such difference</u>"

The words underlined are to cover the situation where there is more than one insurance against excess liabilities and the total sum insured under the policies exceeds the amount of the excess valuation. In such circumstances the sums insured are added together and each policy bears its proportionate share of any excess liability.

Clause 1.2 limits the total liability under each section of the policy, in respect of any one claim, to the amount insured.

The balance of the clause contains the Returns Clause and the paramount War, Strikes, Malicious Acts and Nuclear Exclusions, which are the customary clauses considered in detail previously.

B. Institute Time Clauses — Hulls — Disbursements and Increased Value (Total Loss only, including Excess Liabilities) (1/10/83)

This insurance is subject to English law and practice

1 **NAVIGATION**

  1.1 The subject-matter insured is covered subject to the provisions of this insurance at all times and the Vessel has leave to sail or navigate with or without pilots, to go on trial trips and to assist and tow vessels or craft in distress, but it is warranted that the Vessel shall not be towed, except as is customary or to the first safe port or place when in need of assistance, or undertake towage or salvage services under a contract previously arranged by the Assured and/or Owners and/or Managers and/or Charterers. This Clause 1.1 shall not exclude customary towage in connection with loading and discharging.

  1.2 In the event of the Vessel being employed in trading operations which entail cargo loading or discharging at sea from or into another vessel (not being a harbour or inshore craft) no claim shall be recoverable under this insurance in respect of loss of or damage to the subject-matter insured or for liability to any other vessel arising from such loading or discharging operations, including whilst approaching, lying alongside and leaving, unless previous notice that the Vessel is to be employed in such operations has been given to the Underwriters and any amended terms of cover and any additional premium required by them have been agreed.

  1.3 In the event of the Vessel sailing (with or without cargo) with an intention of being (a) broken up, or (b) sold for breaking up, no claim shall be recoverable under this insurance in respect of loss or damage to the Vessel occurring subsequent to such sailing unless previous notice has been given to the Underwriters and any amendments to the terms of cover, amount insured and premium required by them have been agreed.

2 **CONTINUATION**

  Should the Vessel at the expiration of this insurance be at sea or in distress or at a port of refuge or of call, the subject-matter insured shall, provided previous notice be given to the Underwriters, be held covered at a pro rata monthly premium to her port of destination.

3 **BREACH OF WARRANTY**

  Held covered in case of any breach of warranty as to cargo, locality, trade, towage, salvage services or date of sailing, provided notice be given to the Underwriters immediately after receipt of advices and any amended terms of cover and any additional premium required by them be agreed.

4 **TERMINATION**

  This Clause 4 shall prevail notwithstanding any provision whether written typed or printed in this insurance inconsistent therewith.

  Unless the Underwriters agree to the contrary in writing, this insurance shall terminate automatically at the time of

4.1 change of the Classificiation Society of the Vessel, or change, suspension, discontinuance, withdrawal or expiry of her Class therein, provided that if the Vessel is at sea such automatic termination shall be deferred until arrival at her next port. However where such change, suspension, discontinuance or withdrawal of her Class has resulted from loss or damage which would be covered by an insurance of the Vessel subject to current Institute Time Clauses Hulls or Institute War and Strikes Clauses Hulls-Time such automatic termination shall only operate should the Vessel sail from her next port without the prior approval of the Classification Society,

4.2 any change, voluntary or otherwise, in the ownership or flag, transfer to new management, or charter on a bareboat basis, or requisition for title or use of the Vessel, provided that, if the Vessel has cargo on board and has already sailed from her loading port or is at sea in ballast, such automatic termination shall if required be deferred, whilst the Vessel continues her planned voyage, until arrival at final port of discharge if with cargo or at port of destination if in ballast. However, in the event of requisition for title or use without the prior execution of a written agreement by the Assured, such automatic termination shall occur fifteen days after such requisition whether the Vessel is at sea or in port.

A pro rata daily net return of premium shall be made.

5   ASSIGNMENT

No assignment of or interest in this insurance or in any moneys which may be or become payable thereunder is to be binding on or recognised by the Underwriters unless a dated notice of such assignment or interest signed by the Assured, and by the assignor in the case of subsequent assignment, is endorsed on the Policy and the Policy with such endorsement is produced before payment of any claim or return of premium thereunder.

6   PERILS

6.1   This insurance covers total loss (actual or constructive) of the subject-matter insured caused by

6.1.1   perils of the seas rivers lakes or other navigable waters

6.1.2   fire, explosion

6.1.3   violent theft by persons from outside the Vessel

6.1.4   jettison

6.1.5   piracy

6.1.6   breakdown of or accident to nuclear installations or reactors

6.1.7   contact with aircraft or similar objects, or objects falling therefrom, land conveyance, dock or harbour equipment or installation

6.1.8   earthquake volcanic eruption or lightning.

6.2   This insurance covers total loss (actual or constructive) of the subject-matter insured caused by

6.2.1   accidents in loading discharging or shifting cargo or fuel

6.2.2   bursting of boilers breakage of shafts or any latent defect in the machinery or hull

6.2.3   negligence of Master Officers Crew or Pilots

6.2.4   negligence of repairers or charterers provided such repairers or charterers are not an Assured hereunder

6.2.5   barratry of Master Officers or Crew,

provided such loss or damage has not resulted from want of due diligence by the Assured, Owners or Managers.

6.3   Master Officers Crew or Pilots not to be considered Owners within the meaning of this Clause 6 should they hold shares in the Vessel.

6.4   This insurance covers:

6.4.1   **General Average, Salvage and Salvage Charges** not recoverable in full under the insurances on hull and machinery by reason of the difference between the insured value of the Vessel as stated therein (or any reduced value arising from the deduction therefrom in process of adjustment of any claim which law or practice or the terms of the insurances covering hull and machinery may have required) and the value of the Vessel adopted for the purpose of contribution to general average, salvage or salvage charges, the liability under this insurance being for such proportion of the amount not recoverable as the amount insured hereunder bears to the said difference or to the total sum insured against excess liabilities if it exceed such difference.

6.4.2   **Sue and Labour Charges** not recoverable in full under the insurances on hull and machinery by reason of the difference between the insured value of the Vessel as stated therein and the value of the Vessel adopted for the purpose of ascertaining the amount recoverable under the insurances on hull and machinery, the liability under this insurance being for such proportion of the amount not recoverable as the amount insured hereunder bears to the said difference or to the total sum insured against excess liabilities if it exceed such difference.

6.4.3   **Collision Liability (three-fourths)** not recoverable in full under the Institute 3/4ths Collision Liability and Sistership Clauses in the insurances on hull and machinery by reason of such three-fourths liability exceeding three-fourths of the insured value of the Vessel as stated therein, in which case the amount recoverable under this insurance shall be such proportion of the difference so arising as the amount insured hereunder bears to the total sum insured against excess liabilities.

6.5   The Underwriters' liability under 6.4.1, 6.4.2 and 6.4.3 separately, in respect of any one claim, shall not exceed the amount insured hereunder.

7   POLLUTION HAZARD

This insurance covers total loss (actual or constructive) of the Vessel caused by any governmental authority acting under the powers vested in it to prevent or mitigate a pollution hazard, or threat thereof, resulting directly from damage to the Vessel caused by a peril covered by this insurance, provided such act of governmental authority has not resulted from want of due diligence by the Assured, the Owners, or Managers of the Vessel or any of them to prevent or mitigate such hazard or threat. Master, Officers, Crew or Pilots not to be considered Owners within the meaning of this Clause 7 should they hold shares in the Vessel.

8   NOTICE OF CLAIM

In the event of accident whereby loss or damage may result in a claim under this insurance, notice shall be given to the Underwriters prior to survey and also, if the Vessel is abroad, to the nearest Lloyd's Agent so that a surveyor may be appointed to represent the Underwriters should they so desire.

9   CONSTRUCTIVE TOTAL LOSS

9.1   In ascertaining whether the Vessel is a constructive total loss, the insured value in the insurances on hull and machinery shall be taken as the repaired value and nothing in respect of the damaged or break-up value of the Vessel or wreck shall be taken into account.

9.2   No claim for constructive total loss based upon the cost of recovery and/or repair of the Vessel shall be recoverable hereunder unless such cost would exceed the insured value in the insurances on hull and machinery. In making this determination, only the cost relating to a single accident or sequence of damages arising from the same accident shall be taken into account.

9.3   Provided that the Constructive Total Loss Clause in the current Institute Time Clauses Hulls or a clause having a similar effect is contained in the insurances on hull and machinery, the settlement of a claim for constructive total loss thereunder shall be accepted as proof of the constructive total loss of the Vessel.

9.4   Should the Vessel be a constructive total loss but the claim on the insurances on hull and machinery be settled as a claim for partial loss, no payment shall be due under this Clause 9.

10   COMPROMISED TOTAL LOSS

In the event of a claim for total loss or constructive total loss being settled on the insurances on hull and machinery as a compromised total loss the amount payable hereunder shall be the same percentage of the amount insured as is paid on the said insurances.

11   RETURNS FOR LAY-UP AND CANCELLATION

11.1   To return as follows:

11.1.1   Pro rata monthly net for each uncommenced month if this insurance be cancelled by agreement.

11.1.2   For each period of 30 consecutive days the Vessel may be laid up in a port or in a lay-up area provided such port or lay-up area is approved by the Underwriters (with special liberties as hereinafter allowed)

   (a).............................per cent net not under repair

   (b).............................per cent net under repair.

If the Vessel is under repair during part only of a period for which a return is claimable, the return shall be calculated pro rata to the number of days under (a) and (b) respectively.

11.2 PROVIDED ALWAYS THAT

11.2.1   a total loss of the Vessel, whether by insured perils or otherwise, has not occurred during the period covered by this insurance or any extension thereof

11.2.2   in no case shall a return be allowed when the Vessel is lying in exposed or unprotected waters, or in a port or lay-up area not approved by the Underwriters but, provided the Underwriters agree that such non-approved lay-up area is deemed to be within the vicinity of the approved port or lay-up area, days during which the Vessel is laid up in such non-approved lay-up area may be added to days in the approved port or lay-up area to calculate a period of 30 consecutive days and a return shall be allowed for the proportion of such period during which the Vessel is actually laid up in the approved port or lay-up area

11.2.3   loading or discharging operations or the presence of cargo on board shall not debar returns but no return shall be allowed for any period during which the Vessel is being used for the storage of cargo or for lightering purposes

11.2.4   in the event of any amendment of the annual rate, the above rates of return shall be adjusted accordingly

11.2.5   in the event of any return recoverable under this Clause 11 being based on 30 consecutive days which fall on successive insurances effected for the same Assured, this insurance shall only be liable for an amount calculated at pro rata of the period rates 11.1.2(a) and/or (b) above for the number of days which come within the period of this insurance and to which a return is actually applicable. Such overlapping period shall run, at the option of the Assured, either from the first day on which the Vessel is laid up or the first day of a period of 30 consecutive days as provided under 11.1.2(a) or (b), or 11.2.2 above.

The following clauses shall be paramount and shall override anything contained in this insurance inconsistent therewith.

12   WAR EXCLUSION
In no case shall this insurance cover loss damage liability or expense caused by
12.1 war civil war revolution rebellion insurrection, or civil strife arising therefrom, or any hostile act by or against a belligerent power
12.2 capture seizure arrest restraint or detainment (barratry and piracy excepted), and the consequences thereof or any attempt thereat
12.3 derelict mines torpedoes bombs or other derelict weapons of war.

13   STRIKES EXCLUSION
In no case shall this insurance cover loss damage liability or expense caused by
13.1 strikers, locked-out workmen, or persons taking part in labour disturbances, riots or civil commotions
13.2 any terrorist or any person acting from a political motive.

14   MALICIOUS ACTS EXCLUSION
In no case shall this insurance cover loss damage liability or expense arising from
14.1 the detonation of an explosive
14.2 any weapon of war
and caused by any person acting maliciously or from a political motive.

15   NUCLEAR EXCLUSION
In no case shall this insurance cover loss damage liability or expense arising from any weapon of war employing atomic or nuclear fission and/or fusion or other like reaction or radioactive force or matter.

These clauses are designed to give cover for:

1.   Disbursements and increased value, the sum insured being payable only in the event of the vessel being settled under the hull policy as for a total or constructive total loss.
2.   Excess liabilities.

We have already considered the I.T.C. Hulls — Total Loss only (including salvage, salvage charges, and sue and labour) and the Institute Time Clauses — Hulls Excess Liabilities 1/10/83 (see pages 141 and 161). The above clauses are an amalgam of these two sets of conditions, without the cover against salvage, salvage charges and sue and labour, and it is only necessary therefore to consider any special wording which appears only in these clauses.

9. *Constructive total loss*

Clause 9.3 contains the proviso that if the Constructive Total Loss Clause in the current I.T.C. Hulls 1/10/83 or a clause of similar effect, is contained in the hull and machinery policy, the settlement of a claim for constructive total loss under the hull policy will be accepted as proof of the constructive total loss of the vessel. This clause is necessary because some policies contain entirely different provisos, or are subject to different laws or practices as to the criteria for assessing a constructive total loss. For example in several countries it is only necessary for the cost of repairs to exceed 75 per cent of the insured value in the hull policy in order to prove a constructive total loss. In such circumstances, Clause 9.3 cannot be invoked and the test to establish whether a claim under the disbursements and increased value policy has been triggered is the one laid down in Clause 9.2.

Clause 9.4 makes it clear that if the vessel is a constructive total loss, but the claim on the hull policy is settled as a claim for partial loss, no payment will be made under Clause 9. Upon initial examination its appears to be difficult to envisage circumstances where an assured would elect to claim for a partial loss when the vessel is a constructive total loss. This can happen however where for example the vessel is of an unusual type required for a special trade, which could not be replaced easily or at least only at a figure far in excess of the insured value. In such circumstances the assured may decide to repair and claim for a 100 per cent partial loss under the hull policy. The assured would then be unable to recover a total loss under the disbursements and increased value policy.

10. *Compromised total loss*

It is not uncommon for a claim for total or constructive total loss to be settled under the hull policy as a compromised total loss. If this is the case, the amount payable under the disbursements and increased value policy is reduced proportionately.

3. EXTENDED CONDITIONS

Institute Additional Perils Clauses — Hulls (1/10/83)
(For use only with the Institute Time Clauses — Hulls, 1/10/83)

Whilst it was never an Institute Clause, the forefather of the above clause, the Liner Negligence and Additional Perils Clause, was in common use from its introduction in the 1930s. Although it was included in many policies, particularly those of the major liner operators, and was subject to many differences of interpretation during its history, its wording was never tested in the courts.

With the major revision of the Institute Hull Clauses culminating in the October 1983 editions, the opportunity was taken to issue an Institute Additional Perils Clause.

The Institute Clause now reads as follows:

1   In consideration of an additional premium this insurance is extended to cover
   1.1   the cost of repairing or replacing
   1.1.1   any boiler which bursts or shaft which breaks
   1.1.2   any defective part which has caused loss or damage to the Vessel covered by Clause 6.2.2 of
            the Institute Time Clauses — Hulls 1/10/83,
      1.2   loss of or damage to the Vessel caused by any accident or by negligence, incompetence or error of
            judgement of any person whatsoever.
2   Except as provided in 1.1.1 and 1.1.2, nothing in these Additional Perils Clauses shall allow any claim
   for the cost of repairing or replacing any part found to be defective as a result of a fault or error in
   design or construction and which has not caused loss of or damage to the Vessel.
3   The cover provided in Clause 1 is subject to all other terms, conditions and exclusions contained in this
   insurance and subject to the proviso that the loss or damage has not resulted from want of due diligence
   by the Assured, Owners or Managers. Master Officers Crew or Pilots not to be considered Owners within
   the meaning of this Clause should they hold shares in the Vessel.

"In consideration of an additional premium this insurance is extended to cover"

These words make it clear that the clause is designed to provide an extension of cover, the consideration for which is the payment of an additional premium.

"1.1   the cost of repairing or replacing
1.1.1   any boiler which bursts or shaft which breaks
1.1.2   any defective part which has caused loss or damage to the Vessel
*   covered by Clause 6.2.2 of the Institute Time Clauses —*
*   Hulls 1/10/83"*

Clause 6 of the I.T.C. Hulls, 1/10/83 provides cover against consequential loss or damage caused by, *inter alia*, bursting of boilers breakage of shafts or any latent defect in the machinery or hull, but does not cover the cost of repairing or replacing the boiler, shaft or latently defective part (unless it was damaged as the result of the operation of one of the other insured perils). The Institute Additional Perils Clauses extend the insurance to cover the cost of repairing or replacing any boiler which has burst, any shaft which has broken or any latently defective part which has caused loss or damage covered by Clause 6.2.2 of the I.T.C. Hulls 1/10/83. The practice is to treat these words as giving a coverage simpliciter — in other words to make the cost of repairing or replacing the burst boiler, broken shaft or latently defective part recoverable irrespective of cause (subject to Clause 3). The word "breakage" should be given a natural commonsense meaning and a complete severance is not necessary to constitute a breakage. What constitutes bursting of a boiler has not been judicially considered in England but guidance can be gained from the American courts which have held that the discovery of fractures in a boiler is insufficient and where because of its deteriorated condition the wall of an exhaust line gave way through the normal action of the engine exhaust this did not constitute "bursting" (*Presti* v. *Fireman's Fund Insurance Co.*[2]).

> "*1.2   loss of or damage to the Vessel caused by any accident or by negligence, incompetence or error of judgement of any person whatsoever.*
> 2   *Except as provided in 1.1.1 and 1.1.2, nothing in these Additional Perils Clauses shall allow any claim for the cost of repairing or replacing any part found to be defective as a result of a fault or error in design or construction and which has not caused loss of or damage to the Vessel.*"

The cover granted by this clause is extremely wide. The classic definition of the word "accident" is that given by Lord Lindley in *Fenton* v. *Thorley*[3]: "any unintended and unexpected occurrence which produces hurt or loss". In the light of this definition the cover granted by the Institute Additional Perils Clauses is analogous to the cover provided by an insurance against "all risks" in that fortuitous events are covered but ordinary wear and tear and inherent vice are not. By section 55 of the Marine Insurance Act 1906 "unless the policy otherwise provides, the insurer is not liable for ordinary wear and tear ...". It should be noted that this exclusion relates to wear and tear itself and does not deal with consequential loss and damage. Let us take an example of a pipe on a tanker which has been weakened by internal corrosion at an inaccessible elbow, which in spite of the exercise of due diligence by all concerned, is not discovered. It is submitted that the sudden failure of that pipe in service, resulting in the ingress of oil into the pump room would consititute an "accident" and would give rise to a claim under the Institute Additional Perils Clauses for the consequential damage, the cost of replacing the worn pipe being excluded. The cover against "any accident" effectively includes all occurrences which are fortuitous from the point of view of the assured, other than those resulting from some deliberate infliction of damage.

The cover against loss of or damage to the vessel caused "by negligence, incompetence or error of judgement of any person whatsoever" is qualified by Clause 2, the intention being to exclude claims for parts found to be defective but which have not resulted in any loss or damage. The intention of the clause is that parts which are or have become defective as a result of a fault or error in design or construction will only be paid for if there is a failure or breakdown in service resulting in consequential damage, and the part will not be paid for if it has been condemned in anticipation of failure

2. (1972) A.M.C. 1220.
3. (1903) House of Lords.

or breakdown or simply found to be defective without any other damage having been caused. For example, an engine manufacturer may issue a circular advising operators of their engines that experience has shown that a particular part is prone to fatigue failure due to a combination of design factors and incorrect assembly during manufacture and should be checked as a matter of priority. The cost of replacing or repairing any part found to be defective as a result of such an examination would not be covered. If, however, the part had failed in service before the manufacturer's warning had been received, the cost of its replacement would be covered. Similarly, if after the failure of a part in service, subsequent investigation proves it to have been badly designed, the cost of any improvement in the design and manufacture of the replacement part would not be recoverable under the policy. The expression "faulty design" was considered judicially in *Queensland Government Railways* v. *Manufacturers' Mutual Insurance Co.*[4] by the Supreme Court of Queensland, Australia, and on appeal to the Australian High Court.

The claim was for the cost of rebuilding piers for a bridge which was in the course of construction and had been overturned by flood waters after exceptionally heavy rain. The insurance was in a form of "Contractors All Risks policy" which provided, *inter alia*:

"... this insurance shall not apply to or include:-
(vii) cost of making good faulty workmanship or construction ...
...
(xi) loss or damage arising from faulty design and liabilities resulting therefrom."

Insurers denied liability, contending that loss was due to faulty design of the piers. It was found by the arbitrator that in the state of engineering knowledge at that time, the design of the new piers was satisfactory, but investigation following the accident showed that these piers were subject to greater transverse forces in floods than had been realised.

The judgment of the court of first instance was given by Hoare J. who found that insurers were liable. The judge said:

"It appears to me that in their context the words 'faulty design' do imply some element of blameworthiness or negligence, which has been negatived by the arbitrator's findings. Further, having regard to the findings made by the arbitrator, it seems to me that in the state of engineering knowledge at the time, if, when the contract of insurance was made (i.e., before the tests were made to determine the precise cause of the disaster), someone had inquired of a competent engineer, 'Is the design of the piers faulty?', the answer would clearly have been, 'No'. The fact that subsequently acquired knowledge reveals that the design was not strong enough to withstand transverse forces which it is now known might be expected from a severe flood, cannot, in my opinion, on the

4. [1969] 1 Lloyd's Rep. 214.

true construction of exclusion (xi), convert a design which would at the time have been accepted by responsible and competent engineers into a 'faulty design'."

On appeal it was held that the loss was due to faulty design, it being incorrect to limit the expression "faulty design" to cases involving personal error or non-compliance with standards which would be expected of designing engineers. The majority judgment delivered by Barwick C.J. included this passage:

"We think it was an error [on the judge in the court below] to confine 'faulty design' to the personal failure or non-compliance with standards which would be expected of designing engineers and on the part of the designing engineers responsible for piers. To design something that will not work simply because at the time of its designing insufficient is known about the problems involved and their solution to achieve a successful outcome is a common enough instance of faulty design. The distinction which is relevant is that between 'faulty', i.e. defective, design and design free from defect. ... The exclusion is not against loss from 'negligent designing'; it is against loss from 'faulty design' and the latter is more comprehensive than the former."

A separate judgment was given by Windeyer J. who considered that the derivation of the word "fault" explains its two different meanings:

"When used in relation to a person, a fault is a falling short in conduct or behaviour, some act or omission which, whether wilful or negligent, predicates blame."

"[When] descriptive of an inanimate thing, the words 'fault' and 'faulty' have a different sense ... they designate an objective quality of a thing. It is not up to a required standard. It is 'faulty' because it has defects, flaws, or deficiencies. ... Dr. Johnson defined 'faulty' in this sense as meaning: 'defective, bad in any respect, not fit for the use intended.' The word can be applied not only to concrete things, but also to plans or designs to be used to produce intended results."

Clause 3 incorporates all other terms, conditions and exclusions in the insurance and contains the customary due diligence provision, which has already been considered (see page 99).

4. ADDITIONAL DEDUCTIBLES FOR MACHINERY DAMAGE

Institute Machinery Damage Additional Deductible Clause
(For use only with the Institute Time Clauses — Hulls 1/10/83)

For many years underwriters had become increasingly concerned at their worsening experience of claims which in their opinion was attributable in the main to the poor quality of personnel employed on the vessels. In 1969, with the major revision of the I.T.C. Hulls, we saw the introduction of the

Negligence Co-insurance Clause (Clause 11) under which the assured became co-assurers for a proportion (10 per cent) of claims for loss of or damage to any boiler shaft machinery or associated equipment which was attributable in part or in whole to negligence of master, officers or crew. The philosophy behind the introduction of this clause was the hope that if the shipowners were made co-insurers in respect of certain crew negligence claims they would be encouraged to improve the quality of the crew, particularly engine room personnel, which they employed.

In practice the interpretation of this clause gave rise to many problems of interpretation and in the next major revision of the clauses in 1983 it was omitted from the main body of clauses, with few people lamenting its passing. Concurrently with the issue of the new I.T.C. Hulls in 1983 the Institute Machinery Damage Additional Deductible Clause was also introduced, the intention being that this should only be incorporated into policies covering vessels or fleets where factors such as the age of the tonnage and/or previous claims experience warranted its inclusion. The present clause reads as follows:

Notwithstanding any provision to the contrary in this insurance a claim for loss of or damage to any machinery, shaft, electrical equipment or wiring, boiler condenser heating coil or associated pipework, arising from any of the perils enumerated in Clauses 6.2.2 to 6.2.5 inclusive of the Institute Time Clauses — Hulls 1/10/83 or from fire or explosion when either has originated in a machinery space, shall be subject to a deductible of .... Any balance remaining, after application of this deductible, with any other claim arising from the same accident or occurrence, shall then be subject to the deductible in Clause 12.1 of the Institute Time Clauses — Hulls 1/10/83.
The provisions of Clauses 12.3 and 12.4 of the Institute Time Clauses — Hulls 1/10/83 shall apply to recoveries and interest comprised in recoveries against any claim which is subject to this Clause.
This Clause shall not apply to a claim for total or constructive total loss of the Vessel.

Like Clause 12 of the I.T.C. Hulls 1/10/83, the clause does not specify a figure for the additional deductible and this has to be agreed at the time of effecting the insurance and then entered into the clause.

Before the additional deductible comes into operation all of the following requirements must be met:

(1) The claim must be for "loss of or damage" to any of the enumerated parts of the vessel (so that it would not apply to any claim for say salvage of the vessel, necessitated by the failure of one of the designated parts).

(2) "to any machinery, shaft, electrical equipment or wiring, boiler condenser heating coil or associated pipework". It should be noted that the machinery is not limited to engine room machinery and in appropriate circumstances the additional deductible could apply to a claim for loss of or damage to deck machinery for example winches, windlass etc.

(3) "arising from any of the perils enumerated in Clauses 6.2.2 to 6.2.5 inclusive of the Institute Time Clauses — Hulls (1/10/83) or from fire or explosion when either has originated in a machinery space". Any

claim, therefore, for loss of or damage to the specified items arising from any of the perils in Clause 6.1 of the I.T.C Hulls would not attract the additional deductible, subject to the exception of a fire or explosion originating in a machinery space.

What is a machinery space within the context of this clause? There is no agreed definition but it would almost certainly include the engine room, generator flat, steering flat and pump room. It could be argued that it also includes spaces used for the storage of machinery, e.g. forecastle and deckhouse but in the opinion of the authors this would be too wide an interpretation.

After the application of the additional deductible provided for in the clause, the balance of the claim is then subject to the deductible in the hull policies.

The provisions of Clauses 12.3 and 12.4 of the I.T.C. Hulls, 1/10/83, are imported into the clause to ensure that the treatment of any recovery and interest against any claim which has been subject to the additional deductible will be on the same basis as the main policy.

Like Clause 12 of the I.T.C. Hulls, 1/10/83, the additional deductible does not apply to a claim for total or constructive total loss of the vessel.

Institute Machinery Damage Additional Deductible Clause
(For use only with the Institute Voyage Clauses — Hulls 1/10/83)

Notwithstanding any provision to the contrary in this insurance a claim for loss of or damage to any machinery, shaft, electrical equipment or wiring, boiler condenser heating coil or associated pipework, arising from any of the perils enumerated in Clauses 4.2.2 to 4.2.5 inclusive of the Institute Voyage Clauses — Hulls 1/10/83 or from fire or explosion when either has originated in a machinery space, shall be subject to a deductible of .... Any balance remaining, after application of this deductible, with any other claim arising from the same accident or occurrence, shall then be subject to the deductible in Clause 10.1 of the Institute Voyage Clauses — Hulls 1/10/83.

The provisions of Clauses 10.3 and 10.4 of the Institute Voyage Clauses — Hulls 1/10/83 shall apply to recoveries and interest comprised in recoveries against any claim which is subject to this Clause.

This Clause shall not apply to a claim for total or constructive total loss of the Vessel.

This clause is for all practical purposes identical to the clause for use with the Institute Time Clauses — Hulls, 1/10/83.

Additional Deductible Adaptation Clause (For use
whenever the Institute Machinery Damage Additional Deductible
Clause and the Institute Additional Perils Clauses 1/10/83
(For use only with the Institute Time Clauses, 1/10/83) are
included in the same insurance)

The Institute Machinery Damage Additional Deductible Clause 1/10/83 shall also apply to any claim or part thereof in respect of any machinery, shaft, electrical equipment or wiring, boiler condenser heating coil or associated pipework, where such claim or part thereof is recoverable hereunder solely by reason of the inclusion of the Institute Additional Perils Clauses — Hulls 1/10/83 in this insurance.

This clause simply applies the provisions of the Institute Machinery Damage Additional Deductible Clause to any claim recoverable under the policies solely by reason of the inclusion of the Institute Additional Perils Clauses — Hulls, 1/10/83.

5. FREIGHT INSURANCE

Freight insurance is a complex and difficult branch of the law. When considering ships and cargoes one is dealing with tangible property. Freight, on the other hand, is far more difficult to denote and has been described as "the benefit derived by the ship-owner from the employment of his ship" (*Flint* v. *Flemyng*[5]).

Rule 16 of the Rules of Construction of the Policy (Schedule 1, Marine Insurance Act 1906) defines freight as follows:

> "The term "freight" includes a profit derivable by a ship-owner from the employment of his ship to carry his own goods or movables, as well as freight payable by a third party, but does not include passage money".

The charterer or cargo owner may well have an insurable interest in advance freight, in so far as it is not repayable in case of loss, and this is recognised in section 12 of the Marine Insurance Act 1906. Such advances of freight are not intended to be the subject of insurances on the Institute Freight Clauses and are more properly covered as part of the valuation of the cargo.

Institute Time Clauses — Freight 1/10/83

This insurance is subject to English law and practice.

The effect of this provision is considered in the review of the Institute Time. Clauses, Hulls, 1/10/83 (see page 84).

1   **NAVIGATION**
   The Vessel has leave to dock and undock, to go into graving dock, to sail or navigate with or without pilots, to go on trial trips and to assist and tow vessels or craft in distress, but it is warranted that the Vessel shall not be towed, except as is customary or when in need of assistance, or undertake towage or salvage services under a contract previously arranged by the Assured and/or Owners and/or Managers and/or Charterers. This Clause 1 shall not exclude customary towage in connection with loading and discharging.

Clause 1 is similar to Clause 1.1 of the I.T.C. Hulls 1/10/83 which has been considered earlier (see page 85). The only difference is that instead of expressly covering the vessel "at all times", as in the I.T.C. Hulls, the vessel is expressly given "leave to dock and undock, to go into graving dock".

5. (1830) 1 B. & Ad. 45.

2 CRAFT RISK
Including risk of craft and/or lighter to and from the Vessel.

The partial or total loss of the cargo whilst in transit to or from the vessel can result in a loss of freight to the shipowner and the risk "of craft and or lighter" is expressly covered. In these days of LASH vessels etc. these words can be of considerable importance.

3 CONTINUATION
Should the Vessel at the expiration of this insurance be at sea or in distress or at a port of refuge or of call, the subject-matter insured shall, provided previous notice be given to the Underwriters, be held covered at a pro rata monthly premium to her port of destination.

Identical to Clause 2 of the I.T.C. Hulls 1/10/83 which is considered in detail on page 87.

4 BREACH OF WARRANTY
Held covered in case of any breach of warranty as to cargo, trade, locality, towage, salvage services or date of sailing, provided notice be given to the Underwriters immediately after receipt of advices and any amended terms of cover and any additional premium required by them be agreed.

Identical to Clause 3 of the I.T.C. Hulls which is considered in detail on page 88.

5 TERMINATION
This Clause 5 shall prevail notwithstanding any provision whether written typed or printed in this insurance inconsistent therewith.

Unless the Underwriters agree to the contrary in writing, this insurance shall terminate automatically at the time of
5.1 change of the Classification Society of the Vessel, or change, suspension, discontinuance, withdrawal or expiry of her Class therein, provided that if the Vessel is at sea such automatic termination shall be deferred until arrival at her next port. However where such change, suspension, discontinuance or withdrawal of her Class has resulted from loss or damage covered by Clause 7 of this insurance or which would be covered by an insurance of the Vessel subject to current Institute War and Strikes Clauses Hulls-Time such automatic termination shall only operate should the Vessel sail from her next port without the prior approval of the Classification Society,
5.2 any change, voluntary or otherwise, in the ownership or flag, transfer to new management, or charter on a bareboat basis, or requisition for title or use of the Vessel, provided that, if the Vessel has cargo on board and has already sailed from her loading port or is at sea in ballast, such automatic termination shall if required be deferred, whilst the Vessel continues her planned voyage, until arrival at final port of discharge if with cargo or at port of destination if in ballast. However, in the event of requisition for title or use without the prior execution of a written agreement by the Assured, such automatic termination shall occur fifteen days after such requisition whether the Vessel is at sea or in port.
A pro rata daily net return of premium shall be made.

Identical to Clause 4 of the I.T.C. Hulls which is considered in detail on page 88.

6 ASSIGNMENT
No assignment of or interest in this insurance or in any moneys which may be or become payable thereunder is to be binding on or recognised by the Underwriters unless a dated notice of such assignment or interest signed by the Assured, and by the assignor in the case of subsequent assignment, is endorsed on the Policy and the Policy with such endorsement is produced before payment of any claim or return of premium thereunder.

Identical to Clause 5 of the I.T.C. Hulls which is considered in detail on page 90.

7   PERILS

7.1   This insurance covers loss of the subject-matter insured caused by

7.1.1   perils of the seas rivers lakes or other navigable waters

7.1.2   fire, explosion

7.1.3   violent theft by persons from outside the Vessel

7.1.4   jettison

7.1.5   piracy

7.1.6   breakdown of or accident to nuclear installations or reactors

7.1.7   contact with aircraft or similar objects, or objects falling therefrom, land conveyance, dock or harbour equipment or installation

7.1.8   earthquake volcanic eruption or lightning.

7.2   This insurance covers loss of the subject-matter insured caused by

7.2.1   accidents in loading discharging or shifting cargo or fuel

7.2.2   bursting of boilers breakage of shafts or any latent defect in the machinery or hull

7.2.3   negligence of Master Officers Crew or Pilots

7.2.4   negligence of repairers or charterers provided such repairers or charterers are not an Assured hereunder

7.2.5   barratry of Master Officers or Crew,

 provided such loss has not resulted from want of due diligence by the Assured, Owners or Managers.

7.3   Master Officers Crew or Pilots not to be considered Owners within the meaning of this Clause 7 should they hold shares in the Vessel.

Apart from the omission of the words "or damage" this clause is identical to Clause 6 of the I.T.C. Hulls which is considered in detail on pages 91.

8   POLLUTION HAZARD

This insurance covers loss of the subject-matter insured caused by any governmental authority acting under the powers vested in it to prevent or mitigate a pollution hazard, or threat thereof, resulting directly from a peril covered by this insurance, provided such act of governmental authority has not resulted from want of due diligence by the Assured, the Owners, or Managers of the Vessel or any of them to prevent or mitigate such hazard or threat. Master, Officers, Crew or Pilots not to be considered Owners within the meaning of this Clause 8 should they hold shares in the Vessel.

Identical to Clause 7 of the I.T.C. Hulls which is considered in detail on page 101.

9   FREIGHT COLLISION

9.1   It is further agreed that if the Vessel shall come into collision with any other vessel and the Assured shall in consequence thereof become liable to pay and shall pay by way of damages to any other person or persons any sum or sums in respect of the amount of freight taken into account in calculating the measure of the liability of the Assured for

9.1.1   loss of or damage to any other vessel or property on any other vessel

9.1.2   delay to or loss of use of any such other vessel or property thereon

9.1.3   general average of, salvage of or salvage under contract of, any such other vessel or property thereon,

 the Underwriters will pay the Assured such proportion of three-fourths of such sum or sums so paid applying to freight as their respective subscriptions hereto bear to the total amount insured on freight or, if greater, to the gross freight at risk at the time of the collision.

9.2   Provided always that:

9.2.1   liability of the Underwriters in respect of any one such collision shall not exceed their proportionate part of three-fourths of the total amount insured hereon on freight, and in cases in which, with the prior consent in writing of the Underwriters, the liability of the Vessel has been contested or proceedings have been taken to limit liability, they will also pay a like proportion of three-fourths of the costs, appertaining proportionately to the freight portion of damages, which the Assured shall thereby incur or be compelled to pay;

9.2.2   no claim shall attach to this insurance:

9.2.2.1   which attaches to any other insurances covering collision liabilities

9.2.2.2   which is, or would be, recoverable in the terms of the Institute 3/4ths Collision Liability Clause if the Vessel were insured in the terms of such Institute 3/4ths Collision Liability Clause for a value per ton of her gross registered tonnage not less than the equivalent in pounds sterling, at the time of commencement of this insurance, of 66.67 Special Drawing Rights as defined by the International Monetary Fund;

9.2.3   this Clause 9 shall in no case extend or be deemed to extend to any sum which the Assured may become liable to pay or shall pay for or in respect of:

9.2.3.1   removal or disposal, under statutory powers or otherwise, of obstructions, wrecks, cargoes or any other thing whatsoever

9.2.3.2   any real or personal property or thing whatsoever except other vessels or property on other vessels

9.2.3.3   pollution or contamination of any real or personal property or thing whatsoever (except other vessels with which the insured Vessel is in collision or property on such other vessels)

9.2.3.4   the cargo or other property on or the engagements of the Vessel

9.2.3.5   loss of life, personal injury or illness.

Under several jurisdictions, of which the United States is the prime example, the limitation fund of a vessel is calculated as the sum of her value, plus her pending freight at the time of the collision. In certain circumstances, therefore, damages will be payable by the shipowner in respect of his freight and such damages may exceed the cover granted by the three-fourths collision liability clause in the hull policy. The above clause is designed to cover the proportion of any such liability payable in respect of the insured freight.

"It is further agreed"

These words make the Freight Collision Clause a supplemental agreement, any claim thereunder being payable in addition to any indemnity available under the rest of the policy.

"It is further agreed that if the vessel should come into collision with any other vessel and the assured shall in consequence thereof become liable to pay and shall pay by way of damages to any other person or persons any sum or sums"

The above wording is discussed in detail when considering the I.T.C. Hulls 1/10/83 (see page 101).

"In respect of the amount of freight taken into account in calculating the measure of liability of the assured for"

To substantiate a claim under this clause evidence will be required as to how the liability of the assured was assessed and it would have to be shown quite conclusively that the amount of freight definitely had been taken into account.

Clauses 9.1.1, 9.1.2. and 9.1.3 are identical to the equivalent provisions in the I.T.C. Hulls 1/10/83 considered in detail on page 101.

Underwriters' liability is limited to three-fourths of the sum so paid as applying to freight, pro-rated down to take account of the ratio of the underwriters' subscriptions to the greater of:

1. The total amount insured on freight, or
2. the gross amount at risk at the time of the collision.

The gross freight at risk would be net of any advance freight received.

> **9.2** Provided always that:
> **9.2.1** liability of the Underwriters in respect of any one such collision shall not exceed their proportionate part of three-fourths of the total amount insured hereon on freight, and in cases in which, with the prior consent in writing of the Underwriters , the liability of the Vessel has been contested or proceedings have been taken to limit liability, they will also pay a like proportion of three-fourths of the costs, appertaining proportionately to the freight portion of damages, which the Assured shall thereby incur or be compelled to pay;

Underwriter's liability is expressedly limited to three-fourths of the total sum insured on freight under the policy but in addition underwriters agree to pay three-fourths of the collisions costs attaching to freight, providing that they have given their prior consent in writing to the institution of legal proceedings.

> **9.2.2** no claim shall attach to this insurance:
> **9.2.2.1** which attaches to any other insurances covering collision liabilities
> **9.2.2.2** which is, or would be, recoverable in the terms of the Institute 3/4ths Collision Liability Clause if the Vessel were insured in the terms of such Institute 3/4ths Collision Liability Clause for a value per ton of her gross registered tonnage not less than the equivalent in pounds sterling, at the time of commencement of this insurance, of 66.67 Special Drawing Rights as defined by the International Monetary Fund;

These provisions make it clear that the freight insurance is not intended to "soak up" any collision liabilities attaching to any other insurances. It is not intended that the claim on the freight policy should be increased in some way by reason of the vessel being uninsured or inadequately insured for collision liability under the hull policy. The practical effect of this clause therefore, is to exclude any claim which would be recoverable if the vessel was insured on the standard 3/4ths Collision Liability Clause on a valuation which equates to the English Statutory Limitation Fund for property claimants as laid down in the Merchant Shipping (Liability of Ship Owners and Others) Act 1958. The sterling equivalent of the Special Drawings Rights is published in the *Financial Times*.

The exclusions in Clause 9.2.3 are the customary exclusions in the 3/4ths Collision Liability Clause.

10 SISTERSHIP

Should the Vessel named herein come into collision with or receive salvage services from another vessel belonging wholly or in part to the same Owners, or under the same management, the Assured shall have the same rights under this insurance as they would have were the other vessel entirely the property of Owners not interested in the Vessel named herein; but in such cases the liability for the collision or the amount payable for the services rendered shall be referred to a sole arbitrator to be agreed upon between the Underwriters and the Assured.

Identical to Clause 9 of the I.T.C. Hulls 1/10/83 which is considered in detail on page 107.

11 GENERAL AVERAGE AND SALVAGE

11.1 This insurance covers the proportion of general average salvage and/or salvage charges attaching to freight at risk of the Assured, reduced in respect of any under-insurance.

11.2 Adjustment to be according to the law and practice obtaining at the place where the adventure ends, as if the contract of affreightment contained no special terms upon the subject; but where the contract of affreightment so provides the adjustment shall be according to the York-Antwerp Rules.

11.3 No claim under this Clause 11 shall in any case be allowed where the loss was not incurred to avoid or in connection with the avoidance of a peril insured against.

Freight at the risk of the shipowner can be a contributory interest in both salvage and general average and this clause covers freight's proportion, subject to reduction to take account of any under-insurance. It should also be noted that freight can be a contributing interest in general average even when the vessel is in ballast at the time of the casualty. Rule of Practice B26 of the Association of Average Adjusters provides as follows:

B26 VESSEL IN BALLAST AND UNDER CHARTER: CONTRIBUTING INTERESTS

For the purpose of ascertaining the liability of Underwriters on British policies of insurance, the following provisions shall apply:—

When a vessel is proceeding in ballast to load under a voyage charter entered into by the shipowner before the general average act, the interests contributing to the general average shall be the vessel, such items of stores and equipment as belong to parties other than the owners of the vessel (e.g. bunkers, wireless installation and navigational instruments) and the freight earned under the voyage charter computed in the usual way after deduction of contingent expenses subsequent to the general average act. Failing a prior termination of the adventure, the place where the adventure shall be deemed to end and at which the values for contribution to general average shall be calculated is the final port of discharge of the cargo carried under the charter but in the event of the prior loss of the vessel and freight, or either of them, the general average shall attach to any surviving interest or interests including freight advanced at the loading port deducting therefrom contingent expenses subsequent to the general average act.

When a vessel is proceeding in ballast under a time charter alone or a time charter and a voyage charter entered into by the time charterer, the general average shall attach to the vessel and such items of stores and equipment as are indicated above. Failing a prior termination of the adventure, the adventure shall be deemed to end and the values of contribution to general average calculated at the first loading port upon the commencement of loading cargo.

When the charter to which the shipowner is a party provides for York/Antwerp Rules, the general average shall be adjusted in accordance with those Rules and British law and practice and without regard to the law and practice of any foreign port at which the adventure may terminate; and in the interpretation of Rule XI it shall be immaterial whether the extra period of detention takes place at a port of loading, call or refuge, provided that the detention is in consequence of accident, sacrifice or other extraordinary circumstance occurring whilst the vessel is in ballast.

In practice neither time charter hire, as such, nor time charterer's voyage freight shall contribute to general average.

Clauses 11.2 and 11.3 are identical to Clauses 11.2 and 11.4 of the I.T.C. Hulls 1/10/83 which are considered on page 110.

12 FRANCHISE

This insurance does not cover partial loss, other than general average loss, under 3% unless caused by fire, sinking, stranding or collision with another vessel. Each craft and/or lighter to be deemed a separate insurance if required by the Assured.

This is one of the few insurances still subject to a franchise. Once the franchise is attained the loss is recoverable in full. The franchise is "opened up" when the partial loss is caused by fire, sinking, stranding or collision with another vessel.

A general average loss is not subject to the franchise. The option for the assured to treat each craft and/or lighter as a separate insurance can be of benefit to the assured when the partial loss may not attain the 3 per cent franchise when applied to the whole, but the loss on separate craft and/or lighters may attain 3 per cent.

13 MEASURE OF INDEMNITY

13.1 The amount recoverable under this insurance for any claim for loss of freight shall not exceed the gross freight actually lost.

13.2 Where insurances on freight other than this insurance are current at the time of the loss, all such insurances shall be taken into consideration in calculating the liability under this insurance and the amount recoverable hereunder shall not exceed the rateable proportion of the gross freight lost, notwithstanding any valuation in this or any other insurance.

13.3 In calculating the liability under Clause 11 all insurances on freight shall likewise be taken into consideration.

13.4 Nothing in this Clause 13 shall apply to any claim arising under Clause 15.

Section 70 of the Marine Insurance Act 1906 provides as follows:

70. Partial loss of freight

Subject to any express provision in the policy, where there is a partial loss of freight, the measure of indemnity is such proportion of the sum fixed by the policy, in the case of a valued policy, or of the insurable value, in the case of an unvalued policy, as the proportion of freight lost by the assured bears to the whole freight at the risk of the assured under the policy.

Clause 13.1 limits the indemnity for loss of freight to the gross freight actually lost. The method of applying Clause 2 is quite simple; having established the gross freight lost this is then apportioned over all insurances on freight at the time of the loss, each policy bearing its proportionate share of the loss.

Clause 13.3 places the calculation of the policies' liability for general average and salvage upon the same basis as that for a partial loss of freight. The provisions as to measure of indemnity are expressly excluded by Clause 14.4 from having any effect on a claim for total loss.

14   LOSS OF TIME

This insurance does not cover any claim consequent on loss of time whether arising from a peril of the sea or otherwise.

In providing that the insurer is not liable for any loss proximately caused by delay, even though the delay may have been caused by a peril insured against, section 55(2) of the Marine Insurance Act 1906 only mentions the insurer on ship or goods and does not mention freight. The potential implications of delay were brought home to freight underwriters in the case of *Jackson* v. *Union Marine Insurance Company*.[6] In this case the vessel stranded during the ballast passage to a port where she was fixed to load a cargo. Due to the delay resulting from the casualty the charterers were entitled to throw up the charter as having been frustrated and it was held that the shipowners had therefore suffered a loss of freight by reason of the operation of an insured peril and were entitled to recover under their policy.

There then followed the case of *Inman Steamship Company Limited* v. *Bischoff*.[7] Under the charter in this case the charterers had the right to put the vessel off hire or of making such abatement by way of deduction from the freight as they should adjudge fit in the event of her becoming inefficient. This in fact is what happened when the vessel's performance was affected by perils of the seas. The shipowners who had insured "freight outstanding" under a time policy which covered, *inter alia*, perils of the seas claimed under their policy. The Court of Appeal held that the loss of freight was not caused directly by perils of the seas but by the exercise of the charterers of their discretionary powers. This judgment was unanimously approved by the House of Lords although the Law Lords gave greater emphasis to the argument that there had been no loss of freight, properly speaking, at all. One of the main points to come out in the judgments, was that the position would probably have been different if there had been a stipulation in the charter-party that freight should automatically cease upon the happening of the contingencies mentioned.

This was then confirmed in the two subsequent cases of *The "Alps"*[8] and *The "Bedouin"*.[9] In both of these cases the charter-parties provided for the payment of hire/freight to cease in certain specified circumstances. It was

6. (1873) 23 W.R. 169; 2 Asp.M.L.C. 435.
7. (1882) 31 W.R. 141; 5 Asp.M.L.C. 6.
8. (1893) 41 W.R. 527; 7 Asp.M.L.C. 337.
9. (1894) 42 W.R. 292; 7 Asp.M.L.C. 391.

held that in as much as the clauses in the charter-parties had been brought into operation by the immediate action of insured perils, underwriters were liable for the loss of freight/hire so caused.

The liability imposed upon underwriters as a result of the above cases was wider than they were ready to bear and the above clause was introduced to exclude all claims consequent upon loss of time, including loss of time arising from insured perils.

The clause first came before the courts in *Bensaude* v. *Thames and Mersey Marine Insurance Company Limited.*[10] The freight, which was only payable on arrival, was insured. The ship was damaged by an insured peril and as a result of the delay required for repairs, the charterers cancelled the freight contract. It was held that the claim under the freight policy was consequent upon loss of time and therefore failed.

There then followed several leading cases which can be divided in two separate categories. In *Roura and Forgas* v. *Townend,*[11] *Carras* v. *London & Scottish Assurance Company*[12] and *Robertson* v. *Nomikos*[13] the freight had been lost because the vessels had become constructive total losses and it was held that the loss of freight was not caused by loss of time. On the other hand, in *Atlantic Maritime* v. *Gibbon*[14] the vessel was prevented from loading by restraint of princes and the adventure was consequently frustrated. Here it was held that the claim was barred by the loss of time clause. The distinction between these two categories of cases was brought out in *Nomikos* v. *Robertson*[15]: "the exception would bar any claim whenever it is necessary for the assured to assert the lapse of time as one of the facts establishing his cause of action".

Finally, the clause came before the courts in *Naviera de Canarias S.A.* v. *Nacional Hispanica Aseguredora S.A.* (*The Playa de las Nieves*).[16] In this case it was held that the plain meaning of the clause is to exclude claims for chartered freight lost under an off-hire clause in a time charter.

For the shipowner who wishes to insure loss of hire or earnings arising from the operation of insured perils there are special insurances available, but there are no Institute Clauses for Loss of Hire and/or Earnings insurance.

15   TOTAL LOSS

15.1   In the event of the total loss (actual or constructive) of the Vessel named herein the amount insured shall be paid in full, whether the Vessel be fully or partly loaded or in ballast, chartered or unchartered.

10. (1897) 46 W.R. 78; 8 Asp.M.L.C. 315; 2 Com.Cas. 33.
11. (1919) 14 Asp.M.L.C. 397; 24 Com.Cas. 71; 35 T.L.R. 88.
12. (1936) 40 Com.Cas. 288; 41 Com.Cas. 120; 52 Ll.L.Rep. 34; 53 Ll.L.Rep. 131.
13. [1938] 2 K.B. 603.
14. [1953] 1 Lloyd's Rep. 278; 2 Lloyd's Rep. 294.
15. (1939) 43 Com.Cas. 109; 59 Ll.L.Rep. 182; 61 Ll.L.Rep. 105.
16. [1976] 2 Lloyd's Rep. 80.

15.2 In ascertaining whether the Vessel is a constructive total loss, the insured value in the insurances on hull and machinery shall be taken as the repaired value and nothing in respect of the damaged or break-up value of the Vessel or wreck shall be taken into account.

15.3 Should the Vessel be a constructive total loss but the claim on the insurances on hull and machinery be settled as a claim for partial loss, no payment shall be due under this Clause 15.

Clause 15.1 effectively makes the policy on freight an increased value insurance on the vessel. To invoke payment under the freight policy it is only necessary to show that the vessel has been an actual or constructive total loss and the assured is not put to any proof as to the amount of freight at risk at the relevant time.

Clause 15.2 lays down the "test" for establishing whether the vessel is a constructive total loss and places it on the same basis as provided for in the I.T.C. Hulls 1/10/83.

Clause 15.3 was introduced following the case of *Petros M. Nomikos Ltd.* v. *Robertson*.[17] In that case the policies incorporated the then Institute Time Clauses (Freight) which provided, *inter alia*, as follows:

5. In the event of the total loss, whether absolute or constructive of the steamer the amount underwritten by this policy shall be paid in full, whether the steamer be fully or only partly loaded or in ballast, chartered or unchartered.

6. In ascertaining whether the vessel is a constructive total loss the insured value in the policies on ship shall be taken as the repair value.

After the vessel had been chartered there was an explosion and fire on board and the charter was abandoned. Although the cost of repairs exceeded the insured value in the hull and machinery policies the shipowners elected to repair and claim for a partial loss which was paid by hull underwriters. The shipowners claimed under the freight policy on ground of constructive total loss of steamer, based on Institute Time Clauses (Freight), Clause 5. The freight underwriters countered that the shipowners were not entitled to recover on the ground that there was no constructive total loss of the vessel because there had been no notice of abandonment by the shipowners. The House of Lords held that the claim under the freight policy succeeded due to the fact that the vessel was a constructive total loss within the definition of section 60 of the Marine Insurance Act 1906, notwithstanding that she was never abandoned in any sense of the word. The House of Lords held that abandonment to underwriters is not an essential ingredient of a constructive total loss, but only for a claim therefor.

16   RETURNS FOR LAY-UP AND CANCELLATION
  16.1 To return as follows:
  16.1.1   Pro rata monthly net for each uncommenced month if this insurance be cancelled by agreement.

17. (1939) 43 Com.Cas. 109; 59 Ll.L.Rep. 182; 61 Ll.L.Rep. 105.

16.1.2 For each period of 30 consecutive days the Vessel may be laid up in a port or in a lay-up area provided such port or lay-up area is approved by the Underwriters (with special liberties as hereinafter allowed)

(a)....................................per cent net not under repair

(b)....................................per cent net under repair.

If the Vessel is under repair during part only of a period of which a return is claimable, the return shall be calculated pro rata to the number of days under (a) and (b) respectively.

16.2 PROVIDED ALWAYS THAT

16.2.1 a total loss of the Vessel, whether by insured perils or otherwise, has not occurred during the period covered by this insurance or any extension thereof

16.2.2 in no case shall a return be allowed when the Vessel is lying in exposed or unprotected waters, or in a port or lay-up area not approved by the Underwriters but, provided the Underwriters agree that such non-approved lay-up area is deemed to be within the vicinity of the approved port or lay-up area, days during which the Vessel is laid up in such non-approved lay-up area may be added to days in the approved port or lay-up area to calculate a period of 30 consecutive days and a return shall be allowed for the proportion of such period during which the Vessel is actually laid up in the approved port or lay-up area

16.2.3 loading or discharging operations or the presence of cargo on board shall not debar returns but no return shall be allowed for any period during which the Vessel is being used for the storage of cargo or for lightering purposes

16.2.4 in the event of any amendment of the annual rate, the above rates of return shall be adjusted accordingly

16.2.5 in the event of any return recoverable under this Clause 16 being based on 30 consecutive days which fall on successive insurances effected for the same Assured, this insurance shall only be liable for an amount calculated at pro rata of the period rates 16.1.2(a) and/or (b) above for the number of days which come within the period of this insurance and to which a return is actually applicable. Such overlapping period shall run, at the option of the Assured, either from the first day on which the Vessel is laid up or the first day of a period of 30 consecutive days as provided under 16.1.2(a) or (b), or 16.2.2 above.

The following clauses shall be paramount and shall override anything contained in this insurance inconsistent therewith.

17 WAR EXCLUSION

In no case shall this insurance cover loss damage liability or expense caused by

17.1 war civil war revolution rebellion insurrection, or civil strife arising therefrom, or any hostile act by or against a belligerent power

17.2 capture seizure arrest restraint or detainment (barratry and piracy excepted), and the consequences thereof or any attempt thereat

17.3 derelict mines torpedoes bombs or other derelict weapons of war.

18 STRIKES EXCLUSION

In no case shall this insurace cover loss damage liability or expense caused by

18.1 strikers, locked-out workmen, or persons taking part in labour disturbances, riots or civil commotions

18.2 any terrorist or any person acting from a political motive.

19 MALICIOUS ACTS EXCLUSION

In no case shall this insurance cover loss damage liability or expense arising from

19.1 the detonation of an explosive

19.2 any weapon of war

and caused by any person acting maliciously or from a political motive.

20 NUCLEAR EXCLUSION

In no case shall this insurance cover loss damage liability or expense arising from any weapon of war employing atomic or nuclear fission and/or fusion or other like reaction or radioactive force or matter.

The above clauses are identical to Clauses 22–26 of the Institute Time Clauses, Hulls 1/10/83 which are considered in detail on pages 130 to 134.

PART V

War and Strikes Risks Forms

1. HISTORICAL PERSPECTIVE

From men of war to the terrorists of today

If we look at the list of perils which by Lloyd's form of policy the under-writers were "contented to bear and do take upon us in this voyage", we find that prominence is given to the warlike and hostile acts which might befall the adventure. Those perils were:

> "... of the seas, *men of war*, fire, *enemies, pirates, rovers, thieves*, jettisons, *letters of mart and countermart, surprisals, takings at sea, arrests, restraints, and detainments of all Kings, Princes, and people, of what nation, condition, or quality so ever*, barratry of the Master and Mariners, and of all other perils, losses, and misfortunes, that have or shall come to the hurt, detriment, or damage of the said goods and merchandises, and ship, etc., or any part thereof." (Emphasis added by the authors)

After reading this list it is not difficult to appreciate how hazardous a maritime adventure was in the days when Lloyd's form of policy was evolving, and how much of that hazard arose from the hostile acts of men. Of course, in those days every merchantman was armed, and the gunner was as important a member of the crew as the boatswain. Even so, a heavily laden merchantman was no match, either in sailing ability or fire power, for a man of war or a pirate cutter, and many were the losses which underwriters had to bear from these causes in the 17th and 18th centuries.

During the Napoleonic Wars both England and France came to appreciate the economic dimension of the conflict, and it was about this time that underwriters, wishing to exempt themselves from the consequences of economic blockade, began to insert into their policies of insurance the "free of capture and seizure" clause (or the F.C. & S. Clause, as it came to be known). Merchants who wanted this cover had to take out a separate insurance to cover the risks excluded by the F.C. & S. Clause, which would, of course, be rated separately by the underwriters prepared to run these risks, according to the best available intelligence as to the strength of the enemy's blockade.

During the American Civil War it became common to add to the F.C. & S. warranty "... all consequences of hostilities".[1] By the time of the First World War, the standard form of the F.C. & S. Clause had been extended to exclude the consequences not only of hostilities, but also "war-like operations whether before or after declaration of war".

During both the First and Second World Wars, the ships requisitioned by the United Kingdom Government were engaged under charter-parties by which the Government bore the risks excluded by the F.C. & S. Clause, so that, in effect, the Government were the war risk underwriters for those vessels.

Many were the law cases finely argued as a result of casualties occurring during both World Wars, in order to decide whether or not the losses occurred "in consequence of hostilities or war-like operations". This line of legal authority culminated in the well-known case of The "Coxwold", in which the House of Lords held that the stranding of the vessel near a dimmed light, whilst steaming on a course set by the naval officer in charge of a convoy, was the consequence of a war-like operation. This decision was considered by many to have upset the balance between marine and war risk underwriters, to the extent that the F.C. & S. Clause should be further revised. This was done, and the form of words in use from 1943, and for some forty years thereafter, read as follows:

> "Warranted free of capture, seizure, arrest, restraint or detainment, and the consequences thereof or of any attempt thereat; also from the consequences of hostilities or warlike operations, whether there be a declaration of war or not; but this warranty shall not exclude collision, contact with any fixed or floating object (other than a mine or torpedo), stranding, heavy weather or fire unless caused directly (and independently of the nature of the voyage or service which the vessel concerned or, in the case of a collision, any other vessel involved therein, is performing) by a hostile act by or against a belligerent power; and for the purpose of this warranty 'power' includes any authority maintaining naval, military or air forces in association with a power. Further warranted free from the consequences of civil war, revolution, rebellion, insurrection, or civil strife arising therefrom, or piracy."

It has also to be observed that the reinstatement of the risks excluded by the F.C. & S. Clause, if this is all that is undertaken by the war risks policy, merely reverts to the cover granted by Lloyd's S.G. form. It does not enlarge the risks in any way. In order to meet this, it became usual for war risk insurances to express the cover granted in two different ways, viz:

— the risks excluded by the F.C. & S. Clause, and
— the "positive" cover.

---

1. "all consequences of hostilities". As to the meaning of this term, see *Ionides* v. *Universal Marine Insurance Co.* (1863) 10 Jur. (N.S.) 18, and the remarks of Lord Wright in *Yorkshire Dale Steamship Co. Ltd.* v. *Minister of War Transport* (*The "Coxwold"*) (1942) 73 Ll.L.Rep. 1.

An example of a clause providing such positive cover was:

"This insurance covers loss of or damage to the property hereby insured caused by —

(a) hostilities, warlike operations, civil war, revolution, rebellion, insurrection or civil strife arising therefrom;

(b) mines, torpedoes, bombs or other engines of war."

The new clauses introduced in 1982 and 1983 have done away with all this convoluted draftsmanship. The risks covered by the War Clauses are described in new terms. Gone entirely are "the consequences of hostilities or warlike operations", and so, at a stroke, all the law cases and learned commentaries dealing with the interpretion of those words have become merely of academic interest.

To complete our historical review, insurance is now available to cover loss or damage caused by terrorists — although, rather oddly so far as cargo insurances are concerned, the cover is provided not under the War Clauses, but under the Strikes Clauses. So, before looking at the clauses in detail, we note that for reasons which will shortly appear, there are separate forms for War Risks and for Strikes Risks so far as goods are concerned, whereas for hulls both War and Strikes Risks are covered under the same policy form.

2. CARGO INSURANCES

The reason why, in the London insurance market, the insurances on goods are covered by different forms for war risks and for strikes risks is something of an anomaly. This is because of an agreement between various underwriters in the London market relating to transit insurances, called the "Waterborne Agreement", whereby underwriters in the marine market will not in general cover war risks in respect of goods on land. Thus the Transit Clause, which regulates the duration of the risk, differs according to the risks which are covered.

This distinction does not apply to the covers available for hulls and for freight.

A. INSTITUTE WAR CLAUSES (CARGO)

RISKS COVERED

The risks covered by this form are set out in Clauses 1 and 2.

Clause 1 — Risks Clause

1   This insurance covers, except as provided in Clauses 3 and 4 below, loss of or damage to the subject-matter insured caused by

    1.1   war civil war revolution rebellion insurrection, or civil strife arising therefrom, or any hostile act by or against a belligerent power

    1.2   capture seizure arrest restraint or detainment, arising from risks covered under 1.1 above, and the consequences thereof or any attempt thereat

    1.3   derelict mines torpedoes bombs or other derelict weapons of war.

"war"

"War" involves the employment of force between States or entities having, at least *de facto*, the characteristic of a State. In some respects the fact that a state of war has been declared may be significant, for example by rendering illegal the voyage by a ship carrying goods belonging to the declared enemy — see *British and Foreign Marine Insurance Co. v. Sanday.*[2] As Lord Wrenbury said in that case:

> "A declaration of war by the Sovereign is a political or executive act, done by virtue of his prerogative, which creates a state of war. A state of war is a lawful state, and is one in which every subject of his Majesty becomes an enemy of the nation against which war is declared."

However, a declaration of war is no longer (if it ever was) an essential ingredient: an undeclared war may exist *de facto* between sovereign States, as it can between quasi-sovereign entities. For example, the invasion of China by Japanese armies in 1937 was held in *Kawasaki K.K.K. v. Bantham Steamship Co.*[3] to amount to an outbreak of war within a clause of a charter-party entitling the shipowner to cancel the charter, even though there was no declaration of war and both countries continued to maintain diplomatic relations with each other.

In comparison with the old forms of war risk clauses, the term "war" by itself may be narrower than "hostilities", but not greatly so. As Lord Atkinson said in *Britain Steamship Co. v. The King*[4]: "Hostilities connotes the idea of belligerents, properly so called, enemy nations at war with one another". Accordingly, when "war" is considered together with the other perils listed in this Clause 1.1, the total effect is probably much the same as "consequences of hostilities" under the old form of words, as construed by the English courts.[5]

2. *British & Foreign Marine Insurance Co. v. Sanday* (1916) 21 Com.Cas. 154.
3. *Kawasaki K.K.K. v. Bantham Steamship Co.* (1939) 44 Com.Cas. 170.
4. *Britain Steamship Co. v. The King* [1921] 1 A.C. 99.
5. See the interesting discussion on the interpretation of the word "consequences" in *Templeman on Marine Insurance*, 5th edn., at p. 172, and the cases there cited.

"civil war"

"Civil war" denotes the state of hostilities between different sections or groups in the same State, each exercising at least quasi-governmental authority.

During the Spanish Civil War, in a case involving the requisition of trawlers and the confiscation of their gear by an organised body known as the "Basque Militia", the House of Lords concluded that the loss of the trawlers and their gear was proximately caused by "civil war", and it was said that "the word 'war' in a policy of insurance includes civil war unless the context makes it clear that a different meaning should be given to the word".[6]

"revolution", "rebellion", "insurrection"

In inverse order these words suggest a rising scale in the development of civil disorder. In an American case involving the hijacking of an airliner by two avowed members of the Popular Front for the Liberation of Palestine,[7] counsel and the court agreed that if the loss was not caused by an "insurrection", then it could not have been caused by a rebellion or a revolution. In that case it was held that the word "insurrection" means a violent uprising by a group or movement acting for the specific purpose of overthrowing the constituted government and seizing its powers.

"Rebellion" and "revolution" are terms so similar that one may need to go to a dictionary to ascertain what distinction there is between them. The *Universal English Dictionary* offers the following:

> "Rebellion:— A state of organised armed and open resistance against the authority and Government or Sovereign of the country to which one is in allegiance; distinguished from Civil War, usually by the smaller number of the rebels."

> "Revolution:— Complete subversion of established political authority and establishment of a new form of government; overthrow of existing political conditions."

One is tempted to sum this up by saying that a rebellion becomes a revolution at the moment it becomes successful.

"civil strife arising therefrom"

These words cover civil strife or unrest which arises in consequence of any of the preceding risks. They have to be contrasted with "riots or civil commotions", for which cover is provided in the Institute Strikes Clauses (Cargo). In practice the dividing line may be hard to find between civil strife

6. *Pesquarias y Secaderos de Bacalao de Espana* v. *Beer* (1949) 82 Ll.L.Rep. 501.
7. *Pan American World Airways Inc.* v. *The Aetna Casualty & Surety Co.* [1975] 1 Lloyd's Rep. 77.

arising from an insurrection and a civil commotion which does not. It is submitted that the factor which would bring the loss within the War Clauses is the existence of an intent on the part of the rebels or insurrectionists to overthrow the established government. So in the case of loss or damage by looters, one would have to enquire into the reason for the breakdown of law and order, and if that had arisen, say in consequence of a severe bombing attack by an enemy or of an attempt by a group of people to overthrow the government, the loss would fall under the War Clauses.

"any hostile act by or against a belligerent power"

These words are a great deal narrower than the words which they replace, "hostilities or warlike operations", on the interpretation of which so much legal energy had been expended in past years. They are probably narrower even than "hostilities" alone, since to bring a claim within these words it would have to be shown:

(a) that the loss or damage had been proximately caused by an act (that is to say, some action on the part of somebody)
(b) which was "hostile" (which may or may not involve a question of intent)
(c) directed either by or against a "power" which is "belligerent".

"Power" includes a state and probably also an entity exercising quasi-governmental authority.

"Belligerent" has not yet been defined in this context. The expression has two possible meanings, one restricted, and one much wider. A restricted definition is provided in the *Dictionary of English Law*: "... carrying on war according to the law of nations". In vernacular usage, the term probably applies to anyone engaged in armed conflict.

However, the use of the words "by or against" does ensure that the property of neutrals which are subject to armed attack either by the forces of a State at war, or of one in opposition to it, is protected by the clause.

"1.2 capture seizure arrest restraint or detainment, arising from risks covered under 1.1 above, and the consequences thereof or any attempt thereat"

"capture" and "seizure"

In *Cory* v. *Burr*[8] Lord Fitzgerald said:

> "In the construction of this warranty [the F.C. & S. Clause] it is observable that capture and seizure do not mean the same thing. 'Capture' would seem properly to include every act of seizing or taking by an enemy or belligerent. 'Seizure'

8. *Cory* v. *Burr* (1883) 5 Asp.M.L.C. 109.

seems to be a larger term than 'capture', and goes beyond it, and may reasonably be interpreted to embrace every act of taking forcible possession, either by a lawful authority, or by overpowering force."

In that case, a ship was seized by the Spanish Revenue Authorities because the master was barratrously engaged in smuggling. The House of Lords held that this was a "seizure" in terms of the F.C. & S. clause. It is however to be noted that a loss of cargo from the same cause would not give rise to a claim under the present Institute War Clauses (Cargo), since the seizure would not have arisen from one of the risks covered under Clause 1.1.

"arrest", "restraint" or "detainment"

In Lloyd's form of policy these perils were described by the words "arrests, restraints and detainments of all Kings, Princes, and people, of what nation, condition or quality so ever ..." In the Rules for Construction of Policy contained in the Marine Insurance Act 1906, Rule 10 states "the term 'arrests, etc. of Kings, Princes and people' refers to political or executive acts, and does not include a loss caused by riot or by ordinary judicial process".

It is settled law that the arrest or restraint does not have to be accompanied by force. In *British & Foreign Marine Insurance Co.* v. *Sanday*,[2] goods insured under a policy covering war risks were held to be a constructive total loss by "restraint of Princes", when, being loaded on a British ship, they were diverted from their original destination (Hamburg) and taken to a port in the United Kingdom, in consequence of the declaration of war between Great Britain and Germany. As Lord Atkinson said, "the declaration carries with it all the force of a law prohibiting intercourse with the enemy save with licence of the Sovereign. It has the executive forces of the Crown behind it to enforce obedience to it".

Likewise, in *Miller* v. *Law Accident Insurance Co.*,[9] the restraint consisted merely of a general decree of the Argentine Government prohibiting the landing of cattle from the United Kingdom at any Argentine port: "... the issuing of the decree ... was an act of State and comes within the words within the body of the policy ..."

"... arising from risks covered under 1.1 above ..."

These are new words of qualification which limit the cover in respect of capture, etc. to instances which arise as a result of the war or "war-like" perils listed in Clause 1.1. For example, in the cases referred to above, it will be seen that in *Sanday's* case the restraint arose from the declaration of war, whereas in *Miller's* case the restraint had nothing to do with war or any of the risks now covered in Clause 1.1.

9. *Miller* v. *Law Accident Insurance Society* (1903) 8 Com.Cas. 161.

"and the consequences thereof or any attempt thereat"

In the previous forms of the F.C. & S. and War Risks Clauses these words appeared in juxtaposition to "capture, seizure, arrest, restraint or detainment", which risks they qualify and expand. Despite their now being separated by the intervening phrase "arising from etc. ... " they should receive the same interpretation.

"1.3   derelict mines torpedoes bombs or other derelict weapons of war"

These words replace "mines, torpedoes, bombs or other engines of war", which were the words appearing in previous forms of **War Risks Clauses**. The word "derelict" has presumably been added in order to reverse the effect of the decision in *Costain-Blankevoort (U.K.) Dredging Co. v. Davenport*,[10] in which it was held that damage sustained by a dredger which sucked up ammunition which had been dumped after the end of the Second World War was not the consequence of a "warlike operation".

So, if derelict engines of war are within the cover granted by the Institute War Clauses, can it be said that all loss or damage caused by an active engine of war will also be covered, as was the case under the previous clauses? Alas, this appears not to be so. On the contrary, it appears to be necessary to enquire by whom or on whose orders the mine was sown, the torpedo fired or the bomb thrown. If that arose in the course of a war or as a result of one of the "war-like" perils listed in Clause 1.1, the claim will be covered by the War Clauses; conversely, if the weapon had been discharged in the course of a civil commotion (not amounting to an insurrection) or, say, by a terrorist, then, as we shall see, there will be claim under the Institute Strikes Clauses.

Clause 2 — General Average Clause

2   This insurance covers general average and salvage charges, adjusted or determined according to the contract of affreightment and/or the governing law and practice, incurred to avoid or in connection with the avoidance of loss from a risk covered under these clauses.

This clause is very similar to the General Average Clause contained in the Institute Cargo Clauses (A), (B) and (C), but it must be observed that the cover is, of course, limited to general average and salvage charges incurred in order to avoid a loss which would fall within the War Clauses.

An interesting old case[11] illustrates a general average sacrifice made in order to avoid a loss by capture. The master of a ship being pursued by an enemy extinguished the ship's lights at nightfall, and instead placed a light

10. *Costain-Blankevoort (U.K.) Ltd. v. Davenport (The "Nassau Bay")* [1979] 1 Lloyd's Rep. 395.
   11. Cited in Emerigon, *Des Assurances et des Contrats a La Grosse*, c. xii, s. 41, p. 606.

upon the masthead of the ship's boat, which he set adrift in a different direction: the enemy chased the empty boat, and the ship got away.

For the meaning of the words "adjusted or determined according to the contract of affreightment and/or the governing law and practice", see the commentary under Clause 2 of the Institute Cargo Clauses (A), above on page 14.

EXCLUSIONS

The exclusions are contained in Clauses 3 and 4.

Clause 3 — General Exclusions Clause

3   In no case shall this insurance cover
   3.1 loss damage or expense attributable to wilful misconduct of the Assured
   3.2 ordinary leakage, ordinary loss in weight or volume, or ordinary wear and tear of the subject-matter insured
   3.3 loss damage or expense caused by insufficiency or unsuitability of packing or preparation of the subject-matter insured (for the purpose of this Clause 3.3 "packing" shall be deemed to include stowage in a container or liftvan but only when such stowage is carried out prior to attachment of this insurance or by the Assured or their servants)
   3.4 loss damage or expense caused by inherent vice or nature of the subject-matter insured
   3.5 loss damage or expense proximately caused by delay, even though the delay be caused by a risk insured against (except expenses payable under Clause 2 above)
   3.6 loss damage or expense arising from insolvency or financial default of the owners managers charterers or operators of the vessel
   3.7 any claim based upon loss of or frustration of the voyage or adventure
   3.8 loss damage or expense arising from any hostile use of any weapon of war employing atomic or nuclear fission and/or fusion or other like reaction or radioactive force or matter.

The first six of these exclusions correspond with the exclusions contained in Institute Cargo Clauses, as follows:

Exclusions per Institute War Clauses (Cargo) and Institute Strikes Clauses (Cargo)		*Exclusions per Institute Cargo Clauses (A), (B) and (C)*
3.1	corresponds to	4.1
3.2		4.2
3.3		4.3
3.4		4.4
3.5		4.5
3.6		4.6

For commentary, see the observations under the Institute Cargo Clauses (A) on pages 17 to 20 above.

Exclusions which do not appear in the Institute Cargo Clauses

"3.7 Any claim based upon loss of or frustration of the voyage or adventure"

In the words of Lord Wright, this clause was "undoubtedly invented from a desire to abrogate the effect of *Sanday's* case where only the adventure was affected by the peril, the goods being unaffected". *Sanday's*[2] case is commented upon on page 191, and it will be remembered that the declaration of war operated to make the adventure *ipso facto* illegal; in other words, the restraint frustrated that adventure.

The clause will also have the effect of excluding such a claim as arose in the case of *Rodocanochi* v. *Elliott*.[12] In that case goods were insured from the Far East to the United Kingdom, with an overland transit through France. The goods got as far as Paris at about the time when that city became invested by the Prussian army in 1870, with the result that it became impossible to remove the goods from Paris and send them on to their destination. It was held that their detention within Paris was brought about "by the immediate and direct action of the German army", and since "this was not a mere retardation of the voyage, but a breaking up of the whole adventure" the assured was entitled to abandon the goods to the underwriters and claim for a constructive total loss.

However, the words of Clause 3.7 do *not* mean that any claim which involves the loss or frustration of the voyage or adventure will be excluded. The exception applies only to claims which are "based upon" such loss or frustration, that is to say, such claims as, in the absence of the exclusion, would only be recoverable by virtue of a loss or frustration of the voyage. So, in a set of test cases which were taken to the House of Lords in 1941, it was held that when goods on board a number of German ships were diverted from their voyages by the actions of the German captains obeying the orders of their Government, there was a physical restraint upon the goods as well as a loss of adventure.[13] Lord Wright said: "What happened here was that the master, being in possession of the goods as a carrier ... seized them in the sense that he ceased to hold them as carrier and changed the character of his possession by taking and controlling them as agent for the German Government ..." Thus, despite the inclusion of the "frustration clause" in the War Risk insurances, the owners of the goods were able to recover for their loss in each case.

---

12. *Rodocanochi* v. *Elliott* (1874) 2 Asp.M.L.C. 399.
13. *Middows Ltd.* v. *Robertson* and other cases (H.L.) (1941) 70 Ll.L.Rep. 173.

"3.8   Loss damage or expense arising from any hostile use of any weapon of war employing atomic or nuclear fission and/or fusion or other like reaction or radioactive force or matter."

The wording of this clause differs from the atomic/nuclear weapon exclusion contained in the Institute Cargo Clauses, Institute Strikes Clauses (Cargo) and other similar forms, but only by the inclusion of the one additional word "hostile". This would seem to suggest that a loss by a "non-hostile" use of such a weapon, such as by its explosion whilst being deployed by friendly forces, would result in a claim for which underwriters under the Institute War Clauses (Cargo) would respond.

Clause 4 — Unseaworthiness and Unfitness Exclusion Clause

4   4.1   In no case shall this insurance cover loss damage or expense arising from
   unseaworthiness of vessel or craft,
   unfitness of vessel craft conveyance container or liftvan for the safe carriage of the subject-matter insured,
   where the Assured or their servants are privy to such unseaworthiness or unfitness, at the time the subject-matter insured is loaded therein.

   4.2   The Underwriters waive any breach of the implied warranties of seaworthiness of the ship and fitness of the ship to carry the subject-matter insured to destination, unless the Assured or their servants are privy to such unseaworthiness or unfitness.

The wording of the clause and its effect is the same as in the Institute Cargo Clauses (A), (B) and (C). See commentary on page 20.

DURATION

Clause 5 — Transit Clause

5   5.1   This insurance
   5.1.1   attaches only as the subject-matter insured and as to any part as that part is loaded on an oversea vessel
   and
   5.1.2   terminates, subject to 5.2 and 5.3 below, either as the subject-matter insured and as to any part as that part is discharged from an oversea vessel at the final port or place of discharge,
   or
   on expiry of 15 days counting from midnight of the day of arrival of the vessel at the final port or place of discharge,
   whichever shall first occur;
   nevertheless,
   subject to prompt notice to the Underwriters and to an additional premium, such insurance
   5.1.3   reattaches when, without having discharged the subject-matter insured at the final port or place of discharge, the vessel sails therefrom,
   and
   5.1.4   terminates, subject to 5.2 and 5.3 below, either as the subject-matter insured and as to any part as that part is thereafter discharged from the vessel at the final (or substituted) port or place of discharge,
   or
   on expiry of 15 days counting from midnight of the day of re-arrival of the vessel at the final

port or place of discharge or arrival of the vessel at a substituted port or place of discharge, whichever shall first occur.

5.2 If during the insured voyage the oversea vessel arrives at an intermediate port or place to discharge the subject-matter insured for on-carriage by oversea vessel or by aircraft, or the goods are discharged from the vessel at a port or place of refuge, then, subject to 5.3 below and to an additional premium if required, this insurance continues until the expiry of 15 days counting from midnight of the day of arrival of the vessel at such port or place, but thereafter reattaches as the subject-matter insured and as to any part as that part is loaded on an on-carrying oversea vessel or aircraft. During the period of 15 days the insurance remains in force after discharge only whilst the subject-matter insured and as to any part as that part is at such port or place. If the goods are on-carried within the said period of 15 days or if the insurance reattaches as provided in this Clause 5.2

5.2.1 where the on-carriage is by oversea vessel this insurance continues subject to the terms of these clauses,
or

5.2.2 where the on-carriage is by aircraft, the current Institute War Clauses (Air Cargo) (excluding sendings by Post) shall be deemed to form part of this insurance and shall apply to the on-carriage by air.

5.3 If the voyage in the contract of carriage is terminated at a port or place other than the destination agreed therein, such port or place shall be deemed the final port of discharge and such insurance terminates in accordance with 5.1.2. If the subject-matter insured is subsequently reshipped to the original or any other destination, then *provided notice is given to the Underwriters before the commencement of such further transit and subject to an additional premium*, such insurance reattaches

5.3.1 in the case of the subject-matter insured having been discharged, as the subject-matter insured and as to any part as that part is loaded on the on-carrying vessel for the voyage;

5.3.2 in the case of the subject-matter not having been discharged, when the vessel sails from such deemed final port of discharge;

thereafter such insurance terminates in accordance with 5.1.4.

5.4 The insurance against the risks of mines and derelict torpedoes, floating or submerged, is extended whilst the subject-matter insured or any part thereof is on craft whilst in transit to or from the oversea vessel, but in no case beyond the expiry of 60 days after discharge from the oversea vessel unless otherwise specially agreed by the Underwriters.

5.5 *Subject to prompt notice to Underwriters, and to an additional premium if required*, this insurance shall remain in force within the provisions of these Clauses during any deviation, or any variation of the adventure arising from the exercise of a liberty granted to shipowners or charterers under the contract of affreightment.

(For the purpose of Clause 5

"arrival" shall be deemed to mean that the vessel is anchored, moored or otherwise secured at a berth or place within the Harbour Authority area. If such a berth or place is not available, arrival is deemed to have occurred when the vessel first anchors, moors or otherwise secures either at or off the intended port or place of discharge

"oversea vessel" shall be deemed to mean a vessel carrying the subject-matter from one port or place to another where such voyage involves a sea passage by that vessel)

This clause, although it appears to be extremely complicated, says little more than that the risk does not attach until the goods are loaded on to the overseas steamer and does not extend beyond fifteen days after arrival of the vessel at the final port or place of discharge. Furthermore, if there is a discharge of the goods at an intermediate port or place (even a port or place of refuge), the assured can obtain continuation of the cover (under this insurance) only on payment of an additional premium if required.

The same applies in the event that the contract of carriage is terminated at a port or place other than the destination named in the bill of lading or charter-party. The provision in Clause 5.3 is in this respect to be contrasted with the terms of Clause 9 of the Institute Cargo Clauses — see page 25.

Re-attachment of the insurance is provided for:

— after discharge at an intermediate port or place, on loading into either the original or a forwarding vessel;

— after discharge at a port or place where the contract of carriage is terminated, on reshipment to an on-carrying vessel, but only if notice is given to the underwriters "before the commencement of such further transit" and subject to an additional premium. It is not entirely clear what is intended by the words "before the commencement of such further transit". However, if it had been intended to mean prior to reshipment, it would have been much simpler to say so, and it is therefore submitted by the authors that the words employed imply that the notice is to be given before the on-carrying vessel sails.

Sub-Clause 5.4 provides for an extension of the risks of "mines and derelict torpedoes, floating or submerged" whilst the goods are on craft in transit to or from the ocean steamer: in transit to the ocean steamer there is no limitation on the period of extension, but the period of extension whilst in transit from the ocean steamer to destination will not extend beyond 60 days after discharge from the ocean steamer unless the underwriters specially agree. It is to be noted that the risks for which this extension of time is granted are not precisely the same as the perils listed in Clause 1.3.

Sub-Clause 5.5 is more stringent than the corresponding clause in the Institute Cargo Clauses (Clause 8.3), and requires prompt notice to be given to the underwriters, and payment of an additional premium if required, for continuation of the cover in the event of a deviation or any variation of the adventure arising from the exercise of the liberty granted to the carrier under the contract of affreightment.

Clause 6 — Change of Voyage Clause

6   Where, after attachment of this insurance, the destination is changed by the Assured, *held covered at a premium and on conditions to be arranged subject to prompt notice being given to the Underwriters.*

This clause is the same as Clause 10 in the Institute Cargo Clauses, and like that clause, it is considerably more restricted than its predecessor which, subject to prompt notice and an additional premium, held the assured covered in the event of a change of voyage by the shipowner or carrier — see page 26.

Clause 7

7   **Anything contained in this contract which is inconsistent with Clauses 3.7, 3.8 or 5 shall, to the extent of such inconsistency, be null and void.**

This clause is printed in bold type to draw attention to it. It is of the type of clause called a "Clause Paramount" which is intended to prevail notwith-standing anything to the contrary. The protected clauses are exclusions 3.7 and 3.8, and also the Transit Clause (Clause 5), variation of the terms of which would breach the "Waterborne Agreement".

CLAIMS

Clause 8 — Insurable Interest Clause

8 8.1 In order to recover under this insurance the Assured must have an insurable interest in the subject-matter insured at the time of the loss.

8.2 Subject to 8.1 above, the Assured shall be entitled to recover for insured loss occurring during the period covered by this insurance, notwithstanding that the loss occurred before the contract of insurance was concluded, unless the Assured were aware of the loss and the Underwriters were not.

This clause is the same as Clause 11 in the Institute Cargo Clauses. See commentary on page 27.

Clause 9 — Increased Value Clause

9 9.1 If any Increased Value insurance is effected by the Assured on the cargo insured herein the agreed value of the cargo shall be deemed to be increased to the total amount insured under this insurance and all Increased Value insurances covering the loss, and liability under this insurance shall be in such proportion as the sum insured herein bears to such total amount insured.

In the event of claim the Assured shall provide the Underwriters with evidence of the amounts insured under all other insurances.

9.2 **Where this insurance is on Increased Value the following clause shall apply:**

The agreed value of the cargo shall be deemed to be equal to the total amount insured under the primary insurance and all Increased Value insurances covering the loss and effected on the cargo by the Assured, and liability under this insurance shall be in such proportion as the sum insured herein bears to such total amount insured

In the event of claim the Assured shall provide the Underwriters with evidence of the amounts insured under all other insurances.

This clause is the same as Clause 14 in the Institute Cargo Clauses. See commentary on page 31.

Clause 10 — Not to inure

10 This insurance shall not inure to the benefit of the carrier or other bailee.

This is the standard clause found in all cargo insurances.

Clause 11 — Duty of Assured Clause

11　It is the duty of the Assured and their servants and agents in respect of loss recoverable hereunder
　　11.1　to take such measures as may be reasonable for the purpose of averting or minimising such loss, and
　　11.2　to ensure that all rights against carriers, bailees or other third parties are properly preserved and exercised
　　and the Underwriters will, in addition to any loss recoverable hereunder, reimburse the Assured for any charges properly and reasonably incurred in pursuance of these duties.

This clause is in the same terms as Clause 16 of the Institute Cargo Clauses. However, it has to be borne in mind that underwriters will only reimburse the assured under this insurance for expenses incurred under this clause "in respect of loss recoverable hereunder", that is to say, in connection with a claim brought about by one of the "war perils" listed in Clause 1.

As to the clause generally, see the commentaries on pages 32 and 46.

Clause 12 — Waiver Clause

12　Measures taken by the Assured or the Underwriters with the object of saving, protecting or recovering the subject-matter insured shall not be considered as a waiver or acceptance of abandonment or otherwise prejudice the rights of either party.

This is the same as Clause 17 in the Institute Cargo Clauses. See commentary on page 34.

AVOIDANCE OF DELAY

Clause 13 — Reasonable Despatch Clause

13　It is a condition of this insurance that the Assured shall act with reasonable despatch in all circumstances within their control.

This is the same as Clause 18 in the Institute Cargo Clauses. It is of considerable antiquity and its purpose is self-evident.

LAW AND PRACTICE

Clause 14 — English Law and Practice Clause

14　This insurance is subject to English law and practice.

This clause appears in all the new standard forms of cargo insurance. See commentary on page 35.

There then follows the Note which appears at the foot of all the standard forms for cargo insurances (see page 35).:

NOTE:— It is necessary for the Assured when they become aware of an event which is "held covered" under this insurance to give prompt notice to the Underwriters and the right to such cover is dependent upon compliance with this obligation.

B. INSTITUTE STRIKES CLAUSES (CARGO)

RISKS COVERED

The risks covered by this form are set out in Clauses 1 and 2.

Clause 1 — Risks Clause

1   This insurance covers, except as provided in Clauses 3 and 4 below, loss of or damage to the subject-matter insured caused by
   1.1   strikers, locked-out workmen, or persons taking part in labour disturbances, riots or civil commotions
   1.2   any terrorist or any person acting from a political motive.

"Strikers, locked-out workmen, or persons taking part in labour disturbances"

These words, it is submitted, have to be construed in the ordinary everyday sense in which they are understood. If this is correct, then perhaps the daily newspapers will provide us with a better illustration of the risks covered by these words than would be available from any academic analysis of them.

Conversely, it would seem from the recent case of *Athens Maritime Enterprises Corporation* v. *Hellenic Mutual War Risks Association*[14] that the term "riots" has to be construed as a term of art. Following previous authority, the learned judge in that case adopted the definition of a riot set out in *Field* v. *The Receiver of Metropolitan Police*,[15] which was as follows:

"In order to constitute a riot five elements are necessary:—
1. A number of persons not less than three;
2. A common purpose;
3. Execution or inception of the common purpose;
4. An intent on the part of the number of persons to help one another, by force if necessary, against any person who may oppose them in the execution of the common purpose;
5. Force or violence, not merely used in and about the common purpose, but displayed in such a manner as to alarm at least one person of reasonable firmness and courage."

14. *Athens Maritime Enterprises Corporation* v. *Hellenic Mutual War Risks Association* (*The "Andreas Lemos"*) [1982] 2 Lloyd's Rep. 483.
15. *Field* v. *The Receiver of Metropolitan Police* [1907] 2 K.B. 853, *per* Phillimore J. at p. 860.

This highly technical definition has not commended itself to the courts in the United States of America. In *Pan American World Airways Inc.* v. *The Aetna Casualty and Surety Co.* the U.S. Court of Appeals, without deciding the matter, remarked that in accordance with some of the authorities, a common law riot must be accompanied by tumult or commotion, and that there was also a respectable body of opinion that in insurance policies the term "riot" takes its meaning from common speech, in the sense of a tumultuous assembly of a multitude of people.

While noting the tendency to divergence between the opinions expressed in recent cases in England and the United States of America, it must be borne in mind that this insurance is, by Clause 14, subject to English law and practice, and consequently for the purpose of interpreting the word "riots" in this insurance, the rule in *Field's* case will, for the time being, prevail.

"civil commotions"

In a recent case it was held that a civil commotion need not involve a revolt against the Government, but there must be disturbances with sufficient cohesion to prevent them from being the work of a "mindless mob".[16] At the same time it was recognised that a "civil commotion" borders very closely on an "insurrection", but in the case referred to, the learned judge was not obliged to make this distinction. If such a borderline case were to arise under the terms of the Institute Strikes Clauses (Cargo), the distinction would have to be made, the more particularly since "insurrection" is specifically excluded under Clause 3.10.

"1.2 Any terrorist or any person acting from a political motive"

These words replace the rather vague expression which appeared in the previous clauses, namely "persons acting maliciously".

"terrorist"

One may be tempted to believe that anyone may recognise a terrorist from his actions, particularly in today's climate of "terrorist" activities. There have been recent cases involving loss and damage caused by terrorists,[17] but, unfortunately from the point of view of legal definition, the word "terrorist" did not appear in the policy conditions, either as a peril insured or excluded.

16. *Spinney's* v. *Royal Insurance* [1980] 1 Lloyd's Rep. 406, *per* Mustill J.
17. For example, see *Pan American World Airways Inc.* v. *The Aetna Casualty & Surety Co.* [1975] 1 Lloyd's Rep. 77.

"any person acting from a political motive"

This covers the phenomenon of the "gentle terrorist", who does not wish to do anyone any harm, but wishes merely to demonstrate his objection to somebody or some cause by doing some physical damage to some property associated with the object of his objection. The authors have some knowledge of this class of case, having dealt with claims for damage to a ship and her cargo on board caused by a refugee group having placed a bomb against the side of the ship.

Clause 2 — General Average Clause

2   This insurance covers general average and salvage charges, adjusted or determined according to the contract of affreightment and/or the governing law and practice, incurred to avoid or in connection with the avoidance of loss from a risk covered under these clauses.

In order to constitute a claim under these clauses, the general average act or the salvage service must be performed with the object of avoiding a loss from one of the perils insured in Clause 1. For general observations on the subject of general average and salvage, and the meaning of the words "adjusted or determined according to the contract of affreightment and/or the governing law and practice", see the commentary under the Institute Cargo Clauses (A) on page 13.

EXCLUSIONS

The exclusions are contained in Clauses 3 and 4.

Clause 3 — General Exclusions Clause

3   In no case shall this insurance cover
    3.1   loss damage or expense attributable to wilful misconduct of the Assured
    3.2   ordinary leakage, ordinary loss in weight or volume, or ordinary wear and tear of the subject-matter insured
    3.3   loss damage or expense caused by insufficiency or unsuitability of packing or preparation of the subject-matter insured (for the purpose of this Clause 3.3 "packing" shall be deemed to include stowage in a container or liftvan but only when such stowage is carried out prior to attachment of this insurance or by the Assured or their servants)
    3.4   loss damage or expense caused by inherent vice or nature of the subject- matter insured
    3.5   loss damage or expense proximately caused by delay, even though the delay be caused by a risk insured against (except expenses payable under Clause 2 above)
    3.6   loss damage or expense arising from insolvency or financial default of the owners managers charterers or operators of the vessel
    3.7   loss damage or expense arising from the absence shortage or withholding of labour of any description whatsoever resulting from any strike, lockout, labour disturbance, riot or civil commotion

3.8 any claim based upon loss of or frustration of the voyage or adventure

3.9 loss damage or expense arising from the use of any weapon of war employing atomic or nuclear fission and/or fusion or other like reaction or radioactive force or matter

3.10 loss damage or expense caused by war civil war revolution rebellion insurrection, or civil strife arising therefrom, or any hostile act by or against a belligerent power.

The first six of these exclusions (Clauses 3.1–3.6 inclusive) are the same as those which appear in the Institute Cargo Clauses (A) (B) and (C). See the commentary on pages 17 to 19.

Clause 3.7 is specific to the Strikes Clauses. The same words appeared in previous forms, and they make it clear that while the insurance will pay for loss or damage caused by the violent behaviour of strikers, the underwriters will not respond for any claim which arises merely from the withdrawal of the strikers' labour. So, for example, if workmen, about to shift goods from the quay into a warehouse, are called out on strike, and as a result the goods left on the quayside sustain damage in consequence of their exposure to the elements, this is not such a loss or damage as is covered by the policy.

Exclusion 3.8 is common to both the War Clauses and the Strikes Clauses. For commentary see page 194.

Exclusion 3.9 is one which appears in all Institute Clauses for cargo. See page 20.

Exclusion 3.10 is designed to take out the claims which would be covered by the Institute War Clauses. The meaning of the words in this exclusion is examined on pages 188 to 190, but it may be noted again how fine is the dividing line between a "civil commotion", the consequences of which are covered by the Institute Strikes Clauses, and an "insurrection", or civil strife arising from an insurrection, which is excluded from the Strikes Clauses but covered in the War Clauses. As stated above, it appears that the distinction lies in the motive of the insurgents. If their objective is the overthrow of the Government or some part of the established order, the claim will fall on the War Clauses, and if not, it will lie under the Strikes Clauses.

Clause 4 — Unseaworthiness and Unfitness Exclusion Clause

4   **4.1** In no case shall this insurance cover loss damage or expense arising from
unseaworthiness of vessel or craft,
unfitness of vessel craft conveyance container or liftvan for the safe carriage of the subject-matter insured,
where the Assured or their servants are privy to such unseaworthiness or unfitness, at the time the subject-matter insured is loaded therein.

   4.2 The Underwriters waive any breach of the implied warranties of seaworthiness of the ship and fitness of the ship to carry the subject-matter insured to destination, unless the Assured or their servants are privy to such unseaworthiness or unfitness.

This clause is in the same terms as Clause 5 of the Institute Cargo Clauses. See commentary on page 20.

DURATION

Clauses 5, 6 and 7 — Duration of the Risk, Termination of the Contract of Carriage and Change of Destination

5   **5.1**   This insurance attaches from the time the goods leave the warehouse or place of storage at the place named herein for the commencement of the transit, continues during the ordinary course of transit and terminates either

   5.1.1   on delivery to the Consignees' or other final warehouse or place of storage at the destination named herein,

   5.1.2   on delivery to any other warehouse or place of storage, whether prior to or at the destination named herein, which the Assured elect to use either

   5.1.2.1   for storage other than in the ordinary course of transit or

   5.1.2.2   for allocation or distribution,
      or

   5.1.3   on the expiry of 60 days after completion of discharge overside of the goods hereby insured from the oversea vessel at the final port of discharge,
   whichever shall first occur.

   5.2   If, after discharge overside from the oversea vessel at the final port of discharge, but prior to termination of this insurance, the goods are to be forwarded to a destination other than that to which they are insured hereunder, this insurance, whilst remaining subject to termination as provided for above, shall not extend beyond the commencement of transit to such other destination.

   5.3   This insurance shall remain in force (subject to termination as provided for above and to the provisions of Clause 6 below) during delay beyond the control of the Assured, any deviation, forced discharge, reshipment or transhipment and during any variation of the adventure arising from the exercise of a liberty granted to shipowners or charterers under the contract of affreightment.

6   If owing to circumstances beyond the control of the Assured either the contract of carriage is terminated at a port or place other than the destination named therein or the transit is otherwise terminated before delivery of the goods as provided for in Clause 5 above, then this insurance shall also terminate *unless prompt notice is given to the Underwriters and continuation of cover is requested when the insurance shall remain in force, subject to an additional premium if required by the Underwriters,* either

   6.1   until the goods are sold and delivered at such port or place, or, unless otherwise specially agreed, until the expiry of 60 days after arrival of the goods hereby insured at such port or place, whichever shall first occur,
      or

   6.2   if the goods are forwarded within the said period of 60 days (or any agreed extension thereof) to the destination named herein or to any other destination, until terminated in accordance with the provisions of Clause 5 above.

7   Where, after attachment of this insurance, the destination is changed by the Assured, *held covered at a premium and on conditions to be arranged subject to prompt notice being given to the Underwriters.*

These clauses are the same as Clauses 8, 9 and 10 in the Institute Cargo Clauses. See pages 23 to 27. Contrast, however, the restricted duration clauses which apply in the Institute War Clauses (Cargo) which are the subject of commentary on pages 196/7.

CLAIMS

Clause 8 — Insurable Interest Clause

8   **8.1**   In order to recover under this insurance the Assured must have an insurable interest in the subject-matter insured at the time of the loss.

8.2 Subject to 8.1 above, the Assured shall be entitled to recover for insured loss occurring during the period covered by this insurance, notwithstanding that the loss occurred before the contract of insurance was concluded, unless the Assured were aware of the loss and the Underwriters were not.

This is the same as Clause 11 in the Institute Cargo Clauses. See page 27.

Clause 9 — Increased Value Clause

9 **9.1** If any Increased Value insurance is effected by the Assured on the cargo insured herein the agreed value of the cargo shall be deemed to be increased to the total amount insured under this insurance and all Increased Value insurances covering the loss, and liability under this insurance shall be in such proportion as the sum insured herein bears to such total amount insured.
In the event of claim the Assured shall provide the Underwriters with evidence of the amounts insured under all other insurances.
9.2 **Where this insurance is on Increased Value the following clause shall apply:**
The agreed value of the cargo shall be deemed to be equal to the total amount insured under the primary insurance and all Increased Value insurances covering the loss and effected on the cargo by the Assured, and liability under this insurance shall be in such proportion as the sum insured herein bears to such total amount insured.
In the event of claim the Assured shall provide the Underwriters with evidence of the amounts insured under all other insurances.

This clause is the same as Clause 14 in the Institute Cargo Clauses. See page 31.

BENEFIT OF INSURANCE

Clause 10 — Not to Inure Clause

10 This insurance shall not inure to the benefit of the carrier or other bailee.

This is the same as Clause 15 in the Institute Cargo Clauses.

MINIMISING LOSSES

Clause 11 — Duty of Assured Clause

11 It is the duty of the Assured and their servants and agents in respect of loss recoverable hereunder
11.1 to take such measures as may be reasonable for the purpose of averting or minimising such loss, and
11.2 to ensure that all rights against carriers, bailees or other third parties are properly preserved and exercised
and the Underwriters will, in addition to any loss recoverable hereunder, reimburse the Assured for any charges properly and reasonably incurred in pursuance of these duties.

While this clause is in the same terms as Clause 16 in the Institute Cargo Clauses, it has to be noted that the right of the assured to recover for the expenses reasonably incurred in averting or minimising a loss is restricted to those instances where the loss or damage averted or minimised has arisen, or would have arisen in consequence of the perils listed in Clause 1.

Bills of lading are frequently claused in such a way as to grant the shipowner or carrier a liberty to avoid calling at a strike-bound port and instead to discharge cargo at an alternative port where labour is working. This would constitute a permitted variation of the adventure under the contract of affreightment, and thus, by Clause 5.3, the insurance would remain in force without the assured having to give notice to the underwriters (as would be the case, under Clause 7, if it were the assured himself who had changed the destination). If, consequent upon the exercise of that liberty, the shipowner or carrier claims the extra cost of proceeding to the alternative port and discharging the cargo there, as a special charge on the goods concerned, will this be recoverable from the underwriters insuring those goods under the Institute Strikes Clauses (Cargo)?

It is submitted that the answer depends upon the conditions in the strike-bound port. If the withdrawal of labour is peaceful, then all that has been averted is a loss of time, and the assured's claim would be caught by exclusion 3.7 (see above). However, if there was such a condition of unrest in the strike-bound port that there was a real risk of loss or damage occurring in consequence of a "civil commotion" then the authors submit that a claim can properly be brought under this Clause 11 for the extra cost involved in diverting the cargo.

Clause 12 — Waiver Clause

12   Measures taken by the Assured or the Underwriters with the object of saving, protecting or recovering the subject-matter insured shall not be considered as a waiver or acceptance of abandonment or otherwise prejudice the rights of either party.

This is the same as Clause 17 in the Institute Cargo Clauses.

Clause 13 — Reasonable Dispatch Clause

13   It is a condition of this insurance that the Assured shall act with reasonable despatch in all circumstances within their control.

This is the same as Clause 18 in the Institute Cargo Clauses.

Clause 14 — English Law and Practice Clause

14   This insurance is subject to English law and practice.

This is the same as Clause 19 in the Institute Cargo Clauses. See commentary on page 35.

Under this is printed:

NOTE:— It is necessary for the Assured when they become aware of an event which is "held covered" under this insurance to give prompt notice to the Underwriters and the right to such cover is dependent upon compliance with this obligation.

This is the note which appears at the foot of all Institute Clauses covering goods. See the observations on page 35.

C. SPECIAL WAR AND STRIKES FORMS FOR PARTICULAR COMMODITIES

Appropriate forms have been created for the commodity trades by marrying the special terms agreed with those trades (see examples and commentary on pages 48 to 78) with the Institute War Clauses and the Institute Strikes Clauses.

Up to the time of writing, the following forms have been issued in their new (post 1/1/82) format:

Institute War Clauses (Commodity Trades)	5/9/83
Institute War Clauses (FOSFA Trades)	1/7/85
Institute Strikes Clauses (Bulk Coal)	1/10/82
Institute Strikes Clauses (Bulk Oil)	1/2/83
Institute Strikes Clauses (Commodity Trades)	5/9/83
Institute Strikes Clauses (Jute)	1/1/84
Institute Strikes Clauses (Natural Rubber)	1/1/84
Institute Strikes Clauses (FOSFA Trades)	1/7/85
Institute Strikes Clauses (Frozen Food)	1/1/86
Institute Strikes Clauses (Frozen Meat)	1/1/86

3. INSTITUTE WAR AND STRIKES CLAUSES, HULLS — TIME (1/10/83)

This form combines war risks and strikes risks in one document.

In common with all Hull forms, the following words appear in the heading: "This insurance is subject to English law and practice". See page 84 for the authors' observations on these words.

Clause 1 — Perils

Subject always to the exclusions hereinafter referred to, this insurance covers loss of or damage to the Vessel caused by

1.1 war civil war revolution rebellion insurrection, or civil strife arising therefrom, or any hostile act by or against a belligerent power

1.2 capture seizure arrest restraint or detainment, and the consequences thereof or any attempt thereat

1.3 derelict mines torpedoes bombs or other derelict weapons of war

1.4 strikers, locked-out workmen, or persons taking part in labour disturbances, riots or civil commotions

1.5 any terrorist or any person acting maliciously or from a political motive

1.6 confiscation or expropriation.

Clause 1.1 lists the war and war-like risks in the same words as appear in the Institute War Clauses (Cargo), and the observations made on pages 188 to 190 apply equally to them.

Clause 1.2 is however wider than the corresponding clause in the Institute War Clauses (Cargo), in that the perils of capture, seizure, arrest, restraint or detainment are not limited to those which arise in consequence of the war and war-like risks set out in Clause 1.1. Subject therefore to the exclusions, and particularly those set out in Clauses 4.1.3, 4.1.4, 4.1.5 and 4.1.6 (see below), a seizure, arrest or restraint exercised in time of peace by the political or executive arm of a Government or power will be covered, equally with such acts performed in war or war-like circumstances.

Clause 1.3 is the same as in the Institute War Clauses (Cargo). See commentary on page 192.

Clause 1.4 is the same as Clause 1.1 in the Institute Strikes Clauses (Cargo). See page 200.

Clause 1.5 retains the risk of loss or damage of persons "acting maliciously", and adds, by way both of clarification and expansion, the risks of loss or damage caused by a terrorist or a person acting from a political motive. The cover is therefore wider than that provided in the Cargo Clauses.

"Maliciously" means "out of spite, or ill-will", and as an insured peril it may well overlap with acts performed with a political motivation or in the course of a civil commotion. Sabotage is a malicious act. So are many acts of barratry, but as barratry is one of the perils insured under the Institute Time Clauses, Hulls, a loss from this cause will be excluded from the War and Strikes cover by reason of Clause 4.2 of the Institute War and Strikes Clauses, Hulls — Time, unless the act of barratry involved the detonation of an explosive, in which event it would be excluded from the marine risks cover by virtue of Clause 25 of the Institute Time Clauses, Hulls.

"1.6   confiscation or expropriation"

These seemingly "new" perils do not appear to the authors to be wider than the kind of political or executive acts of a Government or a power which, under Rule 10 for the Rules for Construction of Policy contained in the Marine Insurance Act 1906, are comprehended within the words "arrests, restraints and detainments of all Kings, Princes and People ..." as they appeared in Lloyd's form of policy. However, whether listed in the Institute War and Strikes Clauses, Hulls — Time merely for clarification or by way of expansion of the perils insured, it is to be noted that they were not among the listed perils in the old forms of War and Strikes Clauses for Hulls, neither do they appear in the current Institute War Clauses (Cargo).

A dictionary definition of "confiscation" is:

"Appropriation to the public treasury (by way of penalty)", with the additional colloquial meaning of "legal robbery with the sanction of the ruling power".

"Expropriation" suggests an executive act of dispossession, not necessarily by way of a penalty.

Clause 2 — Incorporation

The Institute Time Clauses — Hulls 1/10/83 (including 4/4ths Collision Clause) except Clauses 1.2, 2, 3, 4, 6, 12, 21.1.8, 22, 23, 24, 25 and 26 are deemed to be incorporated in this insurance in so far as they do not conflict with the provisions of these clauses.

Held covered in case of breach of warranty as to towage or salvage services provided notice be given to the Underwriters immediately after receipt of advices and any additional premium required by them be agreed.

The first part of this clause incorporates the relevant provisions of the Institute Time Clauses — Hulls, particularly those relating to General Average and Salvage, Sue and Labour Charges and the clauses dealing with the adjustment of claims, namely Clauses 14, 15, 16, 17, 18, 19 and 20. It is to be noted that in one respect the cover granted by the Institute War and Strikes Clauses, Hulls — Time is wider than provided in the Institute Time Clauses. This is in respect to collision liability, which is granted in full (4/4ths) under the War and Strikes Clauses, whereas it is normal to limit the cover to 3/4ths in the insurances covering marine risks. So, for example, if a ship insured with the Institute War and Strikes Clauses is taken over by a party of hijackers acting for a political motive, and whilst under their control, collides with and does damage to another vessel, then any collision liability which attaches to the owner of the ship (in spite of his temporary dispossession) will be met in full.

The second part of this Clause 2 holds the assured covered in the event of a breach of warranty as to towage or salvage services, with the usual proviso regarding notice and the payment of any additional premium. By implication therefore, breaches of warranty as to cargo, trade, locality and date of sailing will not be held covered.

Clause 3 — Detainment

In the event that the Vessel shall have been the subject of capture seizure arrest restraint detainment confiscation or expropriation, and the Assured shall thereby have lost the free use and disposal of the Vessel for a continuous period of 12 months then for the purpose of ascertaining whether the Vessel is a constructive total loss the Assured shall be deemed to have been deprived of the possession of the Vessel without any likelihood of recovery.

This is an important new clause and requires some explanation.

By section 60(2) of the Marine Insurance Act 1906, there is a constructive total loss where, *inter alia*, the assured is deprived of the possession of his ship by a peril insured against, and it is unlikely that he can recover it. On the outbreak of the war between Iraq and Iran, a number of ships were trapped in the Shatt-al-Arab by the outbreak of hostilities, and even those which were physically able to sail were prohibited from so doing by the Iraqi authorities. While clearly subject to restraint, underwriters questioned whether the assured had been deprived of the possession of their ships, and if they had, whether they were likely or unlikely to recover them. A test case, *The "Bamburi"*[18] was selected for the arbitration of a judge arbitrator, who found in favour of the claimants. In his reasons, the arbitrator dealt with the following points:

1. Was the detention of the vessel proximately caused by perils insured?

The arbitrator found that the order preventing the vessel from sailing emanated from an executive organ of the Government of Iraq, and that this constituted a "restraint of princes". It was not a mere restriction on navigation.

However, the arbitrator considered that if there had been no restraint or detainment by the Iraqi Government, he would not have been able to find that the vessel's detention constituted a loss by "hostilities or war-like operations", merely an apprehension of loss by those perils.

2. Have the owners been deprived of possession?

The arbitrator held that it was irrelevant to this question that the owners continued to receive payment of hire during the first year that the vessel was detained. There was a real distinction between physical loss of use and financial loss of reward.

The arbitrator found that the owners had been wholly deprived of the "free use and disposal" of the ship. He made a lengthy review of the law in order to deal with the challenge that the deprivation of "free use and disposal" was the right test to apply to answer this question, and concluded that although the "loss of the adventure" theory (which still holds good in the case of a policy of insurance on goods) had been discarded at least by 1857 as regards claims on policies of insurance on ship, the "free use and disposal" test was still correct.

---

18. *The "Bamburi"* [1982] 1 Lloyd's Rep. 312.

3. Was it "unlikely" that the owners could recover the vessel (within a reasonable time)?

It was not disputed that the words "within a reasonable time" are implicit in subsection (2)(i)(a) of the Act — see *Polurrian Steamship Co.* v. *Young* (1915) 19 Com.Cas. 143; 20 Com.Cas. 152.

The arbitrator judged that a reasonable time in a case of this sort would be twelve months from the notice of abandonment, without taking into account any period before the notice.

This Clause 3 summarises the effect of the arbitrator's decision, and lays down the sensible rule that where the assured has lost the free use and disposal of the vessel for a continuous period of twelve months, then it shall be deemed to be a constructive total loss.

Clause 4 — Exclusions

This insurance excludes

4.1 loss damage liability or expense arising from

4.1.1 any detonation of any weapon of war employing atomic or nuclear fission and/or fusion or other like reaction or radioactive force or matter, hereinafter called a nuclear weapon of war

4.1.2 the outbreak of war (whether there be a declaration of war or not) between any of the following countries:

United Kingdom, United States of America, France,

the Union of Soviet Socialist Republics,

the People's Republic of China

4.1.3 requisition or pre-emption

4.1.4 capture seizure arrest restraint detainment confiscation or expropriation by or under the order of the government or any public or local authority of the country in which the Vessel is owned or registered

4.1.5 arrest restraint detainment confiscation or expropriation under quarantine regulations or by reason of infringement of any customs or trading regulations

4.1.6 the operation of ordinary judicial process, failure to provide security or to pay any fine or penalty or any financial cause

4.1.7 piracy (but this exclusion shall not affect cover under Clause 1.4),

4.2 loss damage liability or expense covered by the Institute Time Clauses — Hulls 1/10/83 (including 4/4ths Collision Clause) or which would be recoverable thereunder but for Clause 12 thereof,

4.3 any claim for any sum recoverable under any other insurance on the Vessel or which would be recoverable under such insurance but for the existence of this insurance,

4.4 any claim for expenses arising from delay except such expenses as would be recoverable in principle in English law and practice under the York-Antwerp Rules 1974.

Clause 4.1.1 reproduces the Nuclear Weapon exclusion, which is also found (as Clause 26) in the Institute Time Clauses — Hulls.

Clause 4.1.2 excludes any claim arising from the outbreak of war involving any two or more of the major powers. In this event the insurance is also automatically terminated by virtue of Clause 5.2.

Clause 4.1.3 excludes "requisition or pre-emption". *"Requisition"* means a demand for use in military service. *"Pre-emption"* is understood to have something of the same meaning in the United States of America. In either case it is presumed that the owner will lose possession only for a temporary period of time, and will have the vessel returned to him by the requisitioning authority when it is no longer required. It is also to be noted that requisition is one of the events which brings about the automatic termination of the insurance.

Clause 4.1.4 excludes the perils of capture, seizure etc. (including confiscation or expropriation) by the government or a public or local authority of the country in which the vessel is owned or registered. It was a supposed rule of English law that a marine insurance policy subject to that law would not cover the risk of British capture, on the grounds of public policy. Since the House of Lords held to the contrary in *British and Foreign Marine Insurance Co.* v. *Sanday*,[2] albeit that this was a case involving cargo, it has been necessary to make some specific exclusion in the policy to revert to what was understood to be the traditional position.

Clause 4.1.5 excludes arrest etc. (including confiscation or expropriation) arising in three circumstances. Two of these, under quarantine regulations, and by reason of infringement of any customs regulations, were excluded under the previous forms of War and Strikes Clauses, but the exclusion of claims arising by reason of infringement of "trading regulations" is new.

The exclusion relating to infringement of customs regulations was considered in *Panamanian Oriental Steamship Corporation* v. *Wright*.[19] In that case the Court of Appeal held that the ship had been confiscated under Vietnamese regulations which provided for that penalty in the event of breach of customs regulations.

Clause 4.1.6 excludes the operation of ordinary judicial process, and those other circumstances which give rise to the vessel being placed under civil arrest at the suit of an aggrieved party. So far as English law is concerned, this exclusion is merely declaratory.

Since piracy has been accepted again by underwriters in the British insurance markets as a marine risk, it is necessary in order to avoid duplication to exclude it from the list of war perils, and this is achieved by Clause 4.1.7. However, as has been noted in our review of the Institute Time Clauses — Hulls (see page 133), Clause 24 of those clauses excludes claims arising from riots or civil commotions which are of course covered by the Institute War and Strikes Clauses (Clause 1.4) as we have noted above. The traditional English law definition of "riot" (see page 200) recently approved in the case of *The "Andreas Lemos"*[14] is sufficiently wide to cover some (although not all) acts of piracy — hence the need for the words (in Clause 4.1.7) to limit the exclusion of piracy to those cases which do not also constitute a "riot".

Clause 4.2 is inserted in order to avoid any duplication of cover with the Institute Time Clauses — Hulls.

19. *Panamanian Oriental Steamship Corporation* v. *Wright (The "Anita")* [1971] 1 Lloyd's Rep. 487.

Clause 4.3 is designed to prevent any claim falling upon the policy containing the Institute War and Strikes Clauses which can or could be recovered under any other insurance on the vessel. In the event of there being such a duplication of cover, it is intended that the other insurance should pay on a "first loss" basis.

Clause 4.4 is the usual clause excluding any claim for expenses arising from delay, except when allowable in general average.

Clause 5 — Termination

5.1 This insurance may be cancelled by either the Underwriters or the Assured giving 7 days notice (such cancellation becoming effective on the expiry of 7 days from midnight of the day on which notice of cancellation is issued by or to the Underwriters). The Underwriters agree however to reinstate this insurance subject to agreement between the Underwriters and the Assured prior to the expiry of such notice of cancellation as to new rate of premium and/or conditions and/or warranties.

5.2 Whether or not such notice of cancellation has been given this insurance shall TERMINATE AUTOMATICALLY

5.2.1 upon the occurrence of any hostile detonation of any nuclear weapon of war as defined in Clause 4.1.1 wheresoever or whensoever such detonation may occur and whether or not the Vessel may be involved

5.2.2 upon the outbreak of war (whether there be a declaration of war or not) between any of the following countries:
United Kingdom, United States of America, France,
the Union of Soviet Socialist Republics,
the People's Republic of China

5.2.3 in the event of the Vessel being requisitioned, either for title or use.

5.3 In the event either of cancellation by notice or of automatic termination of this insurance by reason of the operation of this Clause 5, or of the sale of the Vessel, pro rata net return of premium shall be payable to the Assured.

Clause 5.1 permits either party to give the other seven days' notice before the cancellation becomes effective. The underlying intention of the clause is to enable underwriters to vary the rate of premium and/or the conditions of the insurance in the event of a serious change of circumstances relating to war risks in the vessel's likely trading area.

The second part of the clause relates to the reinstatement of the insurance if underwriters and the assured can agree to the new terms within the period of the seven days' notice. Under the previous clauses, the period of notice used to be fourteen days, so it must be assumed that reinstatement negotiations are much less protracted than they used to be.

Clause 5.2 relating to automatic termination is self-explanatory.

There is also an important caution at the foot of the clauses, which reads as follows:

This insurance shall not become effective if, subsequent to its acceptance by the Underwriters and prior to the intended time of its attachment, there has occurred any event which would have automatically terminated this insurance under the provisions of Clause 5 above.

This is also self-explanatory.

4. INSTITUTE WAR AND STRIKES CLAUSES, FREIGHT — TIME (1/10/83)

This insurance is subject to English law and practice.

1. Perils

Subject always to the exlusions hereinafter referred to, this insurance covers

1.1 loss (total or partial) of the subject-matter insured caused by

1.1.1 war civil war revolution rebellion insurrection, or civil strife arising therefrom, or any hostile act by or against a belligerent power

1.1.2 capture seizure arrest restraint or detainment, and the consequences thereof or any attempt thereat

1.1.3 derelict mines torpedoes bombs or other derelict weapons of war

1.2 loss (total or partial) of the subject-matter insured arising from loss of or damage to the Vessel caused by

1.2.1 strikers, locked-out workmen, or persons taking part in labour disturbances, riots or civil commotions

1.2.2 any terrorist or any person acting maliciously or from a political motive

1.2.3 confiscation or expropriation.

It will be noted that whereas the list of perils covered is the same as appears in the Institute War and Strikes Clauses, Hulls — Time, there is an important difference in the manner of their operation. Any loss of freight, whether total or partial, caused by war or the "war-like" perils listed in Sub-Clauses 1.1.1, 1.1.2 and 1.1.3 will be responded for under this insurance. Contrarily, the "strikes" risks covered by Sub-Clauses 1.2.1, 1.2.2 and 1.2.3 will only be paid for when the loss of freight, whether total or partial, arises from loss of or damage to the ship caused by those perils.

The reason for this limitation is not at all clear to the authors. To take an example, if goods which the shipowner has contracted to carry are destroyed by persons taking part in a labour disturbance whilst they are on the quayside awaiting shipment:

— the owner of the cargo will suffer a loss which is covered by the Institute Strikes Clauses (Cargo), whereas

— the shipowner, who bears the risk of freight, will not be entitled to receive any freight in respect of the goods which he has contracted to carry, but this loss will not be covered under the Institute War and Strikes Clauses, Freight — Time.

Likewise any loss of freight which is at the shipowner's risk "until right and true delivery", which the shipowner may suffer in consequence of a loss of cargo caused by "strikes" perils during the voyage and before delivery of the cargo, falls outside the scope of this insurance.

2. Incorporation

The Institute Time Clauses — Freight 1/10/83 except Clauses 2, 3, 4, 5, 12, 16, 17, 18, 19 and 20 are deemed to be incorporated in this insurance in so far as they do not conflict with the provisions of these clauses.

Held covered in case of breach of warranty as to towage or salvage services provided notice be given to the Underwriters immediately after receipt of advices and any additional premium required by them be agreed.

It will be appreciated that the incorporation of the Institute Time Clauses — Freight is far from complete. The risk of craft and/or lighter to and from the vessel (Clause 2 of the Institute Time Clauses — Freight) is not included, there is no Continuation Clause and the circumstances in which the assured will be held covered in case of breach of warranty are limited to instances when towage or salvage services are provided by the ship, subject to the usual proviso regarding notice and payment of any additional premium required by the underwriters.

On the other hand the Franchise Clause contained in the Institute Time Clauses — Freight is not incorporated in the War and Strikes Clauses, and consequently when there has been a partial loss of freight caused by the war and strikes perils insured under these clauses, the claim will be paid irrespective of percentage.

3. Detainment

In the event that a claim for a constructive total loss of the Vessel is paid on the war risks insurance of the Vessel under Clause 3 (Detainment) of the Institute War and Strikes Clauses — Hulls — Time 1/10/83 or the Institute War and Strikes Clauses — Hulls — Voyage 1/10/83 as a result of the loss of the free use and disposal of the Vessel for a continuous period of 12 months due to capture, seizure, arrest, restraint, detainment, confiscation or expropriation whilst this insurance is in force, the amount insured hereunder shall be paid in full less any claims otherwise arising during the said period of 12 months which have been paid or are recoverable hereunder or under insurances subject to the Institute Time Clauses — Freight 1/10/83 and/or the Institute Voyage Clauses — Freight 1/10/83 and any recoveries made in respect of the said period.

The general effect of this clause is that if the assured has lost the "free" use and disposal of the vessel for a continuous period of twelve months due to capture, seizure, arrest, restraint, detainment, confiscation or expropriation during the currency of the insurance, a claim which is met by the war risks insurance on the ship will be followed for the full amount of the insurance subscribed on the War and Strikes Risks Clauses — Freight. Of course, if any interim payments have been made for losses payable by the War and Strikes Clauses — Freight, they will be deducted in arriving at the overall settlement under this clause.

4. Exclusions

This insurance excludes
4.1 loss (total or partial) or expense arising from
4.1.1 any detonation of any weapon of war employing atomic or nuclear fission and/or fusion or other like reaction or radioactive force or matter, hereinafter called a nuclear weapon of war
4.1.2 the outbreak of war (whether there be a declaration of war or not) between any of the following countries:
     United Kingdom, United States of America, France,
     the Union of Soviet Socialist Republics,
     the People's Republic of China

4.1.3   requisition or pre-emption
4.1.4   capture seizure arrest restraint detainment confiscation or expropriation by or under the order of the government or any public or local authority of the country in which the Vessel is owned or registered
4.1.5   arrest restraint detainment confiscation or expropriation under quarantine regulations or by reason of infringement of any customs or trading regulations
4.1.6   the operation of ordinary judicial process, failure to provide security or to pay any fine or penalty or any financial cause
4.1.7   piracy (but this exclusion shall not affect cover under Clause 1.2.1),
4.2   loss (total or partial) or expense covered by the Institute Time Clauses — Freight 1/10/83 or which would be recoverable thereunder but for Clause 12 thereof,
4.3   any claim (not being a claim recoverable under the Institute War and Strikes Clauses Freight — Voyage 1/10/83) for any sum recoverable under any other insurance on the subject-matter insured or which would be recoverable under such insurance but for the existence of this insurance,
4.4   loss proximately caused by delay or any claim for expenses arising from delay except such expenses as would be recoverable in principle in English law and practice under the York-Antwerp Rules 1974,
4.5   any claim based upon loss of or frustration of any voyage or adventure.

In general the exclusions in sub-clauses 4.1.1 to 4.1.7 are similar to those which are incorporated in the Institute War and Strikes Clauses, Hulls — Time. See commentary on pages 211/2.

Clauses 4.2 and 4.3 exclude any claim which would be recoverable either under the Institute Time Clauses — Freight or any other insurance upon freight, except for claims recoverable in the event that the insurances on freight for War and Strikes risks were supplemented by a voyage insurance on similar terms.

Clause 4.4 is in rather different terms from the corresponding clause which appears in the Institute War and Strikes Clauses, Hulls — Time. Expenses arising from delay are not covered, except for a contribution payable in general average to detention expenses admissible under the York/Antwerp Rules, 1974. In addition, the insurance excludes any loss of freight proximately caused by delay, and this reflects the fact that losses of freight due to this cause are not payable under the policies of insurance covering marine risks (see Clause 14 of the Institute Time Clauses — Freight: "any claim consequent on loss of time") or admitted in general average (see Rule C of the York/Antwerp Rules).

Clause 4.5, which excludes any claim based upon loss of or frustration of any voyage or adventure, has its counterpart in the Institute War and Strikes Clauses for Cargo.

The clause was considered in *Atlantic Maritime Co. Inc. v. Gibbon*.[20] In this case the ship was chartered to load a cargo at a Chinese port, which happened to be in the hands of the Communist forces at the time of the Chinese Civil War. Whilst waiting in that port, the master received a warning from an officer of the Government forces that he should leave the port on account of the dangers which would threaten his ship in the event of a Government attack. The master took heed of this warning; the vessel sailed

20. *Atlantic Maritime Co. Inc.* v. *Gibbon* [1953] 2 Lloyd's Rep. 294.

from the port, and the judges in the Court of Appeal held that the contract to be performed under the charter-party was frustrated. Although the judges were not unanimous as to whether there had been a "restraint of Princes", they all agreed that the claim, if any, was caught by the "Frustration Clause".

5. Termination

5.1 This insurance may be cancelled by either the Underwriters or the Assured giving 7 days notice (such cancellation becoming effective on the expiry of 7 days from midnight of the day on which notice of cancellation is issued by or to the Underwriters). The Underwriters agree however to reinstate this insurance subject to agreement between the Underwriters and the Assured prior to the expiry of such notice of cancellation as to new rate of premium and/or conditions and/or warranties.

5.2 Whether or not such notice of cancellation has been given this insurance shall TERMINATE AUTOMATICALLY

5.2.1 upon the occurrence of any hostile detonation of any nuclear weapon of war as defined in Clause 4.1.1 wheresoever or whensoever such detonation may occur and whether or not the Vessel may be involved

5.2.2 upon the outbreak of war (whether there be a declaration of war or not) between any of the following countries:

United Kingdom, United States of America, France,
the Union of Soviet Socialist Republics,
the People's Republic of China

5.2.3 in the event of the Vessel being requisitioned, either for title or use.

5.3 In the event either of cancellation by notice or of automatic termination of this insurance by reason of the operation of this Clause 5, or of the sale of the Vessel, pro rata net return of premium shall be payable to the Assured.

This clause is in the same terms as Clause 5 of the Institute War and Strikes Clauses, Hulls — Time.

There then appears the caution:

This insurance shall not become effective if, subsequent to its acceptance by the Underwriters and prior to the intended time of its attachment, there has occurred any event which would have automatically terminated this insurance under the provisions of Clause 5 above.

This is also the same as in the Institute War and Strikes Clauses, Hulls — Time.

Index